# Prophetic Authority

# Prophetic Authority

## Democratic Hierarchy and the Mormon Priesthood

MICHAEL HUBBARD MACKAY

UNIVERSITY OF
ILLINOIS PRESS
Urbana, Chicago, and Springfield

Manufactured in the United States of America
1 2 3 4 5 C P 5 4 3 2 1
This book is printed on acid-free paper.

Publication of this book was supported by the
Religious Studies Center at Brigham Young University.

Library of Congress Cataloging-in-Publication Data

Names: MacKay, Michael Hubbard, author.
Title: Prophetic authority : democratic hierarchy and the Mormon priesthood / Michael Hubbard MacKay.
Description: Urbana, Chicago, and Springfield : University of Illinois Press, [2020] | Includes bibliographical references and index.
Identifiers: LCCN 2019041036 (print) | LCCN 2019041037 (ebook) | ISBN 9780252043017 (cloth) | ISBN 9780252084874 (paperback) | ISBN 9780252051876 (ebook)
Subjects: LCSH: Prophets (Mormon theology)—History. | Authority—Religious aspects—Mormon Church—History. | Priesthood—Mormon Church—History.
Classification: LCC BX8643.P7 M33 2020 (print) | LCC BX8643.P7 (ebook) | DDC 262/.80882893—dc23
LC record available at https://lccn.loc.gov/2019041036
LC ebook record available at https://lccn.loc.gov/2019041037

*I dedicate this book to the scholars who made it possible. The brilliant mind and careful analysis of Richard Bushman founded a generation of Mormon studies scholars. Furthermore, the scholarship in antebellum religious authority is insurmountable. In particular, the work of Nathan O. Hatch, Amanda Porterfield, and Kathleen Flake framed this entire work. Furthermore, the scholarly spadework of Gregory Prince, Bill Hartley, and D. Michael Quinn enabled its foundation to be rooted in the archives.*

# Contents

# Acknowledgments

I want to thank the institutions that made my research and writing possible. This project began under my employment at the Joseph Smith Papers Project, where I worked on this research extensively with Gerrit Dirkmaat, who was an ideal research companion. The roots of this book took place during my time at the Church History Library in Salt Lake City, but the project flowered once I took a faculty position at the Department of Church History and Doctrine at Brigham Young University. It was primarily funded by my department and the Religious Studies Center at BYU.

Many careful readers of my manuscript offered important critiques of the research, writing, and arguments. In the early stages of the manuscript, Richard Bushman, Andrew Hedges, and Matthew Godfrey read and offered important formative reviews that took the project in new directions. Nicholas Frederick, one of my finest colleagues at BYU, worked through the manuscript with a careful eye for detail. In its finishing stages, Benjamin Park, Spencer McBride, and the blind reviewers helped develop the final product. I also owe an unpayable debt to Jenny Webb and Jana Reiss, two of the most capable scholars and editors in Mormon studies.

Prophetic Authority

# Introduction

## Antebellum Religious Authority and the Development of Mormon Priesthood

In 2008, Mormon presidential candidate Mitt Romney apologetically addressed the problem of "theocratic tyranny" in the lead-up to the election, declaring, "I will put no doctrine of any church above the plain duties of the office and the sovereign authority of the law." Comparing himself to John F. Kennedy, who faced similar questions about his faith as a Catholic during the presidential election of 1960, Romney acknowledged the issues surrounding the sovereign authority held by the Mormon prophet and president of the Church of Jesus Christ of Latter-day Saints.[1] Conservative talk-show host Hugh Hewitt called the dilemma the "Mormon problem."[2] Romney declared, "Let me assure you that no authorities of my church, or of any other church for that matter, will ever exert influence on presidential decisions."[3] Romney's assurance came nearly two centuries after Mormonism's founding in upstate New York during the Second Great Awakening, and such bold words underscored the pervasiveness of Mormon hierarchical authority. Mormonism's radical roots were planted deeply in US soil, and its determined sense of religious authority blossomed as part of the US landscape. Indeed, the Mormon tradition's emphasis on prophetic authority makes it distinct within US religious culture.[4] From local Mormon leaders to the prophet at the helm, social and religious authority came to be defined by hierarchical structures.

Mormonism emerged as an important example of the ways antebellum America shaped independent religious authority. Smith established his church under competing voices and pressures ranging from the shadow of the Enlightenment to the spirited excesses of revivals. It emerged alongside an upsurge of religious interest, as religions established their own authority in reaction to their mistrust of US politics and civic authority. Mormonism's communitarianism and lay priesthood seemed to be clear signs of a democratic tendency, one that allowed illiterate men—as Nathan O. Hatch has argued—to pursue apostolic authority and the cause of church. Yet the rise and interest in early Mormonism is also an ideal example of a sector of the United States that fostered doubt in government, sectarian churches, and reason and simultaneously sought an independent authority in the wake of disestablishment.[5]

This book will trace the contours of Mormonism's unique claim to religious authority and what such a claim can tell us about the surrounding antebellum context from which Mormonism emerged. Though most of the US public ideologically opposed the idea of monarchy and politically equated it with tyranny and suppression, religion created a space in which individuals could build a kingdom of God. Mormonism can be thus aligned with the post-Revolutionary US "nostalgia for monarchy," its development shaped by the symbiotic relationship of US religion and cultural authority. The religion Joseph Smith created not only established a kingdom of God but positioned him as the authoritative voice of Christ on earth as he formed cities, established economies, and arranged governance.[6]

## A Hierarchical Democracy

At the heart of the early Mormon tradition was that it embodied a paradox of hierarchical authority and populist democratization of religion. Mormonism demonstrates that disestablishment in antebellum America did not resoundingly produce antiauthoritarian religious movements. Rather, in the case of Mormonism, disestablishment actually fostered elements of a democratic impulse, but in an authoritarian and hierarchical way.[7] Hatch argues that Mormonism was populist, in that paupers could become priests, yet does not emphasize Smith's prophetic role that single-handedly affects and sometimes controls Mormon governance, economy, and even everyday life. All authority, priesthood, and governance ultimately began with one person: Joseph Smith, who was both a king and the president of the high priests.[8] Yet that same authority to govern and maintain the Mormon priesthood empowered the poor, founded a lay ministry, and allowed the average US man to govern others within the church. Smith established himself as a type of theological king, yet Mormonism succeeded because his concept of kingdom included the ability to distribute the power of governance to other leaders in a form of hierarchical democracy. Kathleen Flake writes, "The practical effect of these overlapping power structures was to ensure that no individual had ultimate authority in every circumstance, including Smith."[9]

Apt as this administrative concept may have been, the most definitive power within the church structure to authoritatively determine practices, beliefs, and rituals through the revelatory word of God was held by the prophet. Smith's successful formula contrasts with other charismatic movements, which also had prophets but were nonetheless short-lived because of internal disputes and poor governance. Though Smith did not go unchallenged, his church turned to his voice repeatedly to form major civic initiatives and to define the cosmos and priesthood order. This order was the only thing that could unite the doubtful and divided world of US Christianity, at least in the minds of the Mormons.[10]

Joseph Smith used his authority to create not just Mormonism but an American Zion, the kingdom of God on earth. The Book of Mormon warned that the wicked would be destroyed if they did not join with Smith in the gathering of both a spiritual and a literal Israel in the United States. Smith's revelations commanded baptism and called for believers to uproot themselves from their established communities to join him in a new society called "Zion" or the "New Jerusalem." Smith's initiatives were always ambitious and included social, political, and even military action—acquiring land, establishing cities, making alliances, establishing independent courts, and protecting the rights of the citizens of the Mormon Zion.

Along with other radical social and religious reformers of antebellum America, like the Shakers and the Harmonists, Smith disconnected from America—moving from New York to Ohio to Missouri and finally to Illinois after an armed war against the Missouri state militia. Even though Mormons esteemed the United States as the promised land, following the lead of early colonists, they also fostered their own understanding of a nation dedicated to God where they would establish the New Jerusalem for the gathering of Israel. Smith believed that Native Americans and Gentiles would form a literal and adopted tribe of Israel to usher in the Second Coming of Christ. In the process, Smith's political and social ambitions created cities and formed "the Law" of Zion, an Israelite government, and an organized kingdom intended to replace the US government as a whole.

How did Smith garner the religious authority necessary for such ambitious actions? This was not a religious society formed by a government, nor was it trying to form a mutually supportive relationship with politics to maintain its authority. Smith controlled Mormonism, eventually through the influence of a well-established lay priesthood, with the commanding voice of a prophet who had the tendency to either drive people away or create devout followers. In this way, Mormon religious authority centered on the concepts of the prophetic voice of God and the sovereignty of prophethood. That voice is what shaped the Mormon priesthood order, controlling the religion's movements and beliefs.

Mormonism therefore represented a unique sense of religious authority in antebellum America. As Flake does, this book moves away from the position of Nathan Hatch, who used Mormonism as an example of US democratization in its populist and antiauthoritarian trends. The reality was more complex. On the one hand, Joseph Smith was like Charles Finney and other revivalists in his attempt to open the heavens and offer the "fullness of God" but, on the other hand, he differed from the Presbyterian or Methodist clergy in challenging the sovereign authority of the Bible and claiming that his own prophetic declarations should be valued and added to the canonized pages of the Bible. This epistemological change that Smith instituted—a major shift from the Protestant tradition—is at the heart of the thesis of this book. Early Mormonism was neither the unfettered populism suggested by Hatch nor the autocracy that Smith's critics accused it of being. Rather, it was a hierarchical democracy, its new polity tailor-made to meet the needs of a post-Enlightenment United States that struggled to define what religion would be in the wake of disestablishment.

## Disestablishment, Politics, and the Religious "Other"

Smith's religion thrived, protected in a diffuse paradoxical realm in which his church was allowed to exist independently, but state government officials also acted to oppose the Mormons.[11] Although religious disestablishment in the early nineteenth century caused the need for a new kind of religious authority and openness to authoritarian rule,[12] Mormonism did not foster the same kind of growth that evangelicals or Methodists experienced, nor did it maintain political power like these other groups. Amanda Porterfield has shown that doubts about US government allowed evangelicals to provide a "strategy for managing concerns about America and linking idealism about America to evangelical religion."[13] Religious authority developed its influence because religion offered an alternative to the public's doubt about government. This relationship with politics was far less effective for Smith and the early Mormons, however, especially before the 1840s. In that Mormon authority developed in the wake of disestablishment along with the evangelicals—and its authoritarian rule certainly subverted religious doubt—Mormon's framing of evangelicals can apply equally to Mormonism. Yet Mormonism became an example for Americans of what religion was not, and while it may have offered them the ability to cope with doubt, it would not link "idealism about America" to itself, as evangelical religion had. Historian J. Spencer Fluhman has highlighted how secular forces framed Joseph Smith's authority as imposture and Mormonism as a foil against which true US religion could be defined.[14] Anti-Smithism emerged, at least in part, because of Smith's authoritative role in Mormonism. As a religious other, Mormons struggled to maintain a kind of Protestant US idealism.

Therefore, Mormon authority developed in spite of its inability to affect politics, not because of its ability to do so. As evangelical religion manipulated doubt in government and used that "eroding force to their advantage," US identity and idealism became intertwined with evangelical religion as it increasingly affected politics. Mormonism, on the other hand, became the enemy of the state, increasingly finding itself at odds with both local and national government.[15] David Sehat pinpoints this gloomy reality of the Mormons when he writes, "Religious partisans assumed control of law and governance and used those tools to coerce dissenters based on their religiously derived moral convictions."[16] Smith mustered armies against the civic government to protect their land and failed to link US idealism with Mormonism. Furthermore, political and civic discontent with the Mormons only increased with time, which questions how Smith created a long-lasting authoritarian US religion all the while US religion was being defined against the standard of Mormonism.[17]

## Mormon Authority and the Development of the Priesthood

Therefore, this book is about how Smith established religious authority and a long-lasting, complex priesthood structure. The thesis of this book enlivens and builds on three scholars' major ideas about religious authority and Mormonism in antebellum America. In an effort to move the conversation toward politics and its relationship to religion, Porterfield argued that populism constrained that relationship. Though it is true that Mormonism grew, as Hatch shows, from the populist appeal of a lay priesthood and communal living in early Mormonism, Flake demonstrates that the Mormon priesthood was hierarchical. Left just outside the focus of the work of Hatch, Porterfield, and Flake is the role of Joseph Smith defining Mormon authority—a role that has not been fully examined with this literature and its context in mind.

Smith's authority grew both in opposition to the civic and political authority being garnered by evangelicals and as a countertrend to the populist religious movements of the Second Great Awakening. In fact, Smith's prophetic voice and scripture formed a hierarchical priesthood structure that eventually empowered every male member of his church to become a prophet, priest, and king, while they answered to each leader above them within the same structure. Thus this book argues that Smith's prophetic voice became the arbiter of authority. It had the ultimate power to create and guide, and it was used to form a strong lay priesthood order in a stable hierarchical democracy devoid of the kind of political authority that evangelicals fostered.

Chapter 1 establishes the groundwork for Joseph Smith's prophetic voice as the basis of Mormon authority. It creates this foundation by placing him within antebellum culture and comparing him to other prophetic figures of the time. It then examines his production of the Book of Mormon to see how he convinced other people that he was a prophet and considers how immediate his revelations were and how serious the recipients were about following them. Smith's scripture was malleable, allowing him to offer definitive scriptural guidance without the unchanging rigidity of the biblical text that Protestants embraced.

Once that foundation is laid, the next five chapters investigate the primary restoration narratives of Mormonism to demonstrate Smith's central role within all of them. Each chapter is designed to examine the dichotomies and parallels of Mormon constructions of authority within antebellum America, for example, Mormon restorationism versus Protestant biblicism; Mormon kingdom-building versus US democracy; and communal Mormon ecclesiology versus individual prophetic authority. Most of the chapters also demonstrate that the foundational narratives of Mormon restorationism evolved over time, with significant details being added to earlier stories as Smith's vision expanded and his authority grew. Chapters 2, 3, and 4 develop the initial functionality of Smith's authority; chapters 5, 6, and 7 are more analytical, addressing relationships of authority and the balance of power in Mormonism.

Chapter 2 explores baptism as a vehicle Smith used to assert priesthood authority, identity, and community and to perpetuate a particular form of Mormon covenant theology. The kind of citizenship that Smith offered was in his church rather than within the nation or state. Through Mormon restoration narratives and scripture, Smith established authority that derived from God and was channeled through Smith himself. Chapter 3 uses the establishment of apostleship to examine how Smith created and adjusted Mormon initiatives that required deep commitment from the church's membership but were malleable as the church developed and changed over time. This shows that narrative flexibility was central to Smith's prophetic authority, allowing him to adjust his ecclesiology amid change and development within his church. Specifically, he moved from a notion of apostles as charismatic missionaries to one that included institutional authority that was bestowed by heavenly messengers. Chapter 4 examines how Smith established the church, which institutionalized his charismatic leadership and began to offer opportunities for leadership to the members at large, in that they were authorized to lay hands on one another and confer the gift of the Holy Ghost. It demonstrates how Smith transformed spiritual matters into concrete institutions, within the shadow of the US enlightenment, and how his unique role as its ordained prophet guided both enthusiastic behavior and administrative governance.

Chapter 5 addresses the development of Mormon priesthood and its genealogy back to Adam. It shows how this genealogical narrative of holy orders enabled Smith to create a generation of not just priests, but high priests. This new structure created an inevitable hierarchical system of governance and priesthood that challenges Hatch's work and builds upon Flake's arguments. Chapter 6 demonstrates how Smith maintained his prophetic role hierarchically, even though he had just created a kingdom of high priests, by invoking a restoration narrative of administrative keys through Peter, James, and John. The chapter shows how religious and theological narratives balanced the hierarchical structure of Mormon leadership. Chapter 7 then deals with new Mormon rituals and the empowerment of the membership, which created potential challenges for Smith as he maintained his role as prophet. By offering his followers new rituals, such as solemn assemblies and temple anointings, Smith gave them ecclesiastical authority and a tie to an ancient order and simultaneously underscored his own singular right to lead. This peculiar balance of authority has empowered leaders in Mormonism since the nineteenth century. Mormons like Mitt Romney might emphasize the democratic nature of the LDS Church, yet the "Mormon problem" can be exhibited by the members' propensity to maximize the prophet's revelatory voice.

# 1

# Prophetic Authority

## The Prophet of the Burned-Over District

By his death in 1844, Joseph Smith was the president of a well-organized priesthood and even a king within the Mormon kingdom of God. He claimed to possess religious authority that enabled him to build cities, create a Mormon society, and establish governance over thousands of Americans.[1] At the root of his authority were the imposing words of a prophet that took shape on the scrawling pages of his Bible-like canon of Mormon scripture. Like others in the antebellum period, Smith had emerged from the chaotic clamor of sectarian strife, claiming to open the heavens and possess authority from God. Yet the importance of his charismatic experiences was not established through ecstatic camp meetings or public demonstrations, nor did it depend on the certainty of a closed biblical canon. Rather, Smith's authority derived from his efforts to open the Christian canon and add new scripture. This inevitably placed him at the apex of a hierarchy of Mormon religious authority.

To explore the foundations of Mormon religious authority, this chapter will introduce the idea of a Mormon prophet and demonstrate how the production of the Book of Mormon established Smith's claim to authority and how his ongoing revelation created a hospitable environment to maintain his prophetic authority hierarchically within his church.[2] This will lay the foundational concepts for how Smith developed and maintained a hierarchical role while developing a democratic priesthood. It will also set the scene for how an inclusive populist priesthood could eventually embrace a hierarchical ecclesiology, as demonstrated by Kathleen Flake's work.[3] This chapter will begin to define what a Mormon prophet looks like and how Joseph Smith established his prophethood and authority through the charismatic practices of communing with the dead and producing modern revelation and ancient scripture. It will establish that this kind a charisma founds authority and creates a space in which prophetic authority can exist charismatically without the grounding of an institution.

## Prophet of the Burned-Over District

During the first few years of his ministry in the late 1820s, the number of people who believed Joseph Smith was a prophet was limited to dozens instead of hundreds. Yet his religious authority rested on that prophetic identity and his ability to convince others of it. The fertile bed of Americans seeking refuge from sectarian squabbles and partisan conflict caused some to react positively to Smith's unique claims to authority.[4] He rose to power as a "voice from the dust," a prophet restoring ancient order and speaking directly for God.[5] He presented a confident sense of stability in a world of strife. His initial approach did not give poor men church authority or a democratic priestly order (these elements would arrive later); it offered a definitive, certain voice in an environment of competing voices.[6]

Smith found authority within a visionary world. His prophetic mission began three years after his powerful theophany, known as his 1820 "First Vision," in which he claimed to have seen Jesus Christ. This was a claim also made by the revivalist Charles Finney, who lived in Adams, New York, in 1821. Seeing Christ face-to-face was not unheard of in the Burned-over District. Revivalists questioned the Enlightenment preference for emotionless rationality as they expressed excitement for remarkable visionary experiences at revivals across New York State. Authors even began publishing their experiences for others, broadening the impact of the revivals. Joseph Rakestraw's *Extraordinary Instance of Divine Guidance* (1814), for example, marked these kinds of visionary impulses, and Orson Pratt's *Interesting Account of Several Remarkable Visions* (1840) described Joseph Smith's visionary claims in the 1820s and early 1830s in a similar vein. Individuals like Finney saw these experiences as callings to preach or testify, whereas Smith understood them as events that developed his authority to act as a prophet and even deliver new scripture.[7]

Visions of angels and even Christ did not create prophets out of other Christians and certainly did not lead to an open canon. Their visions were evidence for belief, packaged as signs of the restoration of Christ's New Testament church, but Protestants did not see them as evidence of prophethood. Visions generally guided revivalists back to the text of the Bible rather than toward following a modern prophet. So what made Smith different? How did Smith convince others, if they too were having visions, that he was a prophet?

When an open heaven was no longer a singular event, what shifted Smith into an exceptional religious space? The foundations of religious authority, formed by the relationship between religion and politics, had already allowed the public to hear the message of evangelicals and self-declared preachers. Yet the accepted religious boundaries of the nineteenth-century United States placed Smith's claims well outside the standards of Christian orthodoxy.[8]

The appeal to the authority of a prophet also appeared elsewhere in antebellum America. Jemima Wilkinson, Robert Matthews (Matthias), and Mother Ann Lee all represented a type of prophetic figure that emerged from the First and Second Great Awakenings, all of them basing their claims on a kind of messianic mysticism. If they did not directly teach that they were new embodiments of the Messiah, they did little to prevent others from claiming that about them. Their messages found an appreciative audience. As religion began to detach itself from civic authority after the Revolution, it was fueled by democratic zeal and shaped into a more independent kind of authority.[9] Democratic religious groups like Methodists and Baptists grew in the same soil but favored different approaches in order to attract individuals to their congregations.[10] Mistrust of politics and government, along with concern for an unknown future during the early republic, created an environment that refashioned religious authority. At the extreme end of the changes to religion were the prophets of the early nineteenth century, including Wilkinson and Matthews, who capitalized on this notion of being God's single representative on earth, presenting themselves as a solution to the dilemma of competing Christian voices. Matthews, for example, claimed to speak for God when he emerged as a prophet in New York at the same time that Smith began his ministry. Matthews reduced the power and authority of the Bible by teaching his adherents to stop praying and reading the scriptures in exchange for listening to and following his voice.[11]

In this context of visions and prophetic claims, Smith's close friend and supporter William W. Phelps pondered how a prophet would obtain validation. He wrote, "If you start a church with a prophet in it, everybody will be against you, as they were against Ann Lee, Joanna Southcoate, and Jemima Wilkinson."[12] Smith was not the first to claim that he was a prophet, nor would he be the last. Because he came from a family with no firm tradition in any denomination, no sect or local group saw him as a member of their congregation, nor did they lend him their support. The lack of either hereditary or denominational support then raises the question: how did Joseph Smith reinforce his sense of his calling?[13]

The most obvious difference between him and other prophets was the Book of Mormon and the open canon of Mormonism. Smith's claim to be a prophet was not exclusive, but the way that he came to be known as a prophet was that he rooted his claim in the production of the Book of Mormon. Smith's prophetic authority was intimately linked with his production of the Book of Mormon precisely because the narrative of that production—one that involved vision, revelation, purification, translation, and inspiration—witnessed a unique form of divine investiture that was formally recognized by Smith's followers.[14]

## The Practices of a Prophet: Producing the Book of Mormon

To produce another Bible, even a "Gold Bible" from ancient America, made Smith an impostor to many, but to his followers, it made him a prophet. Smith's claim to be a prophet was bolstered by supporting narratives about the recovery and translation of gold plates to produce the text of the Book of Mormon, including supposed interaction with an angel and the retrieval of an ancient record. The possession of gold plates in itself functioned as a supporting narrative for his claims. Smith did not simply act like a prophet: he used material implements to bind himself successfully to a perceived ancient world from which he produced an ancient text.

One can find Smith's first claim to authority within a narrative about an ancient Book of Mormon prophet named Moroni, who visited Smith to offer him power and authority to bring forth a translation of the Book of Mormon.[15] If the translated text were not persuasive enough to outsiders, Smith's claim to have been visited by a long-dead character in the Book of Mormon, appearing as a resurrected being, reinforced the book's authenticity—and his own prophetic importance. One of Smith's earliest revelations explained that Moroni "inspired him from on high and gave unto him power." Smith's revelation states, "God visited [Joseph Smith] by an holy angel." This angel gave Smith "commandments which inspired him from on high, and gave unto him power, by the means of which was before prepared that he should translate a book."[16] Smith described this power as the "gift and power of God" in the preface of the Book of Mormon.[17]

From these records, it is clear that the angel intended to empower and authorize Smith, not simply inspire him to be good or faithful. In one of the earliest accounts describing Smith's angelic visits, a local Palmyra newspaper, the *Palmyra Freeman*, described the exchange between Smith and the angel who transferred the gold plates into his possession. The anti-Masonic editor, Jonathan Hadley, had spoken directly to Smith in the summer of 1829 and given a rare contemporary reaction to Smith's claims. He wrote that Smith "reported that he had been visited in a dream by the spirit of the Almighty [Moroni], and informed that in a certain hill in that town, was deposited this Golden Bible, containing an ancient record of *divine nature and origin*."[18] To Hadley, Smith's claim that he retrieved an ancient record from an angel was preposterous and worth reporting to the public. Smith's earliest claim to authority here invokes "the spirit of the Almighty," who transferred the plates into his possession. The physical plates (whose material presence gestures toward notions of proof and logic so common to the Enlightenment) pointed toward the supernatural delivery and their "divine nature." Hadley declared, "It was said that the leaves of the Bible were plates of gold about eight inches long, six wide, and one eighth of an inch thick, on which were engraved characters or hieroglyphics."[19] Hadley's description of the material reality of the plates represents the way in which Smith cultivated his credibility: if the plates physically existed, then the angel transferred them into Smith's possession, thus marking Smith as one empowered or authorized to receive such a record via divine direction.

The immaterial angelic visit became a physical reality within Smith's story. In 1839 Joseph Smith described a far more elaborate exchange, in which he met with Moroni once every year for four years.[20] In that later account, Smith emphasized the physical reality of the ancient prophet, now an angelic being with physical features: "His hands were naked and his arms also a little above the wrist. . . . His head and neck were also bare. I could discover that he had no other clothing on but this robe as it was open so that I could see in his bosom."[21] While the 1829 version had Moroni appearing to Smith only as a spirit in a dream, Smith's 1839 account is enmeshed within an increasingly material reality. This contrasts with Finney, who had originally described his own vision as being "face to face" but later decided that the vision occurred only in "a mental state."[22] Smith insisted instead that an ancient prophet stood before him, the same prophet (later described in the Book of Mormon) who buried the ancient record more than fifteen hundred years earlier for him to uncover. Smith's 1839 history explains that Moroni directed him to the spot where "under a stone of considerable size, lay the plates deposited in a stone box," which also contained a sacred relic similar to the Urim and Thummim of the Old Testament.[23]

The location of these events held significance. Many in the United States believed their country was a providential place, selected for divine purposes.[24] Joseph Smith likewise believed that the New York landscape itself held an abundance of ancient artifacts that individuals could access in the soil.[25] Some conjectured that Native American populations originated from ancient Israel, an idea disseminated by preachers from the earliest European explorers through the nineteenth century.[26] Even as some in the educated classes began to challenge this theory, scholars at the American Philosophical Society eagerly compared Native American characters to various European languages, Egyptian, and even Hebrew.[27] Smith added a potential physical reality to this idea, quite literally materializing it as he elaborated on the engrained belief in America. To pull an ancient Christian record from the ground would be exhilarating in the sense that it supported a belief already generally established among the US populace.

Like a royal coronation, the plates and the Urim and Thummim crowned Smith as a religious leader. Smith's claim to be a prophet, prior to the publication of the Book of Mormon, rested firmly on the idea that an ancient American prophet had visited him to deliver physical artifacts buried by an exterminated people. As Hadley wrote in 1829, Smith claimed that the plates were "divine in nature and origin," and by such investiture, God sanctioned Smith, "ordained" by way of the physical exchange that occurred between him and the angel God sent.[28] Smith continued to connect his practical world of religious objects to the miraculous metaphysical world of religion. The four years he spent meeting with the angel Moroni in order to prepare to retrieve the plates overlapped with his nocturnal money-digging pursuits, assisted by his seer stones, and Smith drew on these experiences in order to frame and formulate his translation process. Even though the religious elite frowned on folk magic, divining, and money digging, those in the agrarian and lower classes often saw these activities as religious and even associated them with Christian expressions of devotion. The folklore of divining was often linked to the miracles of the Bible, further providing Smith with a foundation to establish himself as a gifted prophet.[29]

Smith's seer stones became a sign of his religious authority, in part from the way he named them: Urim and Thummim held a specific relationship with priestly ordination and authority in that they represented the high priest in the Old Testament. The bases for Smith's claims to authority were far from the rational systems developed within the minds of the clergy who attended the increasing number of seminaries throughout the United States. Rather, Smith tried to identify himself through a nineteenth-century reflection of the Old Testament's high priestly religious material culture. Smith's tools were only as valuable as the religious system he attached them to. The plates defined the purpose of the stones and the stones the purpose of the plates—a mutually reinforcing relationship that simultaneously buttressed Smith's emerging identity as a prophet. In this sense, Smith transformed his previous economic use of seer stones as tools for money digging by shifting his association with them to the sphere of biblical authority and priestly ordination.

The process of translating the Book of Mormon also provided Smith a narrative of prophetic authority. As Moroni placed the seer stone interpreters into Smith's possession, he indicated that God would give Smith the power to use them during the translation.[30] That power from God made Smith a prophet. Those closest to him observed his strange methods and believed he was laboring under some kind of divine power. Emma Smith, his wife, remembered that "day after day" he sat "with his face buried in his hat [to block out the light], with the stone in it, and dictating hour after hour with nothing between us." For hours and days at a time, explained Emma, Smith dictated concepts and ideas that she claimed he could have only read from a book, yet he "had neither manuscript nor book to read from." Each day when they would resume the translation, Smith would "begin where he had left off, without either seeing the manuscript or having any portion of it read to him."[31]

As Emma witnessed, Smith performed within an oracular space, defined by his gift to see words on the stones, without reference to books or a manuscript. The content described as appearing on the stones created a new, meaningful relationship between the plates and Smith. It was the dictation process itself—the simple act of reading words off the seer stone—that presented the most powerful evidence to believers that Smith had an extraordinary prophetic gift. With the gold plates covered with a cloth or in a box, Smith got down to business as a seer and prophet without the plates. He spent months uttering words he supposedly saw illuminated on the seer stones, from early 1828 to the spring of 1829, to five individual scribes.[32] Those who left a record of the translation marveled at the process. Oliver Cowdery, Smith's primary scribe, explained that it was a time "never to be forgotten," stating, "Day after day I continued, uninterrupted, to write from his mouth, as he translated."[33] Without the seemingly impossible (and thus miraculous) process of translation and the context of Smith's relationship to specific items as having an angelic provenance, the seer stones may have been just rocks, the plates fabricated, and Smith an imposter. Yet together they empowered him as a young prophet and confirmed his prophetic calling to those who saw these tangible pieces of evidence as both something distinctly new in the tradition of US religious history and old in their stated connection to Israel itself.

Finally, the gold plates themselves demonstrated Smith's authoritative claims. The translation process legitimized the gold plates, even though they remained a hidden object; they were rarely used or even kept in the same room with Smith when he translated them through the seer stones.[34] Because the translated words presumably appeared on the seer stones, translation could occur via the seer stones while the plates remained apart. But the mere fact of the gold plates themselves instilled confidence in Smith and his scribes that the text appearing on the stones was truly from an ancient record. As Ann Taves argues, even if they were not ancient, they still became sacred and represented something deeply important to Mormonism.[35] Without the translation, the plates were a lump of metal, lifted and hefted by others, yet in context the plates became the object of inspiration—the proof of prophethood—that prompted a belief in the historical reality of the Book of Mormon text. Without the plates, the text of the Book of Mormon was nothing more than modern revelation, but the combination of the translated text, the plates, and the seer stones elevated all three, placing them in a complex relationship that knit the sacred word with an earthly physical reality.

Nevertheless, the text of the Book of Mormon itself provided the most substantial defense of Smith's authoritative claims, offering an ancient narrative that describes why Smith was a prophet. In explicit terms, the Book of Mormon designates prophethood in the same way that it describes Smith: as a seer and a translator. It states that "a seer is a revelator and a prophet also; and a gift which is greater can no man have, except he should possess the power of God, which no man can; yet a man may have great power given him from God."[36] Like the testimonies of Smith's scribes, who witnessed the translation process, the Book of Mormon also equated seemingly distinct terms: the role of seer and revelator *is* the role of a prophet, according to the text. The prophetic authority here was threefold: first, the Book of Mormon declared that the person who possessed the seer stones "is called a seer, after the manner of old times"; second, it asserted that Smith was a literal descendant of the patriarchs of old; and third, it claimed that he possessed the Nephite interpreters who were prepared specifically for him, the prophet who would bring forth the Book of Mormon.[37]

The connection between Joseph Smith and the narrative is explicit in the text of the Book of Mormon itself. In 1835 Smith printed one of his revelations that pointed directly to the Book of Mormon as the source from which to explain the origins of the Book of Mormon interpreters or seer stones.[38] These passages in the book also clarified the relationship between the stones and prophets, foreshadowing Smith's specific use of the seer stones in a process of recovery, understanding, and insight. The stones functioned as mediators through which the process of translation occurred, linking past and present peoples together. The record of this provenance emphasized a sense of connection that was both historical and personal. Declared to be a literal descendant of Joseph of Egypt, Smith could inherit the role of Moses during the last days. Expounding on the resemblance between Moses and Smith as prophets, the Book of Mormon goes on to explain, "I will write unto him my law, by the finger of mine own hand [like Moses's tablets and referencing Smith's seer stones]; and I will make a spokesman for him."[39]

No longer was Smith's practice and possession of the stones the only evidence for his divine calling and authority—the text of the Book of Mormon became a scripture that would endure far beyond his own life. The text forged a new relationship between the translation process, the seer stones, and Smith's prophetic role. This relationship inaugurated, through a mutually reinforcing set of overlapping claims to legitimacy, a concept of prophetic authority in which authority emerged as something with ties to both a material world (e.g., seer stones) and a spiritual one (e.g., revelation). As a religious figure he was not providing the sureness of established orthodoxy in a Protestant nation, but his embrace of prophethood attracted seekers nonetheless.

## Open Canon and the Authority of Joseph Smith's Revelations

The Book of Mormon added to Joseph Smith's authority in yet another way, because its presence demonstrated that he was troubling the waters of how canon would be defined. Like Catholics who "threatened to breach the canonical borders," Joseph Smith expanded the biblical canon by adding the Book of Mormon as another piece of scripture.[40] The Book of Mormon was functionally similar to the addition of the Apocrypha in the Protestant canon, within its liminal nature. No one would continue to add chapters to the Book of Mormon, but Smith expanded the boundaries by delivering authoritative scripture in the form of other revelations that showed very few signs of coming to an end. By opening the canon (again and again) and departing from the principles found in creedal religion, Smith created a different kind of authoritative voice. His translations and ongoing revelations created an alternative way of framing ecclesiastical leadership.[41] If the canon was closed, authority was framed more interpretively within the pages of the Bible, yet when it was open Smith as prophet controlled at least some of the ways of knowing belief by adding definitive statements about authority within his new scripture.

Authority is both necessary for and inherent in maintaining an open canon, especially if one can convince others that he or she is the only person authorized to deliver the word of God. An open canon also can threaten the authoritative clerical interpretation of the Bible, which for many of Smith's early followers was part of the appeal: the heavens were declared open, and a prophet had been chosen to reveal God's new words. Smith's appeal to authority found an eager audience among Americans who were interested in prophetic claims that were tied directly to the Bible. This revealed the fault lines of tension about religious authority in the antebellum era, when sectarian revivalism threatened to undermine the authority of established Protestant clergy to govern the landscape of theology and religious practice. Some US Protestants embraced a closed canon in order to strengthen their rejection of revival enthusiasm. Clergy such as Presbyterian minister John W. Nevin reacted to the fact that the Bible was becoming "a book dropped from the skies for all sorts of men to use their own way."[42] A Bible hermeneutic defined by the populist approach empowered individuals, quacks, and revivalists alike yet also emphasized that self-obtained certainty was available to common people in the early republic. Lay voices interpreting the Bible commonly stood in stark contrast to the authoritative voice of the educated clergy. In Smith's case, he saw the itinerant preachers sowing more sectarian conflict, but he also lost respect for the absolute power of the traditional clergy. As a young teenager, Smith remembered turning to the Bible of his own accord, not to seek democratic religion but rather to discover definitive religious authority.[43] Smith sought something even more reliable and trustworthy than the voice of the clergy.[44]

His own revelations offered the authority he was seeking, while also maintaining the authority of the Bible. Joseph Smith's approach depended on the Bible as a foundational text, but as he garnered answers from his own revelations, he added to or changed the Bible. This connection with the Bible was attractive to some but seemed dangerous to others. Local Palmyrians publicly denounced Smith's new scripture, regardless of their own affinity for religious authority. Abner Cole juxtaposed the publication of Smith's "gold bible" with the potentially canon-expanding publishing endeavors of itinerant preacher Lorenzo Dow, whose autobiography was one of the bestselling books in the United States, second to the Bible. Maintaining a reductionist approach to canon, Cole categorized such publications as "priestcraft."[45] Further satirizing the idea of additional scripture beyond the Bible, Cole mocked: "The 'Gold Bible' is fast gaining *credit*; the *rapid spread* of Islamism was no *touch* to it!" Cole's criticisms were direct and centered on an absolute opposition to a democratic biblical hermeneutic that legitimized an open canon.

Like Cole, many others saw Smith's new revelations as a sign of his imposture and viewed him as no different from others like him in the past.[46] Jonathan Hadley declared, "The Public should not be imposed upon by this work [The Book of Mormon], pronounced as it is, by its proselytes, to be superior in style, and more advantageous to mankind, than the Holy Bible!"[47] Even the Shakers, with whom the Mormons interacted, grounded their movement on immediate revelation.[48] Like the Mormons, their doctrine of revelation differed sharply from the Protestant clergy that surrounded them. Smith reserved official revelation for the Mormon community to be given authoritatively by him alone. He did, however, encourage his followers to seek their own personal revelation and considered such individual spiritual experiences to be important, or even necessary, to a truly converted life. The idea of revelation empowered Protestants and was not unique to Smith's religion. As the Bible was being interpreted by the masses, the idea of personal revelation appealed to the common Christian. Mormon and Shaker revelations often arrived via ecstatic experience and even personal spiritual insights, along with miracles intended for specific individuals. The result was controlled, but not far afield from the experiential revivalism. Smith's earliest revelations were seen by believers as immediate commandments of God that demanded compliance. The fact that they were delivered in the first-person voice of God after the summer of 1828 only enhanced their divine authority.

Yet they were also highly personal. During the earliest years of his ministry, Smith only dictated authoritative revelations to his closest friends and family. Eventually, he published his revelations to the world (first as the Book of Commandments [1833] and then as the Doctrine and Covenants [1835]), but they were originally recorded as Smith sat in front of his family. The setting is important: those closest to him knew Smith was gifted or spiritually inclined, but, significantly, they also were familiar with his human frailty and imperfections. Still, they believed he spoke for God when he was divinely directed to do so. The firm commandments that Smith delivered appeared to be dictatorial, especially when they were given in Kirtland, Ohio, in 1832 to govern his followers in Independence, Missouri, hundreds of miles away. Adherents to the revelations understood them not as Smith's own voice or will; rather, Smith was simply a vessel of divine investiture. The recipients of Smith's revelations had immediate and compliant responses to his commandments, which emerged as if he were reading directly from a well-established biblical text like the King James Bible.[49]

In the winter of 1829, sitting across the table from Joseph Smith Sr., his father, Smith dictated the word of God that reflected both the Gospel of John and passages from Isaiah.[50] That event convinced Smith Sr. that his son had the gift of revelation.[51] Smith Jr. did not ordain his father as a clergyman during this 1829 revelation, but God *did* call Joseph Smith Sr. to the work with apocalyptic urgency: "if ye have desires to serve God ye are called to the work for behold the field is white already to harvest."[52] The revelation ended with a clear reference to the first chapter of 2 Peter. Joseph Smith Sr. not only embraced the revelation but also made a convert of Oliver Cowdery, who was staying at his house in Palmyra and would soon devote months of his life to helping Smith translate the Book of Mormon.[53]

Within the next two years, numerous copies of Smith's revelation to Joseph Smith Sr. were made, including the earliest manuscript copy, which was bundled with eight other revelations by Edward Partridge in 1830.[54] Many of Smith's revelations remained in manuscript form for years, folded and kept in the pockets and journals of believers, but still valued as scripture. Eventually, it would be published in multiple canonized editions of Mormon scripture (the Doctrine and Covenants), Joseph Smith's own published history, and the church's earliest newspaper.[55] Just as the scriptural cadence and thematic consistency of the language was received by individuals sitting across from Smith in a domestic setting, the biblical resonance of the canonized revelations invited listeners to demonstrate faith and belief, immediately taking the revelations as seriously as the Bible. The revelations were in every sense commandments for both major and minor initiatives that would form the theology and structure of Smith's restoration.

Smith's revelations were firm and in the voice of God. In March 1829, Martin Harris quickly made his way to Harmony, Pennsylvania, under the threat of a lawsuit for fraudulently claiming Smith had gold plates when he had never actually seen them.[56] Harris recalled that "In March [1829] the People Rose up & united against the Work gathering testimoney against the Plates & Said they had testimony Enough & if I did not Put Joseph in Jail ["& his father" inserted later] for Deseption they Would me."[57] When Harris arrived, Smith inquired of God and received an authoritative answer to Harris's request to see the gold plates. It stated, "I, the Lord, am God . . . and you have no power over them [the plates] except I grant it unto you."[58] Apparently sitting across the table from Smith, Harris listened to Smith's voice ring out the words of God, commanding obedience and silencing Harris's incessant worry about the possible lawsuit. Even though Harris traveled to Harmony, Pennsylvania, to see the plates, the revelation refused to acquiesce until he had proven his obedience and done his part to build the kingdom of God.

It was as if Harris had stood before the Almighty himself. The words of God were delivered to Harris only after they had been embodied by Smith. Like the gold plates and Smith's seer stones, Smith himself became and embodied the concept of prophet in a very real and physical sense. Experiences such as this demonstrate how Smith's ministry required an explicit connection between heaven and earth. His message about the Book of Mormon translation, open canon, and continuing revelation demanded a material connection in these physical forms. This would lead increasingly toward the importance of the rituals later instituted, compelled by Smith's authoritative voice as the mouth of Christ.

Joseph Smith made his prophethood real by materializing the divine in gestures that reached back to the ancient world, offering physical evidence as a reason to believe in his revelations. Such actions were particularly salient to his audience in the early nineteenth century. The French natural philosopher Georges Cuvier (1769–1832) had redefined the natural world through a careful analysis of ancient shards of buried bones. His new comparative anatomy uncovered a lost world of extinct animals at the beginning of the nineteenth century, known only through archaeology and the reconstruction of ancient bones.[59] Evidence from the natural world was convincing. Though natural history museums like John Hunter's massive collection in London were multiplying, few people saw the bones of these ancient creatures. Still, their existence and entrance into popular understanding marked the creation of whole new worldview.[60] With the idea of evidence of this lost world in mind, Smith produced ancient plates and gathered witnesses to experience them. Three select witnesses claimed to have seen them along with relics (a sword, the Urim and Thummim, a compass, and a breastplate) that provided physical representations of the supposed peoples described within the text of the Book of Mormon.[61] These items acted as the material voices of a forgotten world speaking from the dust. Mormonism may have lacked the aural intensity available in the evangelical ecstatic experience, but, when considered from a material perspective, it presented a veritable cacophony of physical voices, especially when God's voice was embodied within Smith himself.

This kind of physical embodiment attracted a specific kind of believer, people who were devoted to the Bible and a serious study of its contents. These Christians were highly influenced by rationalism and the evidence it produced. Smith tied his authority to visionary experiences, sacred objects, and heavenly messengers to underscore this authority. Like Moses's witness of the burning bush, Smith's earliest revelations were delivered to him during tangible theophany. His first recorded revelation,[62] for example, drew together the power of the Urim and Thummim, angelic visitation, and the delivery of God's word to him personally.[63] After losing the interpreters for nearly a month in 1828,[64] Smith explained that "I was walking out a little distance [from my home in Harmony, Pennsylvania], when Behold the former heavenly messenger appeared and handed to me the Urim and Thummim again."[65] Like Moroni's visits to Joseph Smith from 1823 to 1827, angelic guidance again placed the interpreters into his hands.[66] Once Smith was given the interpreters—physical objects that represented his authority—he "enquired of the Lord through them" in order to see the text of the revelation.[67] Smith's revelations were more than just text; they were visions, angelic experiences, physical expressions, embodied realities, all of which were demonstrated alongside and through objects.

These tangible objects and experiences were important to Smith in the construction of his prophetic mission. When he held the ancient relics in his hands, he possessed the authority of God, just as Cuvier's influence was only as convincing as the fossils in his possession. Like Cuvier, Smith offered his audience reasons to believe in an unseen world. Smith was operating in a religious culture emerging from the Enlightenment that held an expectation of proof yet also retained belief in the supernatural. Experiential religion was convincing to revivalists. Preachers, for example, wanted to be called by God to the work. They all sought an experience that confirmed they had been called to preach.[68] And so it is no surprise that, given the surrounding cultural expectations of and general high value placed on evidence, Smith found confidence in his experience through the physical objects that made his experience real, grounding on an earthly, physical plane what would otherwise be another ecstatic witness. Once Smith was given the interpreters, revelation began to flow again. The physical nature of the exchange represented, to believers, Smith's relationship with God and God's willingness to send his messengers to the young prophet. To see and feel was to believe. Smith claimed the impossible, offering an irrational experience to rational people and then backing the irrational with the obstinately tangible.

## Charismatic Prophet to Democratic Priesthood

Smith (within his prophetic role) and his revelations are inseparable parts of early Mormonism's religious authority. They also formed the heart of the Protestant complaint against Mormonism. Smith's revelations offered a rational approach to religious knowledge via both experiential and intellectual paths, which appealed to religious seekers who were skeptical of the overly emotional revivalists and sectarians yet interested in experiential rationalism. Just as some of the public had experiential knowledge of Cuvier's recovery and possession of the bones of extinct animals, many new Mormon converts were open to the possibility that Smith really possessed gold plates and the biblical Urim and Thummim. The connection between rational materialism and Smith's claim to divine investiture convinced radical seekers as they heard God's voice reverberate from Smith's mouth.

Smith's religious movement began to surge under his authoritative voice. Supernatural experiences and prophetic claims had become a protected realm under which Smith's kingdom of God could develop. The Book of Mormon ushered in the restoration of ancient Israel, both spiritually and physically, and Smith's prophetic voice was established to govern that kingdom. This chapter has demonstrated how a small religious movement like Mormonism could take root in antebellum America and reveal signs of independent religious authority and hierarchy. Smith's scripture and the experiences that produced it cannot be underestimated as the foundations on which Mormonism's hierarchical authority and tradition of prophethood rest. His kingdom would soon be established with a lay priesthood and a democratic tone, but it would also be subject to the authoritarian rule of his revelations and leadership. Smith relied on the foundations he had already established in cementing his prophetic position—an open canon of continuing revelation for the future, tied to ancient relics and scriptural authority from the past to create a Mormon priesthood. The order of priesthood Smith was about to establish can be characterized as a symptom of a deeper, more fundamental sense of religious authority found not in ecclesiastic structure but rather in his revelations and the authority he possessed. Even with his populist appeal to antebellum Americans, his charismatic nature and unorthodox ability to produce new authoritative scripture not only enabled his hierarchic status to emerge but in reality encouraged it to thrive.

# 2

# Authority, Baptism, and Angelic Restoration

As Smith's revelatory voice resonated with early followers, he increased his authority through the establishment of an organized priesthood and church. The foundations of this church were solidified by specific claims to authority that were developmentally constructed and malleable. As Smith faced the pressures of sectarian strife and US politics, not to mention geographical itinerancy and the inevitable pains of change and growth, his revelations and restoration narratives emerged to create and balance his authority within the church, empowering others in leadership while maintaining his prophetic voice. It was through these developments that the stability of Mormon authority and paradoxical concept of democratic hierarchy emerged. After his church was established, Smith's movement perpetuated a lay priesthood and a community of saints who eventually embraced a theology that built them into gods. As a result, Smith's restorations have generally been viewed as empowerments of the lay member. As true as that may be, it underemphasizes the fact that each narrative depended on Smith's growing authority, and each imbued him with divine power to administer, govern, and change all the priesthood orders and church governance. The relationship between prophet, priesthood, and church of the Mormon democratic hierarchy enabled it to survive as a quintessential religious other.

This chapter shows how the evolving narrative about Smith receiving the power to baptize sheds light on his authoritative role in Mormonism. Analyzing Mormon baptism is a great first example of how Smith used his prophetic voice to create religious authority, in which he connected himself to God experientially, defined the meaning of baptism through the restoration scripture of the Book of Mormon, and built an influential restoration narrative in which a heavenly figure directly conferred the authority to baptize. Smith would eventually claim that his authority derived from a direct, divine source: angels, as understood through his revelations. The angels who authorized him were not, this time, those with an ancient American past like Moroni, but rather beings taken from the familiar New Testament narrative. Within this context of restoration, baptismal authority was first tied to a narrative involving John the Baptist, from which began Smith's reconstruction of Christ's ancient church. The example of how Smith received the authority to baptize demonstrates how his prophetic voice began to build a distinct Mormon religious authority almost immediately. His hierarchical position was bolstered and he quickly offered his authority to lay believers, making the first step toward a democratic hierarchy.

## Baptism and the Question of Religious Authority

Baptism was the first ritual test case to mark Smith's new authority over saving ordinances. In Protestant America, baptism was valued and performed more consistently than other sacraments practiced by Roman Catholics and Orthodox churches, yet in Smith's eyes baptism was more than just a sign of conversion or belief: it was an indispensable salvific act that connected believers to an everlasting Mormon covenant. It was efficacious and binding, but only as far as Mormons performed it under the religious authority that Smith claimed to possess. To Smith and his early converts, sacramental ordinances identified Mormonism as a church that offered salvation to humankind and bound individuals to Christ.[1]

Baptism initiated and evidenced a kind of church citizenship that Americans resonated with and therefore was a highly debated and deeply important subject to churches in the antebellum America. As Baptist churches grew at an unprecedented rate in the early nineteenth century, their congregational nature created diversity of opinion even in their own ranks over baptism. Questions arose over the mode and manner of baptism: Should it occur by immersion or sprinkling? Was infant baptism permissible, or was it a rite for adult believers only? Christians also parsed its theological meaning and purpose: did baptism actually confer salvation, or was it only an outward sign of an inward reality? Other debates centered on baptismal practices such as clothing and prayer, or whether individuals baptized in one congregation should be accepted in another congregation.[2]

At the heart of all these questions about baptism lay the larger issue of authority. The idea of churches accepting or rejecting the baptisms of other churches or even sharply disagreeing over the mode of baptism itself shaped religious communities by giving them power to include or exclude individuals and other churches. To restorationist Alexander Campbell, the authority of baptism rested on individual freedom. He believed that no church could baptize "by proxy, or upon another person's confession." If parents baptized their children without the children's consent, it was despotism of the worst kind. Campbell also contended sharply against Presbyterian minister John Walker, arguing that state religions stripped the personal nature of baptism from the individual's hands much in the manner of a parent baptizing an infant. This democratic tone, however, did not deny baptism its inherent authority: through baptism, churches could create a community or even the kingdom of God.[3]

In the context of these ongoing debates about authority and baptism, Joseph Smith began a religious movement. Smith's own ideas on religious authority took root amid a myriad of questions about baptism alongside his need to establish his own position within the plurality of churches. Proclaiming Mormonism's unique authority to perform baptisms functioned to unify the early movement and enable it to define itself against the claims of other churches. One popular Methodist minister from Kirtland, Ohio, Ezra Booth, recognized that baptism successfully differentiated Mormonism from the religions around it. Booth joined the Mormons after witnessing Smith's supposedly miraculous healing of a young woman's decrepit arm.[4] He quickly rose through the ranks of the new religion and was ordained a high priest in the summer of 1831.[5] Booth later wrote, "The Mormonite preachers go forth proclaiming repentance and baptism for the remission of sins. . . . The form of baptism is similar to other orders; only it is prefaced with—'having authority given me of Jesus Christ.'"[6] Booth recognized that baptism revolved around issues of authority, but he separated Mormonism from other churches precisely because of Mormons' claims of provenance: Mormons asserted that their authority came directly from Christ and notably not a community of believers, the episcopacy, or the pope.

Booth focused on demonstrating precisely *how* the Mormon baptism differed from the surrounding religious practices. By examining Smith's unique claim to perform baptisms by the authority of Christ, we can understand more clearly how he attempted to garner religious authority through the rite of baptism. Smith's baptismal emphasis differed from that of other Christians. Evangelicals variously used baptism as an expression of individual belief or conversion, and Baptists in particular distanced baptism from formal priesthood authority. The emergence of baptism in Mormonism (in May 1829), in contrast, originally accentuated the authority required to perform the initiation rite. This authority would prove to be fertile ground for the development of a robust priesthood theology within Mormonism. The ordinance of baptism was important: baptism became a rite of passage that offered citizenship in the kingdom of God and membership within the earthly incarnation of that kingdom, the church. But baptism's importance also stemmed from the way it delineated exactly who had the authority to be that kingdom's gatekeepers. It was through religious ordinances that Smith made his first exclusionary claims to religious authority. Since baptism was required as an entry point to membership in the kingdom, the performance of that rite naturally became a source of authority for the lay clergy.

Like most restorationists, Smith embraced a Protestant sense of succession claims to authority in which he eventually articulated a break in other claims to authority. One of Smith's later revelations would condemn the authority of all other churches to baptize, declaring, "Ye cannot enter in at the straight gait by the law of Moses, neither by your dead works, for it is because of your dead works that I have caused this last covenant and this church to be built up unto me."[7] Smith's claim to exclusivity of authority and saving ordinances chafed at contemporary restorationists. About Smith's argument that no other church possessed the authority to baptize, Thomas Campbell complained, "Re-baptizing believers is making void the ordinance of Christ." He exclaimed that he would "expose the anti-scriptural assertion, that there has been none duly authorized to administer baptism" outside of the Mormon priesthood.[8]

Requiring rebaptism effectively excluded all other religious authority and placed salvation in the hands of the lay Mormon clergy. Years later, Orson Pratt explained, "In the early days of this Church there were certain persons, belonging to the Baptist denomination, very moral and no doubt as good people as you could find anywhere, who came, saying they believed in the Book of Mormon, and that they had been baptized into the Baptist Church, and they wished to come into our Church," but they had no intention of being baptized by Mormon clergy. "This is the reason why the Lord commanded this people—the Latter-day Saints—to re-baptize all persons who come to them professing to have been baptized before."[9]

In Smith's new religious movement, the issue of who would be qualified to perform baptisms pushed larger questions of authority into the foreground. Though some historians have misidentified Smith's lay priesthood order with a strictly democratic sentiment, it was a hierarchical democracy with compartmentalized religious authority: not all Mormon men could baptize. Even before Smith established a church, he created a lay clergy in 1829 that his revelations defined hierarchically by the rituals that each officer could perform.[10] Clergy in other churches performed baptisms as an expression of faith, though some did believe that the rite was necessary to return to

God. Smith's rite of baptism, however, was required to cleanse and save, and thus those able to perform baptism filled an essential (and authoritative) role in the salvation of the Mormon people. This claim to authority, however, depended solidly on a specific and legitimized mode of delivery for the authority: Smith explicitly did not link his authority to a line of popes or bishops, nor did he endorse the priesthood of all believers. The authority Smith inhabited straddled an interesting site of tension between the new and the old, augmented by exclusive scripture, especially the Book of Mormon.

## Baptism, Authority, and the Book of Mormon

As we saw in chapter 1, Smith differed from other restorationists in antebellum America by turning not just to the Bible or to Christian history to restore ancient baptismal rites, but to his own open canon: the Book of Mormon and his own revelations. Without formal creed and liturgy, the ordinance of baptism required a distinct written context for believers to understand what to do and why. This context was found in the Book of Mormon, which contained strong, definitive statements on the purpose and performance of the ordinance and apparently served as an initial guide in instituting baptism as a rite of salvation. Smith used the Bible as an authoritative source for contextualizing baptism, but it was the Book of Mormon that initially established the tradition in the Mormon faith. This source was important because the Book of Mormon itself was an example of lost Israel, or remnant Israel, establishing and maintaining the covenant through baptism.

Under the assumption that baptism was no longer efficacious in the hands of Protestants, the Book of Mormon and Smith's revelations included a pattern for restoration.[11] According to the historical record, Smith became deeply interested in the ordinance of baptism—and the authority to perform it—by the spring of 1829.[12] Just days after he began dictating the translation of the Book of Mormon to Oliver Cowdery, the text began to refer to baptism frequently. For example, it was Cowdery who recorded in the Book of Mormon's original manuscript "Come and go forth, and show unto your God that ye are willing to repent of your sins and enter in to a covenant with him to keep his commandments, and witness it unto him this day by going into the waters of baptism."[13] The divine declaration was clear: citizenship in God's kingdom followed baptism. Day after day as they worked through this section of the translation, Smith and Cowdery produced a text focused on the creation of churches and the need for baptism.[14] The text unequivocally clarified "that whosoever did not belong to the church who repented of their sins were baptized unto repentance, and were received into the church."[15] Along with associating baptism with membership in God's church, the Book of Mormon text explicitly bound the ordinance of baptism with an ecclesiastical ministry. The prophet Nephi, for example, "ordained . . . men unto this ministry that all such as should come unto them should be baptized with water."[16]

Even before Smith established a church or began baptizing, then, the text of the Book of Mormon provided him with a blueprint for how to gain legitimate citizenship in the kingdom of God. As part of the translation process, Smith repeatedly dictated the necessity of baptism, as Cowdery recalled, "day after day" in an "uninterrupted" stream of baptismal narratives that arrived over the course of six weeks from early April to mid-May of 1829.[17] Analyzing the narrative of the Book of Mormon manuscript from the book of Alma to the ministry of Christ in 3 Nephi, Smith likely proclaimed the necessity of baptism nearly every day in April and May.[18] The earliest dictated passages explained that Smith and Cowdery needed divine authority and even provided an example of how they could baptize themselves without any previously authorized individuals there to perform the rite.[19]

Other passages about baptism also centered on questions of religious authority. Before the middle of May, Smith had dictated the Book of Mormon narrative of Christ's postresurrection American ministry, in which Christ bestows the power to baptize on his chosen disciples. Cowdery recorded in the manuscript that Christ spoke to his prophet Nephi: "I give unto you power that ye shall baptize this people when I am again ascended into heaven. And again the Lord called others, and said unto them likewise; and he gave unto them power to baptize. And he said unto them: on this wise shall ye baptize."[20] Christ gave Nephi and others power to baptize and declared that they were the only people to whom he had transmitted this authority.

Christ did not offer a detailed explanation of this power that he offered his disciples, but the term seemed to be synonymous with authority. He offered his divine approval, given only to selected individuals who were then empowered to perform ordinances. The focus of the passage was not on an ecclesiastical order or priesthood—in fact, the word *priesthood* is not mentioned at all—or on the offices of those who were given that power. It was only after Christ established his church, an action described later in the translation, that the supposed compilers of the gold plates associated this power with specific church offices. So, to Smith, the nexus of authority described in the text centered on questions of legitimate performance of an ordinance rather than questions of structure and organization. The book's focus on performance over structure helps to explain Smith's own use of narrative performance as a site for the ongoing construction of priesthood authority. The external application of an ecclesiastical power structure would have foreclosed future flexibility—something that, in Smith's open heavens theology, was unintelligible. By instead grounding priesthood authority within an ongoing narrative performance, Smith effectively constructed a notion of authority that managed to be both exclusive and adaptable.

That adaptability was needed soon. After weeks of translation, both Smith and Oliver Cowdery believed that they needed special authority to perform baptisms.[21] Smith apparently understood that the power to baptize was distinct from his authority to speak for God or the gift to translate. Cowdery explained, "After writing the account given of the Saviour's ministry . . . it was easily to be seen . . . none had authority from God to administer the ordinances of the gospel."[22] What is interesting to note here is that Smith did not *assume* the authority to baptize. Rather, he *constructed* that authority through complex restoration narratives in which God delivered and authorized his power, a pattern that would hold true for future issues as well, such as the establishment of priesthood and apostleship. God may have chosen and sanctioned Smith as his prophet, according to believers, but that role did not automatically include the authority to baptize. Authority, then, was in a certain sense both particular—something composed of discrete, multiple parts—and organic—something structurally open to growth and expansion. Smith described this concept of authority throughout his life through the text of his revelations, to which he continually turned to for direction. It is important to understand that, for Smith, there was never a single event that gave him the completely realized authority of the priesthood. Rather, as described in a letter he wrote in 1842, this authority was provided "line upon line, precept upon precept; here a little, and there a little; giving us consolation by holding forth that which is to come, confirming our hope."[23]

The Book of Mormon was a vital part of that process, giving directions for the formation of ordinances and guiding early Mormon ritual practices as if it were a liturgical text. Though the ritual of baptism would be variously used and repeated in a number of forms—especially in healing—in the Mormon church, the origins of this particular ordinance center on short but important liturgical forms that emerged in 1829 from the pages of the Book of Mormon as revealed to Smith and Cowdery.[24] The narrative provided impetus and form, but it was Smith and Cowdery's own adoption and performance of the narrative that constructed the underlying authority for the rite itself, as well as its exclusionary status.

## Angelic Narratives and John the Baptist

The Book of Mormon was not the only instrument granting Smith and Cowdery the power to baptize; as their understanding grew, they also drew their authority from the heavens in the form of angelic messengers.[25] Remarkably, other individuals also claimed to see angels in this particular time and place. Richard Bushman argues that the Burned-over District's revivals were replete with stories of visions and appearances of heavenly beings. "Too often the visions justified a breach of the moral code or a sharp departure in doctrine," he explains. The only visions the clergy were willing to accept were those similar to Charles Finney's experience, which granted forgiveness, offered grace, and welcomed the believer as a follower of Christ.[26] Joseph Smith's angelic visitations were harder for clergy to swallow because they were wrapped in his claims to exclusive authority and prophetic responsibility. The authority granted by angels to Joseph Smith was exclusionary and claimed to have bypassed any clerical ordination.

Consider the previously discussed demarcation of Mormon baptism by Ezra Booth. Booth described the Mormon baptism as identical to other baptismal rites save for the verbal declaration by which Mormon priesthood holders called upon Christ's authority to perform the ordinance. Landmark Baptists created succession claims through their practice of baptism and community, while others claimed a succession of ordinations authorized them, all of which led back to the New Testament apostles. Smith, on the other hand, claimed to have received his authority from the heavens in a physical visitation that restored the legitimate power to baptize (exclusively) to him. Following his lead, early Mormons often preached that Christ had commissioned them through angelic visitation.

Once Mormon missionaries began sharing this belief more broadly, their exclusion of and disregard for other Christian sacraments quickly became a point of contention. Warren Isham, the proprietor and editor of a Painesville, Ohio, newspaper, the *Observer and Telegraph*, challenged the Church of Christ's authority to baptize in February 1831, making him one of the first to publish Smith's claims to the world. He questioned, "When did Smith [receive it]—and from whom did he receive the Ordinance?" Ostensibly informed, he wrote, "The ordinance originated with these men, and the authority found vested in them to the exclusion of all others."[27] Isham questioned their assertion that an angel gave Smith and Cowdery their authority and focused on the fact that they were not ordained by other clergymen or by an inner calling from God. Isham argued that their authority originated with Smith and Cowdery themselves, while they insisted the authority came from an angel.

Through emergent practices and by word of mouth, Smith and Cowdery had already established a restoration narrative that an angel had restored authority to them. In the fall of 1830, Oliver Cowdery and his missionary companions had found great success for the fledgling Mormon church among Sidney Rigdon's Ohio congregations of reformed Baptists. Within weeks,

Mormon missionaries had baptized Rigdon and more than one hundred of his followers, which alarmed numerous local residents and caused several newspapers to complain about the Mormons in print. Soon after the missionaries' arrival, the editor of the *Telegraph* in Painesville, Ohio, wrote that Oliver Cowdery had told him he had "seen Angels, and assisted in translating the plates." The editor explained that Cowdery "holds forth that the ordinances of the gospel have not been regularly administered since the days of the Apostles, till the said Smith and himself commenced the work."[28] The *Telegraph* recounted an early Mormon narrative of angelic restoration of the "ordinances of the gospel." Just weeks later, on December 7, 1830, the editor declared that Cowdery claimed "that he has credentials, written and signed by the hand of Jesus Christ, with whom he has personally conversed, and as such, said Cowdery claims that he and his associates are the only persons on earth who are qualified to administer in his name. . . . By this authority, they proclaim to the world" that those who are not baptized by them, "must be forever miserable."[29] The elements of the restoration narrative in place by the end of 1830, then, associated authority with baptism in a way that both excluded and delegitimized other Christian practitioners. It utilized legalistic language and visionary rhetoric with a unique, almost surgical precision in order to reinforce Smith's prophetic persona as a man not only inspired by the Holy Spirit but, like an Old Testament prophet, capable of interacting with heavenly beings here on earth. The combination proved equally inspiring and fearsome.

Over time, Smith's restoration narrative about the authority to baptize became more specific and more closely related to the New Testament. Though Cowdery and Smith claimed that an angel authorized them in 1829, there are no records acknowledging the event until they began to evangelize in 1830. It took even longer for them to begin to identify the angel who visited them. Upon Cowdery's return to Kirtland after retrieving a printing press from the East in the fall of 1833, records began appearing on the subject of the restoration of the power to baptize. Just days before Cowdery was chosen to be a member of the Kirtland high council, Smith declared on February 12, 1834, that he acted within his church position only by "the dignity of the office which had been conferred upon me by ministering of the Angel of God, by his own voice, and by the voice of the Church."[30] Smith built upon his statements on April 21, 1834, in a meeting at Norton, Ohio, where he "gave a relation of obtaining and translating the Book of Mormon, the revelation of the Priesthood of Aaron."[31] Smith's New Testament restoration of baptism had taken on an Old Testament form of priesthood by calling the authority the "priesthood of Aaron" (a concept that will be further discussed in subsequent chapters). Unfortunately, Cowdery, who recorded the minutes of that meeting, did not give any historical details, including the identity of the angel. The record emphasized the revelation of the priesthood without connecting the experience explicitly with an angel. In fact, calling it the priesthood of Aaron leaves the identity of the angel open to numerous possible biblical figures back to Aaron. In 1834, Smith was likely describing the origin of his authority by emphasizing his ability to receive the word of God through revelation and translation—modes of authority that were clearly connected with the 1829 angelic visit. But unless Smith was describing the 1829 visit as revelation, the angelic restoration of the authority to baptize was not mentioned in Norton, Ohio.

Early records leave the angel nameless and faceless, but when Smith and Cowdery later began to readdress the importance of the angelic visit, his identity became a primary focus of the narrative. In September 1834, Cowdery wrote a letter to William W. Phelps that initiated a clear tradition that emphasized that the priesthood had been restored by a specific angel on May 15, 1829. Without mentioning the identity of the angel, Cowdery wrote that he and Smith had "received baptism, by the direction of the angel of God . . . when we received under his hand the holy priesthood, as he said 'upon you my fellow servants, in the name of Messiah I confer this priesthood and this authority which shall remain upon earth, that the sons of Levi may yet offer an offering unto the Lord in righteousness!'"[32] This description provided the fullest account of the event up to that point. By September 1835, Smith and Cowdery recorded additional accounts of the angelic visit. For example, Cowdery recorded a patriarchal blessing Smith had given him in 1833. In the introduction, Cowdery described the circumstances in which Smith gave the first five blessings. He wrote that Smith "was ordained by the angel John, unto the lesser or Aaronic priesthood, in company with myself, in the Town of Harmony, Susquehannah County, Pennsylvania, on Fryday, the 15th day of May, 1829, after which we repaired to the water, even to the Susquehannah River, and were baptized, he first ministering unto me and after I to him."[33] This private blessing was the first record from either Smith or Cowdery that identified the angel as John the Baptist. It was an identification of no small significance.[34]

This new narrative provided authoritative validation for Smith and Cowdery's power to baptize: they were ordained to do so by none other than the biblical figure who had baptized Jesus himself. As the last great prophet before Christ, John the Baptist not only symbolized Smith's prophetic role but also represented an important thematic link between the New Testament establishment of Christ's church and the restoration of said church that Smith theologized in 1830. Smith and Cowdery's ordination by John the Baptist formed a clerical order that claimed to supersede the authority of other Christian clergy. This order cut through linear time, connecting ancient biblical authority directly to the modern restoration. By 1835, the Mormons sang

And an angel surely, then,
For a blessing unto men,
Brought the priesthood back again,
In its ancient purity.[35]

Yet Smith's understanding of this visitation by John evolved over time, with further elaborations contributing both to his growing religious authority and to the early Mormons' understanding of the theology of baptism. By 1839, Smith was offering previously unknown details on the John the Baptist restoration narrative as it had been recorded by Cowdery in 1835. In particular, Smith's history added several statements to John's declaration (additions in italics): "Upon you my fellow servants, in the name of Messiah, I confer *the Priesthood of Aaron, which holds the keys of the ministering of angels and of the gospel of repentance, and of baptism by immersion for the remission of sins*, and this *shall never be taken again from the earth, until* the sons of Levi *do offer again* an offering unto the Lord in righteousness." Because there is no record of Smith using the terminology "priesthood of Aaron" until 1832, it seems likely that the additions in the first line were later elaborations on the part of Smith or his scribe James Mulholland once this was officially written down in 1839.[36] On the other hand, Cowdery's original quotation in the patriarchal blessing introduction from 1835 reflects the earliest account of the angelic visit as found in his 1829 Articles of the Church and the 1830 Ohio newspapers, mentioned earlier. Even if Smith's account in his 1839 history accurately relates the specific wording used by the angel, official church records never emphasized the John the Baptist narrative until after 1835. And the wording was not made explicit until 1839, when Smith recorded his experience in the official history. Furthermore, Smith's account in his history was not made public until the fall of 1842, when it was published in the *Times and Seasons*.

During the 1830s, then, the narrative about where Smith and Cowdery had received authorization to perform baptisms matured, their power no longer loosely tied to an unnamed angel but to a specific and powerful New Testament figure. The Mormon narrative explained Smith's priesthood authority in terms of connective restoration. John the Baptist ushered in a new era of authorized baptisms and the gospel of repentance by physically bestowing on Smith and Cowdery an ordination that, by virtue of its provenance, legitimized Mormon baptism. For nonbelievers, Mormonism's literalism about this act of restoration would have been difficult to understand. Restoration held a different meaning for non-Mormons: for example, on the cover of the *Millennial Harbinger*, Alexander Campbell published a passage from the Book of Revelation (14:6) to emphasize the restoration of primitive Christianity. Instead of copying the passage verbatim from the King James version of the Bible, Campbell replaced the vision of an angel restoring the gospel with an image more readily associated with acts of human preaching. He changed the word *angel* to *messenger*. Thus, he revised the passage to say, "I saw another messenger flying through the midst of heaven, having everlasting good news to proclaim to the inhabitants of the earth." The difference between Campbell's rendering of the passage (to broaden the boundaries of its ecclesiastic usage) and Mormonism's literal reading of the same passage (that an actual angel would restore the gospel) marks the Mormon brand of restorationism with a distinctive claim to exclusive religious authority obtained through actual angelic intervention.

Yet Joseph Smith's restoration of authority claimed to be more than just authority that derived from the New Testament era. The New Testament figure, John the Baptist, apparently restored a priesthood that Smith identified with the Old Testament figure Aaron. This was a far more ancient form of authority. This reflected Mormonism's overarching sense of covenant theology that included a continuous line of authority that did not separate the Old and New covenants or uphold a supersessionist claim.[37] John the Baptist was passing authority that apparently originated "before the foundations of the world," which had become identified with a preparatory authority used by the "sons of Levi" that would remain on earth until they returned in the last days at the Second Coming of Christ to "offer again an offering unto the Lord."[38] This connection to a much broader narrative reflected the Book of Mormon narrative, which described remnant Israel in the Americas with the authority of the pre-Abrahamic figure Melchizedek.[39] While this narrative, as will be discussed in later chapters, developed alongside Mormonism, it was distinctly captured in the claim of Joseph Smith to have been authorized by heaven to baptize.

## From Baptism to Apostleship

The John the Baptist restoration narrative demonstrates Smith's determination to obtain and shape a unique religious authority among a plurality of churches that were already using baptism as a form of nonexclusive authority. The identity of John the Baptist aligns Mormonism's origins with other contemporary movements that sought a restoration of the New Testament order, while it also positioned John the Baptist within a far more ancient form of authority. Smith knitted a New Testament restoration narrative to an ancient American narrative that culminated in the empowerment of a nineteenth-century Mormon narrative. This identity was a significant component within the Mormon priesthood restoration narrative that established both Mormonism's claim to exclusive religious authority and a firm foundation for a ritual people. Smith's revelations guided the practices of the religion as it developed, practices that eventually included the command to baptize the dead vicariously. To Smith, the salvific force of the baptismal ordinance was so potent that it would be deemed effective not only for those living on the earth but also for those who, though dead, received baptism via its performance by proxy. Smith's theology necessitated this reach past death in part because he stood firm on the requirement of baptism. He believed that "although a man should be baptized an hundred times it availeth him nothing," if it was done by another church and through another authority.

The John the Baptist narrative also demonstrates Smith's ability to reinterpret and recontextualize past events in new and informed ways as his revelations continued to interpret the restoration. This ability demonstrated a certain ongoing flexibility or even theological mutability at the core of Mormon doctrine: the prophet could clarify, add to, and reinterpret past revelations and theophanies. Reinterpretation happened frequently with Smith's revelations, to the extent that it formed a consistent pattern. Small pieces from earlier revelations appeared to be part of much larger initiatives that came into focus only years later, a pattern that the following chapters will begin to trace.

In some ways, this framing of restoration as an act that cuts through linear temporality to connect with biblical authority makes sense. Smith's upbringing did not provide him with extensive education or biblical training, nor did he receive a sense of authority through a conventional ecclesiastical tradition. Smith had to establish his authority as both a revelator and seer, first through his ongoing translation of the Book of Mormon and then as one with the angelic authorization to perform saving rituals. Yet Smith's revelatory voice and his claims to have obtained exclusive authorization from angels and God would ground Mormon identity for years to come. With sovereign authority from God, delivered by angels, Smith's revelations and translations organized a priesthood order and dictated the governance of God's kingdom. These new revelations also helped him navigate the growing complexities of his priesthood as he attempted to restore an apostleship that was a central feature of the New Testament.

# 3

# Apostleship and the Authority of Change

In addition to baptism, a second foundational narrative that demonstrates Joseph Smith's authority was the establishment of the Mormon apostleship. His translations and revelations called for major initiatives that required increasing amounts of commitment from his adherents, but the revelations also required a certain amount of malleability. Smith established certain forms of authority, such as priesthood and sacraments, through his revelations and then molded and reformed them through additional revelations to meet the evolving needs of his church. In doing this, Smith demonstrated his ability to control the narrative and shape its authority. As his theology developed and his lay ministry expanded, his prophetic leadership adapted. It was the malleability of his leadership that enabled the relationship between hierarchy and democracy to adjust and find stasis on the waves of change. To demonstrate this point, this chapter will explore one of Smith's most radical concepts of authority—namely, apostleship—in its nearly superfluous beginnings and its ultimate importance within Mormonism.

Smith claimed that apostles, like Christ's New Testament apostles, were an essential element of his restoration theology. Protestant America—especially those determined to restore New Testament Christianity—believed that apostles of the New Testament could not be reproduced. Yet even before Smith established his church, he was commanded by revelation to find twelve apostles as part of his restoration. Like many of Smith's revelatory commandments, some of which were initiatives that took years to accomplish, he did not call twelve apostles immediately. In the case of this commandment, he did not ordain twelve apostles for almost six years (in 1835), and it was not until the 1840s that they began acting as a governing and administrative body.[1]

The origins of apostleship demonstrate Smith pursuing an element of the Mormon hierarchy that did not develop until later. The evolution of apostleship offers a window into Smith's earliest efforts to establish authority through apostleship and demonstrates how its development as an institutional hierarchy depended on his earlier prophetic role and his ability to reframe an old initiative. After exploring the context of Christians' interest in restoring apostleship in the antebellum era, this chapter will examine Mormonism's original 1829 directive to establish apostles and analyze its relationship with the actual call of a quorum of apostles in 1835. It will begin to demonstrate that the Book of Mormon juxtaposed Israel in Jerusalem with scattered Israel in America, connecting the two groups through their shared form of leadership: twelve apostles.

## Restoring the Apostles in the Antebellum Era

Creating a set group of official apostles did not initially make sense in antebellum America, but Mormonism was not the only new religion that tried to re-create apostleship. Edward Irving, a radical Scottish clergyman, acted as a kind of John the Baptist for what later became known as the Catholic Apostolic Church, which was founded on the calling of twelve apostles in the early 1830s. As he led his congregations away from Presbyterian orthodoxy, Irving formed independent congregations that embraced Pentecostal expressions of devotion and eventually called for twelve apostles. Though Irving died before all twelve apostles were called, by 1835 his church had chosen twelve apostles to lead it.[2]

This all occurred within the same five years in which Smith developed his own understanding and calling of apostles, but the two movements, divided by the Atlantic Ocean, had almost no effect on each other—though there were several people who came from the Irvingite tradition, some of whom met with the Mormons.[3] The Irvingites believed that apostles should lead the church and that eighteen hundred years had elapsed before God sent apostles to the Gentiles. Irving's movement taught a succession of authority from Peter to its own modern apostles, claiming that the episcopacy and the papacy did not possess the authority of apostleship.[4]

Closer to home in the antebellum United States, tradition, practice, and the Bible formed the structure that supported the authority of the Christian clergy. Other movements fostered a deep sense of restorationism to undergird their religious authority, but the specific contours of the restorationist impulse were often strikingly different. No stable approach or definitive guiding idea gave shape to US restoration movements. Instead, practices and interpretations of the New Testament gospel were fluid and complicated, which created a complexity in Christian ministry in the United States.[5] Methodists, for example, mingled "primitivism and churchliness" and were intimately connected to Wesleyan tradition, though in early-nineteenth-century United States, Francis Asbury slowly excluded much of the European tradition from the church.[6] Evangelicals explained their authority through Martin Luther's notion of the priesthood of all believers, a position that drove a wedge between the Catholic and Protestant churches by discounting the idea of apostolic succession.[7] Evangelicals did not emphasize the keys that Peter possessed, described in Matthew 16:19, or believe that God delivered his authority through a succession of sanctioned clergy. Like many evangelicals, Smith also questioned notions of succession (even though half his family attended the Presbyterian church in Palmyra before his church was established) and embraced authority founded on restorationism. Unlike them, however, he eventually adopted a unique form of restorationism that taught there had been a restoration of authority from the ancient twelve apostles, again conferred by angelic means.

Adding apostleship to the restoration of the ancient church set Smith apart from contemporaries like Alexander Campbell, who tried to restore a primitive church but did not go so far as to include apostles.[8] Campbell and others, like Barton Stone, focused instead on the record of the New Testament, which was an unsurprising response in light of the Protestant reliance on the Bible. To most Protestants, apostles as described in the New Testament could have existed only in the first century, since the Bible defined them according to a specific ministry for which they were ordained by Christ. Yet even in the antebellum United States there were some Christian seekers, like Joseph Smith's uncle, Jesse Smith, who believed there would be another apostleship. Smith's call for a restoration that included a specific, embodied form of apostleship was radical.[9] Smith's restoration, like Irving's, included the audacious claim that the twelve apostles would be reinstitutionalized, despite the fact that Christians almost universally rejected the idea of continually calling apostles since the biblical precedent was for them to be ordained by Christ, which was no longer possible.[10] The tension that came with the audacity to restore twelve apostles who were equivalent to Christ's twelve New Testament apostles slowed Joseph Smith's immediate thoughts of calling twelve in 1829.

## The Sources of Mormon Apostleship, 1829–31

The formation of the Mormon apostleship follows a narrative of development and change. Smith's commandment to call apostles originated in 1829, but there were no ordained apostles until 1835. In the intervening years, his thinking developed as he explored various foundations of apostleship and encountered the challenges of governing his growing church. Smith's initial ideas about apostleship drew on several sources, including direct revelations, biblical precedent, and the Book of Mormon.

First, Smith looked to his own revelations for instructions on apostleship, though this source was not as well developed in the founding years as it would become in the mid-1830s. There are only vague traces of apostleship in 1829, primarily via a single revelatory commandment received in June of that year to call twelve "disciples" (a term used in the Book of Mormon to represent the US counterpart to Christ's twelve apostles in Jerusalem). Oliver Cowdery declared in 1835 that the twelve disciples of this early revelation actually referred to the twelve apostles whom he assisted in calling in 1835. The association of the terms *disciple* and *apostle* has caused a debate among Mormon historians about how radically different the intentions of the 1829 revelation were from Smith and Cowdery's reinterpretation of the revelation once they called the twelve apostles six years later. Sorting through this debate reveals how Smith utilized the idea of modern apostles and restoration to form his own idiosyncratic sense of religious authority from 1829 to 1835.

A second source for Smith was the biblical precedent of the New Testament, specifically the Gospels and the book of Acts. Yet even this is a somewhat confusing and contested witness, for two different kinds of apostleship seem to be present in those texts. The term *apostle* is used to designate both a missionary, like Paul or Barnabas, and one of Jesus's chosen twelve apostles, like Peter.[11] Nineteenth-century Christians puzzled over passages in which the text refers to both Paul and Barnabas as "apostles."[12] As Adam Clarke's 1831 Bible commentary explained, "When they had ordained them elders—Elder seems to be here the name of an office. These were all young or new converts, and yet among them the apostles constitute elders."[13] The implication for nineteenth-century Protestants like Clarke is that Paul and Barnabas received the call to serve as missionaries, but that this call did not include the formal leadership of Christ's church—they were not part of Christ's original apostles. Early Christian leaders were ordained as elders, but apostleship outside the body of the twelve denoted a responsibility to evangelize.

Early Mormons used the terms *elder* and *apostle* in similar ways throughout the nineteenth century, making the distinction between the two hazy at times. Before 1835, it is very difficult to demonstrate the difference between an apostle and a disciple, let alone that between an evangelizing apostle and an apostle ordained to a position of ecclesiastical leadership (that is, part of the Quorum of the Twelve Apostles in 1835 terms). There were clearly evangelizing apostles in the church before 1835, so the debate rests on whether there were also official apostles and whether discipleship and apostleship were synonymous. It is important to sort through the relationship between these two terms: if there were only evangelizing apostles prior to 1835, then Smith's claims to religious authority up to that point were not terribly different from those of most other antebellum Protestants who used the term *apostle* to represent those sent forth to preach. It is possible that Smith and others were struggling with the dual meaning of apostleship as early as 1829.

A third source was hugely important for Smith's growing understanding of apostleship. The concept of apostleship seems to have emerged in the minds of Smith and Cowdery during the translation of the Book of Mormon in the spring of 1829.[14] Smith's new scripture built on the biblical precedent of the New Testament and offered an example of Christ choosing additional apostles outside the New Testament setting (an ancient precedent for modern purposes). The Book of Mormon manuscript provides the earliest Mormon account using the term *apostle* outside the biblical context. From April to June 1829, Smith's translation of the Book of Mormon referred to "apostle(s)" sixteen times, each of which referred specifically to Christ's New Testament apostles. Significantly, none of the references described an individual who was sent forth to preach or serve as a general missionary (as many Christian contemporaries did). Instead, thc Book of Mormon always referred to them as a body of twelve chosen apostles—specifically Christ's apostles.[15] This is perhaps the best background to understand how Smith and Cowdery used the term from April to June 1829 when they were translating the plates. This usage demonstrates that the text they were producing displayed a specific and consistent version of apostleship in 1829—at this time, *apostle* connoted Christ's twelve ordained apostles in the New Testament.

Furthermore, the text of the Book of Mormon does not simply witness what Smith and Cowdery were reading and thinking about in 1829; it served as the textual guide to and even impetus for the establishment of the Mormon church. As we saw in chapter 2, the Book of Mormon encouraged them to ask for the power to baptize, which they did, resulting in not only baptism, but also the significant theological development of the ordinance itself. Following the pattern established with the question of baptism, Smith and Cowdery would eventually copy the offices described in the Book of Mormon into the governing document for their church, attempting to restore the same Christian authority described in the Book of Mormon.[16] Knowing that they used the term *apostle* consistently during that period, they likely did not deviate from the received pattern of the term's usage and definition, at least within the first months after its dictation.

The Book of Mormon, therefore, offers a glimpse into how Smith and Cowdery understood the term *apostle* in 1829. In contrast to the apostles

Christ chose during his ministry, the Book of Mormon describes elders who serve the church and associates them with the related duties of an apostle. The text explains that elders were apostles, a usage that carries the connotation that elders were also missionaries. The usage does not imply that these elder-apostles were like Christ's New Testament apostles. The office of elder and its association with the descriptive position of apostle in the Book of Mormon make it difficult to decipher the normative usage of the term in the early years of the nineteenth-century LDS Church—namely, how to distinguish between those who later claimed to have been ordained to the office of apostle and those who served more generally as missionaries.[17] The Book of Mormon text establishes the term *disciples* as the US counterpart to Christ's New Testament apostles (table 3.1). In 3 Nephi 11, Christ chose twelve men in the New World and laid his hands on them, calling them to preach his gospel. The thematic resonance in this image is clear: these Book of Mormon disciples were meant to evoke their New Testament counterparts, serving with similar responsibilities, yes, but even more, serving under a specific call of ritual authorization and ecclesiastical structure.

In addition, the concept of apostleship that emerged out of the Book of Mormon created an important relationship between Christ's New Testament Israel, remnant Israel in America, and Joseph Smith's nineteenth-century restoration. The Book of Mormon makes the twelve disciples in America and the twelve apostles in Jerusalem highly important factors in God's plan for Israel in the future. Binding the remnant Israel of the Book of Mormon to biblical Israel, the Book of Mormon declares, "wherefore, the twelve ministers of thy seed shall be judged of them; for ye are of the house of Israel."[18] The Book of Mormon thus creates theological continuity for Israel through the concept of apostleship, whether in Jerusalem or lost in the Americas. Further, it calls out for covenant Israel to establish another set of twelve in Smith's restoration. The implications here revise our understanding of Smith's project: Smith's restoration was not just trying to restore the New Testament church or replicate its ecclesiastical structure.[19] Rather, his overarching goal was to restore covenant Israel. The New Testament apostles and the Book of Mormon disciples thus emerge not as solitary aberrations but instead as the culminations of a covenant pattern of adaptive and ongoing apostleship. Smith's reworking of apostolic identity manifests his efforts to create a covenant theology that connected directly to God's covenant people in the Old Testament.

Unlike their Protestant contemporaries in the antebellum era, early Mormons were thus steeped in the possibility that Christ could still call and authorize another set of twelve. Cowdery would later describe the two sets

Table 3.1. Deciphering between apostles and disciples

Twelve apostles

- Called by Jesus Christ in the New Testament
- Nineteenth-century Protestants did not call apostles
- By 1835 Mormons ordained twelve apostles

Evangelizing apostles

- Like Barnabas and Paul
- Nineteenth-century Protestants called apostles, who served as missionaries
- Included with the ordination to the office of elder in Mormonism

Disciples

- Followers who are called by charismatic apostles
- Nineteenth-century Protestants called disciples
- Called within Mormonism as within Protestant denominations

Twelve Book of Mormon disciples

- Called by Jesus Christ in the Book of Mormon (as the New Testament apostles were called)
- 1829 revelation commanded Cowdery to call twelve "disciples"
- By 1835, twelve disciples were synonymous with twelve apostles in Mormonism

of twelve (in Jerusalem and in America) as if they were understood to be indistinguishable as apostles. Yet, if so, the question remains why the Book of Mormon does not call them by the same name in 1829. Both sets of twelve were chosen by Christ, implying an identical authorization, yet both calls resulted in seemingly distinct identities. Unlike Paul and Barnabas, the twelve disciples in the Book of Mormon were chosen by Christ.

For Mormons, these issues of identification, responsibility, and authority were nebulous in the early 1830s. This uncertainty is disconcerting because the question reflects larger issues surrounding Smith's restorationist impulse and the legitimacy of his actions. Establishing modern apostles displays a kind of religious authority that falls outside traditional religious authority in the nineteenth century. Clearly, Mormonism did not institutionalize apostleship until 1835, but there are indications that Mormons were developing a unique kind of authority through apostleship as early as 1829, albeit without being definitive or precise at that time. Still, Mormonism's ability to justify calling an additional set of twelve apostles marks a distinct break from other nineteenth-century religious practices and demonstrates the emerging relationship between text and authority that would come to dominate Mormon religious and cultural practice in the coming years. What marks Mormonism's authority, in this case, is both the revelation to establish apostles and the ability to redefine that revelation at a later point in time, often by building on earlier foundations.

## Early Mormon Priesthood Licenses

With this context in mind, the malleability of Smith's use of the apostleship is most officially demonstrated in priesthood licenses. Like itinerant Methodist preachers, Mormon priesthood leaders traveled throughout upstate New York, but their official licenses at one time called them apostles and were signed by Cowdery and Smith, who were both titled as apostles on each certificate. It is difficult to know, however, exactly how this seal of apostleship was understood at the time, which illustrates the ambiguity of Mormonism's evolving authority narrative. By the first conference of the church on June 9, 1830, Smith and Cowdery signed ecclesiastical licenses. John Whitmer's license characterized him as an evangelizing apostle, declaring that he was an "Apostle of Jesus Christ an Elder of the Church of Christ."[20] Oliver Cowdery wrote out the license at the conference, and both Smith and Cowdery endorsed it as apostles and as the first and second elders of the church. Whitmer received his license along with four other elders, three priests, and two teachers. These declarations were also made in Joseph Smith Sr.'s ministerial licenses, signed by Smith and Cowdery on June 9, 1830.

Whitmer's license, in particular, demonstrates the change that developed over time in the meaning of the term *apostle*. His initial ministerial license indicated that he was an apostle. Someone, however, vigorously scribbled out the title *apostle* to the point that the pencil tore through the paper so that it read, "Given to John Whitmer, signifying and proveing that he is an ~~Apostle of Jesus Christ~~ Elder of this Church of Christ." Unfortunately, it is difficult to know when the redaction was made. Nonetheless, the action seems to be an attempt to reinterpret the license's meaning and to clarify the difference between the two definitions of apostle within the church. The redaction also indicates a radical break within the meaning of *apostle* itself—someone, at some specific point in time, experienced a hermeneutic shift in their approach to apostleship, and that shift was powerful enough to require explicit and unmistakable revision to a textual example of religious authority. It is even possible that this act occurred soon after the license was created in 1830. Pinpointing the moment of the redaction could thus point toward an important realization within the development of Mormon apostleship.

The editor of Whitmer's certificate did not cross out the title *apostle* next to the signatures of Smith and Cowdery. The redaction makes it clear that

Whitmer's apostleship was limited to evangelizing. It is possible, then, that the redactor thought Smith and Cowdery were more than just evangelizing apostles and exercised ecclesiastical authority. Whitmer's title as apostle may have even been crossed out at the conference at which it was created and thus may indicate some sort of readily realized mistake. In the final line of the license, Cowdery originally wrote that John Whitmer was ordained an elder "under the hand of Joseph Smith Jun.," but he apparently returned to the license and included the phrase "who is an Apostle of our Lord." The other extant licenses included "who is an Apostle of our Lord," as if they had standardized the statement at a point in time that required them to return to Whitmer's license to ensure uniformity. As Cowdery standardized the certificates, someone may have felt it was inappropriate to state that John Whitmer was an apostle.[21] Regardless of whether it was crossed out at the conference, it was expunged while Smith's and Cowdery's apostolic titles were preserved below, something that seems to indicate that Smith and Cowdery represented a different kind of apostle. The text clearly identifies Smith and Cowdery as "Apostles of our Lord" and not merely "elders and apostles." The delineation, of course, conveniently matches the story of their retrospective narrative after 1835.

Framing this redaction in terms of a palimpsest (in which one text overwrites another) provides a useful figure for the evolving concept of authority within early Mormonism. The emphatic nature of the redaction, with its heavy black line and accompanying visual force, provides a tangible representation of the importance of apostolic authority within the restoration narrative. Even though someone clearly removed Whitmer's title as an apostle, the trace of that title and its associated authority remains visible to the naked eye. Similarly, despite the eventual consensus that emerged on the role and range of apostolic authority, the underlying open impulse behind the early use of the term remained culturally visible in early Mormonism. Structures of authority remain open to the changing force of evolving revelation, simultaneously resting on a sense of eternal and unchanging restoration.

The mystery here surrounding Whitmer's license concerns whether Smith and Cowdery saw themselves as a different kind of apostle, as a kind distinct from that of the other evangelizing apostles in 1829. Though the narrative is not explicit in the earliest records, there are indications that they thought of themselves as more. In June 1829, Oliver Cowdery wrote, "I am an apostle of Jesus Christ by the will of God the Father and the Lord Jesus Christ" in an early creedal-like statement called the Articles of the Church of Christ. Cowdery wrote this declaration within days of Smith's dictation of Nephi's vision of the New Testament twelve apostles found in the Book of Mormon.[22]

Though Cowdery did not claim that he was identical to those whom Christ chose in the Bible, he felt confident in identifying himself as an apostle, even though the Book of Mormon text utilized the term with unqualified precision. Cowdery did not identify himself as an elder, nor did he claim to be one of the "twelve disciples," but on the other hand, it also is clear that he was not claiming to be only an evangelizing apostle.

Smith and Cowdery certainly exercised more institutional authority than would be characteristic of an evangelizing apostle. They controlled the distribution of priesthood certificates and signed their names as apostles to each one. In fact, the authority attached to their names came from their positions as apostles and first and second elders. Even if they saw themselves acting as leaders and evangelizing apostles (like Paul), they separated the quality or range of their own authority from that of all other apostles in the church on the basis of their authority to distribute priesthood as the first and second elders. Smith and Cowdery were the only individuals who distributed priesthood authority to others within the church. Signing their names to these certificates repeatedly underscored their claim that their authority came not from their own individual identities, but rather through a specific ecclesiastical structure. This role, underdeveloped as it may have been, created an ideal precedent for a later understanding of the twelve apostles that integrated Smith's authority with a seamless narrative that sourced that authority in Peter, James, and John. Although the narrative would certainly need to be reinterpreted and ironed out to meet the later understanding of authority and its relationship to priesthood, the initial impulse for this synthesis is seen here in Smith and Cowdery's self-conception as occupying positions of legitimated apostolic authority.[23]

## Apostles in the Contemporary Written Record, 1829–31

The use of apostleship in these malleable terms shows a reticence to fully embrace the Book of Mormon duplication of Christ's apostles, but it does move us toward the realization that Smith's prophetic authority allowed him to interpret and govern by revelation and appropriate his own sense of administrative and cultural need for apostleship. Outsiders who were acquainted with Mormonism in its first few years were already uncomfortable with the Mormon idea of apostleship, even though its complete development and implementation was yet to be elaborated. Contemporary reactions in print provide some indication that the Mormons were discussing and developing their own ideas about apostleship.

Though the New Testament apostles did not have the same function or role as Smith's apostles, Smith equated them only insofar as they were chosen by Christ as part of a distinct body of twelve. This was publicly discussed in 1829, causing a visceral reaction among other Christian denominations, who claimed the Mormons had called twelve apostles as early as 1829 and 1830. On September 23, 1829, Abner Cole printed, "The number of Gold Bible Apostles is said to be complete. Jo Smith Jr. is about to assign to each, a mission to the *heathen*."[24] Cole's newspaper, the Palmyra *Reflector*, seemed to have an insider's view on Mormonism because Cole used Egbert B. Grandin's press at nights and weekends between the times that the typesetter was preparing the Book of Mormon for printing. Cole even printed passages from the earliest pages of the book in December 1829 and January 1830. Eventually, on June 1, 1830, he wrote, "The apostle to the NEPHITES (Cowdery) has started for the EAST, on board a boat, with a load of 'gold bibles.'"[25] (To put a point on Cole's intimacy with the church, after Joseph Smith's brother Hyrum had a confrontation with a local resident, Willard Chase, Cole printed that "apostles should keep cool" and designated Hyrum as a "Gold Bible apostle.")[26] Those even closer to the early Mormon band thought they were calling twelve apostles. As David Marks, who visited Smith at the Whitmer home in Fayette, New York, in March 1830, wrote, "they further stated that twelve apostles were to be appointed, who would soon confirm their mission by miracles."[27]

Historians Michael Quinn and Gregory Prince find such accounts to be evidence that there were twelve apostles by 1830. Both authors draw from newspaper articles that declared that the Mormons "have therefore sent out twelve Apostles to promulgate its doctrine," in the fall and winter of 1830.[28] This evidence is interesting because it refers to the apostles as a body of twelve—like Abner Cole's September 1829 article—which may in fact make this a reference to ordained apostles rather than evangelizing apostles, or elders sent out to preach. But it is difficult to conclude what the *Ashtabula Journal* and those reprinting their message meant or whether the article's author was simply being polemical. Furthermore, though Smith and Cowdery were demarcating between kinds of apostle, it may have been only among themselves. If so, members of the church may have confused the differences between ordained and evangelizing apostles. Outsider newspapers, under this scenario, would be even further away from Smith and Cowdery's private knowledge about apostles. Either way, it is difficult to unravel the real meaning behind satirical and negative second-hand newspaper accounts. Whether twelve were called in 1829 or 1830 is certainly an arguable point, but whatever the date, there is not enough evidence to conclude that we know who the twelve were.

Among the newspaper accounts that referred to apostleship,[29] those with the highest circulation were the 1831 letters of Ezra Booth in the *Ohio Star*.[30] Booth's sarcasm and acerbic tone ridiculed the Mormon leaders sharply, and his letters were printed and reprinted for months. In the course of his ridicule, Booth began calling some of the Mormon clergy "apostles." In one letter, he challenged the disciplinary measures taken against Ziba Peterson for sexual misconduct, claiming they were unfounded, which seemed all the more hypocritical since he believed that Cowdery was in fact guilty of some kind of sexual misconduct. He wrote, "Ziba was deprived of his elder and apostle. . . . And thus by commandment, poor Ziba, one of the twelve apostles, is thrust down, while Oliver the scribe, also an apostle, who had been guilty of similar conduct, is set on high."[31]

Whether it was just rhetoric or not, when Booth ridiculed the Mormons, he grouped them into a body of twelve men, as if they were claiming to be the New Testament apostles. He did not characterize them as missionaries or simply as Mormon leaders. According to Booth, twelve leaders apparently carried a log "in honor of the twelve tribes of Israel" at a dedication of the land of Zion in Independence, Missouri. They identified twelve men, including Cowdery, on August 2, 1831, to carry the log.[32] Booth wrote, "A shrub oak, about ten inches in diameter at the butt, the best that could be obtained near at hand, was prostrated, trimmed, and cut off at a suitable length, and twelve men, answering to the twelve apostles, by means of handspikes, conveyed it to the place."[33] Here, again, Booth clearly understands the twelve men carrying the log as apostles, with apostleship here associated with participation in official acts of worship, and possibly even ritual.[34] Despite the gaps in records from 1829 to 1831, these contemporary media sources demonstrate an interest in the concept of a restored apostleship that reached beyond the boundaries of belief and membership. Apostles, even in the abstract, were noteworthy both inside and outside Mormonism.

## 1835: The Cementing of Mormon Apostleship through Peter, James, and John

We have seen that although Smith and Cowdery had developed the concept of a restored apostleship sufficiently to actually call twelve apostles in 1829, the historical record suggests that they did not do so. That changed in 1835 when, after years of development and institutional structuring in Mormonism, twelve men were ordained, claiming to be the modern twelve apostles of Christ. What's more, their ordination was associated with the authority of the New Testament apostles Peter, James, and John. Just as we saw in chapter 2 that the Mormon narrative about the authority to perform baptisms expanded over time to include the specific sanction of John the Baptist, so too did evolving LDS understandings about apostleship begin to include the endorsement of important biblical figures.

As recorded in 1832, Smith's story first began making mention of "reception of the holy Priesthood by the ministering of angels to administer the letter of the Gospel"; by 1835, that general discussion of angels had narrowed more specifically on the New Testament figures of Peter, James, and John. Within the same months that the Mormon apostles were ordained, Smith and Cowdery were revising and printing Smith's revelations as official Mormon scripture. Within those revisions were direct references to how apostleship was restored in 1829 and 1830, specifically about the role of Peter, James, and John. By late 1835, Mormons were teaching that Peter, James, and John had visited Smith and Cowdery in 1829 and given them the authority to call additional apostles, even though no additional apostles had been called at that time.

In February 1835, once Cowdery called the twelve apostles, he explained that he had then fulfilled the commandment given to him in 1829 to call twelve *disciples*.[35] It is interesting to note that the 1835 publication of the Doctrine and Covenants was edited so that the call for twelve disciples was changed to a call for twelve "apostles" in the earlier revelation.[36] Smith also mentioned this change in his 1839 history.[37] This textual revision plays into the larger prophetic ethos Smith constructed in which his authority to receive revelation was explicitly ongoing—the role of the prophet was not just to receive new revelation, but to continue to seek and receive better understanding of older revelations. Smith was "translating" his older revelations and building on them with new revelations that would be codified in the 1835 Doctrine and Covenants. Hence, as Smith came to understand the concept of apostleship as involving official ecclesiastical authority conferred through a legitimate ordination, he was then able to utilize his authority to edit past revelations to reflect his expanded understanding. Using both revelation and his official history, Smith created certainty out of vagueness. His understanding of his authority allowed him to behave as if the concept of apostleship had been constant. With retrospection and in the official printed publications of the church, Smith expressed the interpretation that the apostles in the New Testament were no different from the twelve disciples in the Book of Mormon, making the issue seemingly one of mere semantics.

This history of the changing status and understanding of Mormon apostleship offers insight into how Smith developed his own sense of religious authority. In 1829, there was ambiguity about how the apostles and apostleship would function within Smith's restoration—ambiguity that rested in the minds of both Smith and his followers. Yet the records show that he was struggling with a radical idea that did emerge later as a predominant concept of authority within Mormonism. In 1829, Smith was emphasizing his own prophetic authority and used that to sustain his leadership. By 1835, apostleship added another dimension within the ecclesiastical hierarchy. Although high councils had already been introduced as a means to distribute local power and authority, divisions within the high councils in Missouri and Ohio made it clear that an overarching structure also was necessary. Authority needed to be distributed and mobile, and thus potentially geographically accessible, and yet high enough to override local leadership when necessary in order to keep the young church from doctrinal fragmentation. Smith thus fleshed out the dormant concept of apostleship so that it could emerge at the right moment within the current needs of church governance.

## A Seamless Narrative

Smith and Cowdery's seamless narrative about the 1829 and 1835 apostles was also perpetuated in the stories of some of the earliest members. Hiram Page, an early convert who married into the Whitmer family, claimed in 1848 that Cowdery had been an apostle before the church was established. Page was chosen from among the believers in June 1829 to see the gold plates, and he was likely present when Smith founded the Church of Christ on April 6, 1830. Writing about the establishment of the church, Page declared, "In the beginning we find the first ordinations were by Peter, James and John. They ordained Joseph and Oliver. . . . These offices Oliver received from those holy messengers before the 6th of April, 1830."[38] Page effortlessly combined the Peter, James, and John narrative with a claim that these heavenly messengers had ordained Smith and Cowdery to be apostles even before the church was officially established. When Page made this statement in 1848, he had experienced years of development and formation within the restoration narrative, and thus his comments likely represent a later synthesis rather than what he actually knew in 1830. What is remarkable about Page's account is that as an insider to Smith's restoration, he saw no problem with the narrative outcome. There was clearly change and development throughout the restoration process, but not enough to cause Page to question the eventual narrative that reinterpreted the early years of Smith's restoration. Page's account is also unique in that he provided it once he was no longer associated with the Mormon church, a circumstance that could lend itself to a more critical evaluation of the restoration process.

This was also the experience of Orson Pratt, a developing polymath who joined the church in the fall of 1830 and who was ordained as one of the twelve apostles in 1835. As an ordained member of the Quorum of the Twelve Apostles,[39] Orson remembered that he first learned of the difference between an evangelizing apostle and an ordained one in 1830. Soon after his older brother Parley P. Pratt joined the church in September 1830, Orson met Smith and the three witnesses in Fayette, New York. In that meeting, Smith told Orson about the revelation he received in 1829 for Oliver Cowdery and David Whitmer to call twelve apostles. Orson told this story for decades, recalling that the revelation was placed in front of him and he was told to "read it." He then explained, "Joseph said . . . that I should be one of these Twelve."[40] He told this story of his ordination as one of those apostles, explaining that before he was ordained he had acted as an evangelizing apostle. In early December 1831, Smith sent Orson to Colesville, New York, to help Hyrum Smith and Newel Knight, who knew nothing about Pratt. To introduce him, Joseph Smith and John Whitmer wrote a letter to the members in Colesville, New York, that stated, "According to your prayers, the Lord hath called, chosen, ordained, sanctified and sent unto you another servant and apostle."[41] Pratt's later ordination as an apostle and Smith's promise to him in the fall of 1831 that he would be an apostle both indicate that Pratt was aware of the two definitions later in his life and that he could make sense of these definitions even after he joined the ordained body of twelve apostles.[42]

The experiences of Page and Pratt can be positioned within Mormonism's early history as representations of the process of authority being established in its most basic form. This authority resembles its later incarnations only because the complex development of the church caused Joseph Smith to ask new questions and receive diverse revelations that he replaced within a new narrative to make sense of both their past and their present circumstances. Narrative malleability is central to the prophetic authority of Mormonism, for it allows the development of and reliance on the prophet's immediate and contemporary significance.

## From Apostleship to Church

Smith laid a radical seedbed in 1829 through his revelations for the eventual growth of Mormon apostleship. In this he was unusual. The antebellum era was rife with restorationists who wished to bring back the primitive church of the New Testament, but few of them believed that apostleship should be restored alongside that church. Joseph Smith's program of restoring apostleship thus set him apart from his contemporaries and, often, made his movement an object of ridicule in the periodicals of the day. Apostleship was an important issue that emerged from the Book of Mormon in 1829 in a narrative that appears strikingly similar to that of Smith's desire to obtain the authority to baptize. There is also evidence that some individuals were called apostles in Mormonism's earliest years, though that seems to have represented an evangelizing position that was tied to missionary work, rather than an ecclesiastical charge that empowered church governance.

As the concept of apostleship developed, it came to include mention of Peter, James, and John to Smith's associates, an elaboration that was woven into Mormonism's evolving narrative. Smith's initial reference to choosing twelve disciples in 1829 and its subsequent theological development to the actual calling of twelve apostles within a defined ecclesiastic structure in 1835 demonstrate the gradual revelatory refinement at work within early Mormonism. Smith manipulated the Bible's teachings about apostles by reproducing them in the Book of Mormon and creatively establishing the apostleship as an ecclesiastical nineteenth-century Mormon structure. Once the idea was laid, he had the ability to shape it around the needs of his church and empower laymen to the heights of Jesus's chosen apostles. As Smith controlled this process by revelation, he reified his hierarchical position as the Mormon democratic hierarchy took shape. The next step then created a house for Smith's revelations and his developing priesthood through the establishment of a church.

# 4

# Church

## Materializing Authority and Ordaining the Prophet

The third foundational narrative that secured Joseph Smith's religious authority surrounds the founding of his church, the Church of Christ. The founding marked Smith's prophetic voice extending beyond his personal charisma into the institutional realm of an enduring religion. Scholars have observed that Mormonism is a kind of test case for Max Weber's theory of the routinization of charisma, since at Mormonism's founding the religion was heavily tied to Joseph Smith's prophetic power, and such movements do not often survive the death of their founders. Weber insists that charismatic authority can easily falter in its fragile state and that such leaders rarely form long-lasting organizations. Yet Mormonism did not fade after Smith's death in 1844. In fact, Smith was obsessed with organization from the point that he merged his charismatic prophethood with the bureaucracy of church governance in a form of hierarchical democracy. A sustainable and manageable priesthood hierarchy was not possible until he grounded his tradition within an official church where ordinations could be performed and ordinances carried out with the legitimating force of the institution. The church would form its own ecclesiastical structure that was maintained through Smith's prophetic voice and periodically reevaluated with changes in geography, demography, and politics. The long-lasting priesthood order led to a new phase in Mormonism and religious authority in the antebellum United States. This chapter will chart early Mormonism's development into an institutional state, beginning with the initial 1829 charismatic revelations for the design of the church and ending with the 1830 establishment of the church and the official ordination of Joseph Smith as its prophet. This trajectory will demonstrate how Smith's voice maintained its singular value while also securing an institutional status within a church. In doing so, he democratized his gifts as part of priesthood ordination while monopolizing his own prophetic authority.

## Church and Charisma: The Chamber of Old Father Whitmer

Joseph Smith's charismatic authority quickly found institutional backing through the founding of a church. In the antebellum United States, there is no underestimating the authority this structure provided. Americans became devoted to church governments as the disestablishment of religion forced civic authority to protect the right to establish religious governance, though they would function in tandem. By April 6, 1830, Smith's charismatic movement became a church, but the church inevitably depended on Smith's past angelic narratives, which were in turn materialized through the church. Various accounts about these events are revealing about how Smith's authority emerged in this early period.

Traditional Mormon narratives emphasize the visit of John the Baptist and Peter, James, and John as the foundations of the church and the priesthood. The Peter, James, and John narrative eventually became the central narrative for priesthood restoration (as discussed in chapter 6) once ecclesiastical distribution of the authority was associated with that priesthood.[1] Thus this narrative of restoration was important for defining administrative and ecclesiastical authority. When Smith was constructing his own historical narrative in his official history, however, he left the Peter, James, and John story out of his account to emphasize charisma and the construction of the Church of Christ. He ties three events together (the John the Baptist visit, the chamber of Father Whitmer experience, and the establishment of the church) as one narrative, from which they received the power to baptize, the power to confer the gift of the Holy Ghost, the Melchizedek priesthood, the eldership, and the church. This narrative expresses the roots of charisma taking on its earliest form of institutionalization, while the Peter, James, and John narrative starts with administrative authority (later defined by the term *keys*) in a way that doesn't untangle charisma and institution or the other narrative. Put simply, the narrative in his history emphasizes the relationship between Smith's role as a charismatic prophetic and the church, while the Peter, James, and John narrative better defines his later role as the president of the high priesthood. Central to the former narrative, the "chamber of Father Whitmer" served as the connective tissue between religious charisma and the establishment of Smith's church, with its codified ordinances and priesthood. See table 4.1.[2]

Table 4.1. Textual connection between the John the Baptist narrative and the "Chamber of Father Whitmer" (Joseph Smith, History, A-1)

| *John the Baptist*, 17–18 | "Chamber of Father Whitmer," 27–28 |
|---|---|
| *Three Promises* made by John the Baptist in Smith's history and fulfilled in the Chamber. | Transition: "We now became anxious to have that promise realized to us, which the Angel [John the Baptist] that conferred upon us the Aaronick Priesthood had given us" |
| 1. "He said this Aaronic priesthood had not the power of laying on of hands, for the gift of the Holy Ghost, but that this should be conferred on [us] hereafter" | 1. "Authority of the laying on of hands for the gift of the Holy Ghost." |
| 2. Melchizedek "priesthood he said should in due time be conferred on us." | 2. "that provided we continued faithful; we should also have the Melchesidec Priesthood" |
| 3. "And that I should be called the first Elder of the Church and he the second." | 3. "when the word of the Lord, came unto us in the Chamber, commanding us; that I should ordain Oliver Cowdery to be an Elder in the Church of Jesus Christ, and that he also should ordain me to the same office." |

With this in mind, the context for the "chamber of Father Whitmer" is imperative for understanding Smith's narrative. In June 1829, as the translation of the Book of Mormon was coming to an end, Joseph Smith was in Fayette, New York, visiting the home of Peter Whitmer Sr., also called "Father" Whitmer. There he was commanded by the audible voice of Christ in the home's upstairs chamber to start a church and ordain elders. Smith described this event as a charismatic experience, though the revelation's content—to organize a church to offer membership, ordinations, and ordinances within an exclusionary community with laws and structure—was decidedly institutional. The narrative of the voice of Christ, in its truly charismatic character, demanded systematic institutionalization. Examining this event will trace a path to the formalized ordination of Mormon priesthood and the ordination of Joseph Smith himself as the prophet of the church. Most important, it is the ideal example for how Smith's charisma called for and entangled itself within the fledgling Mormon bureaucracy.

This 1829 event is a major narrative of early Mormonism, but it has unfortunately been lost to the twentieth- and twenty-first-century Mormon consciousness. The context of the story is that for nearly two years, Joseph Smith had delivered commandments as revelation and established what David Whitmer called a "church in spirit" without any formal organization. In fact, there is almost no mention of establishing a church until the spring of 1829—two years after Smith claimed to have retrieved the gold plates and six years after his first visit with Moroni. As Smith and Cowdery translated the Book of Mormon and discussed the prophecies therein, one of Smith's revelations told Cowdery to "seek to bring forth and establish the *cause of Zion*."[3] That same commandment was given to two other visitors, Hyrum Smith and Joseph Knight Sr., while still in Harmony, Pennsylvania.[4] In addition, an apocalyptic revelation given to Joseph Smith Sr. declared, "a marvelous work is about to come forth among the children of men."[5] In Fayette, the Whitmer family, who had become enthusiastic about the Book of Mormon, received similar revelations. David Whitmer, Peter Whitmer's son and an early Mormon leader, in particular was commanded to "bring forth and establish my Zion."[6] Smith's revelation to David Whitmer declared, in the voice of God and reflecting the words of the Book of Mormon, "I must bring forth the fullness of my gospel from the Gentiles unto the house of Israel . . . [and] thou art David and thou art called to assist."[7] All these revelations—received by multiple people in 1829, all promising a major new event on the horizon—set the stage for what occurred in Father Whitmer's chamber.

In exploring the context of the Whitmer chamber revelation, it is essential to observe which part of the Book of Mormon Smith and Cowdery were translating in late June 1829, when they asked God for the authority to give the Holy Ghost to other believers.[8] This request was part of the restoration of spiritual gifts and their desire to follow the Book of Mormon in their restoration efforts, yet it began to lead them to the establishment of the Church of Christ. According to Smith's own later history, after this request was made, the Lord authorized him to give the "gift of the Holy Ghost." With the hindsight that came through a decade of Mormon developments from 1829 to 1839, he called that authority the Melchizedek priesthood, which was a term on the periphery in 1829, but represented the highest form of Mormon priesthood in 1839.[9] In one of Smith's Nauvoo revelations, he called this event "the voice of God in the chamber of old Father Whitmer."[10] He marked this event as an important part of the restoration of Mormon authority and claims in his history that it was the first time they were given the power to confer the gift of the Holy Ghost. His history states, "We now became anxious to have that promise realized to us, which the Angel that conferred upon us the Aaronick Priesthood had given us, viz: that provided we continued faithful; we should also have the Melchesidec Priesthood, which holds the authority of the laying on of hands for the gift of the Holy Ghost."[11]

To some, this event was just another revelation guiding the nascent movement, but to Smith, it was the experience that shaped the establishment of the church. His history described what happened in the chamber in terms similar to those of one of his authoritative revelations. His history stated, "the word of the Lord came unto us, in the Chamber," which was similar to the wording in Smith's revelations delivered in the same period.[12] Cowdery's role is not entirely clear. The history uses the phrase "came unto us," in plural form, as if Cowdery were included in the experience in some way, but it neglects to explain whether Cowdery's participation included an auditory experience in which he also heard God's voice. Smith's description from September 1842 that it was the "voice of God in the chamber of old father Whitmer," suggests that it was possibly an auditory experience. Smith included the account among a list of angelic visits and other experiences in which God spoke to him.[13] Nevertheless, in the same passage, Smith's revelation explained that he had heard God's voice "in divers places through all the travels and tribulations of the Church," probably referring to his own revelations—certainly emphasizing his prophetic voice in the restoration. Even though it is unknown whether they heard a voice or the event took the form of other 1829 revelations, such as through seer stones, it is clear that Smith and Cowdery believed God had spoken to them.[14] Either way, in Smith's mind, the experience in Father Whitmer's chamber became part of his restoration narrative. As we will see later in this chapter, its charismatic tone and its similarity to the Book of Mormon narrative make it appear to be historical in nature. That experience is also the connective tissue that joins Smith's early charismatic group (or "spiritual church") in 1829 with his codified institutional church after 1830.

Without the experience in the chamber, Smith's religious authority remains primarily charismatic and malleable, even vulnerable to the threat of new charismatic leaders. Some of the earliest members who eventually formed their own churches, like David Whitmer, emphasized their own charismatic authority by disregarding the establishment of the Mormon church and focusing on the authority acquired before it was institutionalized.[15] In fact, the experience in the chamber was recalled by only a few of the earliest members—especially those who wanted to emphasize the "spiritual church" before 1830. David Whitmer, who was closely involved with Smith and Cowdery, was also staying at his father's house in June 1829, yet he recalled the event only in order to challenge Smith's institutional church much later. Whitmer recalled that the church had been established in 1829 "spiritually."[16] Whitmer was asked by an interviewer in 1885 whether he was present when the Lord told Smith and Cowdery to "ordain each other to the Melchesidek priesthood." Apparently speaking about the chamber of Father Whitmer, the interviewer asked this question as if it was already understood that the priesthood authority was received in the chamber. Whitmer answered, "No I was not," as if he was aware that the experience in the chamber was relevant and part of the narrative describing the Restoration, but confirming he was not present during the event. The interviewer followed up the previous question by asking: "Can you tell why that Joseph and Oliver were ordained to the lesser Priesthood by the hand of an Angel but in receiving the Higher they ordained each other?" Whitmer stated that Cowdery told him in the presence of Smith that "they baptized each other seeking by that to fulfill the command . . . at fathers sometime in June 1829. Smith ordained Cowdery to be an Elder, and Cowdery ordained Smith to be an Elder in the Church of Christ."[17] This vague dialogue, which accepts the earlier experience in the chamber but rejects the later institutionalization, places the chamber experience on the precipice of change.[18] Both Smith and Whitmer spoke about the event to confirm its importance, but they differed in their opinion about its purpose.

Smith's history is the only detailed account and offers a retrospective but important telling of the event. Smith explained that the visit of John the Baptist (see chapter 2 in this book), laid the groundwork for the experience in Father Whitmer's chamber where Christ called for further institutionalization, including a church and ordination.[19] According to Smith's own narrative, the experience in the chamber fulfilled the promise John the Baptist gave Smith and Cowdery on May 15, 1829.[20] Smith's history explains that John the Baptist promised them that they would eventually receive the power to confer the gift of the Holy Ghost. Then, while translating upstairs at the Whitmers' house, Smith and Cowdery asked the Lord for power to confer the gift of the Holy Ghost in fulfillment of John's promise.[21]

This event began the institutionalization of the ordinance to confer the gift of the Holy Ghost and led to the establishment of the church. As Smith reminisced in his history, "And here to our unspeakable satisfaction did we realize the truth of the Saviour's promise; Ask, and you shall receive, seek, and you shall find, knock and it shall be opened unto you" (Mt. 7:7). Taken at face value, it is clear that when he wrote those words, Smith understood the experience in terms of receiving the power and authority to confer the gift of the Holy Ghost in the chamber. It is important to recognize that the necessary elements for a ritualized, institutionalized bestowal of the gift of the Holy Ghost were put in place by this experience in Father Whitmer's chamber. The Holy Ghost was conferred only on those who met certain standards (baptism) and who had thus separated themselves out through an authorized ordinance (again, baptism). The gift of the Holy Ghost continued to demarcate between converts and the unconverted, reinforcing the implicit structure of an inner community set against the outer world.

Smith's history explains that with that authority given to them, he and Cowdery were commanded to ordain each other elders (thus officially connecting this ordinance to an ecclesiastical office) but to delay that ordinance until later. The passage in the history relating these events divides the first part, where they seem to be given the power to confer the gift of the Holy Ghost, and the second part, which contains the delayed command to ordain each other elders, by a semicolon. This punctuation makes it difficult to interpret whether both acts should be delayed, or just the ordination. Smith's history also explicitly describes them asking for the priesthood that John promised them; this was not just a reiteration of the precepts acquired by an earlier restoration, but also an event that initiated the sacramentalization and institutionalization of authoritatively offering the Holy Ghost to baptized believers and a call for the establishment of a church.

The question of priesthood, and in particular the priestly right to confer this gift of the Holy Ghost, provided another level of structural authentication: Smith and Cowdery were given power, but that power was coded in terms of a particular office (elder). Whereas a prophet might operate outside institutional parameters, the designation "elder" functioned not only as a title (identity of the person) but also as a formal, institutionalized role (identity of the position). The church had not been formally established at this point, but the use of the term *elder* indicated that an institutional hierarchy was both implicit and awaited. The experience in Father Whitmer's chamber can thus be read as an anticipatory call for the establishment of a church.

Coupled with these developments, the chamber experience provides a narrative about religious authority and power. The Book of Mormon demonstrates this thematic focus with the role its narrative played in understanding the chamber experience. In particular, it described a similar scenario for receiving the power to confer the gift of the Holy Ghost and emphasized the importance of that power. Smith and Cowdery were compelled to restore what was given to the ancient Americans in the narrative about Christ's ministry. If they were to bring about the "cause of Zion," they would need to establish the same order that Christ did in ancient America. According to the Book of Mormon, just before Christ departed from his American ministry, he laid his hands on each of his disciples. The text read "And it came to pass that when Jesus had made an end of these sayings, he touched with his hand the disciples whom he had chosen, one by one, even until he had touched them all, and spake unto them as he touched them; and the multitude heard not the words which he spake, therefore they did not bear record; *but the disciples bear record that he gave them power to give the Holy Ghost.*[22]

This reflects the basic scenario of the chamber experience because the actual performance of the ordination also happened later. Near the end of the Book of Mormon, a prophet named Moroni reflected on the disciples' experience, indicating that Christ told each of the disciples how to receive the power to confer the gift of the Holy Ghost. That passage stated, "Ye shall call on the Father in my name, in mighty prayer; and after that ye have done this, ye shall have power that on him whom ye shall lay your hands, ye shall give the Holy Ghost; and in my name shall ye give it: for thus do mine apostles."[23] Christ explained that they would receive that power only after he ascended to heaven and after the disciples had prayed for the power. Therefore, according to the Book of Mormon, they had to first ask the Lord in prayer before the authority would be given to them.

The Book of Mormon emphasizes the ability to obtain the godly authority, the authorized power, to confer the gift of the Holy Ghost. Their prayer for that power did not cause the Holy Ghost to exhibit itself in the twelve disciples. Instead, they were seeking authority to distribute the gift of the Holy Ghost to others. Smith too was seeking power and authority in the chamber of Father Whitmer. He dictated a revelation in early June, after John the Baptist told them they would receive additional power, which commanded Cowdery to "Ask the Father in my name in faith believing that you shall receive, and you shall have the Holy Ghost."[24] David Whitmer was also told by one of Smith's revelations that he should pray for the Holy Ghost, in a fashion similar to when Christ commanded his disciples in the Book of Mormon.[25] It was a promise that echoed one of Christ's parting statements in his American ministry and reflected Smith and Cowdery's purpose in the chamber: "And now, behold, my beloved brethren, I suppose that ye ponder somewhat in your hearts concerning that which ye should do after ye have entered in by the way. But, behold, why do ye ponder these things in your hearts? . . . after I have spoken these words, if ye cannot understand them it will be because *ye ask not, neither do ye knock*; wherefore, ye are not brought into the light, but must perish in the dark. (2 Nephi 32:1–4; emphasis added).

As if in response to this passage, Smith's history states that they "had for some time made this matter a subject of humble prayer, and at length we got together in the Chamber of Mr Whitmer's house in order more particularly to seek of the Lord what we now so earnestly desired." Their objective was clear: they sought authority. Smith remembered that, to his "greatest satisfaction," he was given that permission to confer the Gift of the Holy Ghost and they could do so once they met together to organize a church and after they had ordained each other as elders in that church.[26]

## Ordination and the Establishment of the Church

From 1829 until the spring of 1830, Smith and Cowdery followed the commandment given to them in the chamber of Father Whitmer. It told them to "defer this our ordination" until

> such times, as it should be practicable to have our brethren, who had been and who should be baptized, assembled together, when we must have their sanction to our thus proceeding to ordain each other, and have them decide by vote whether they were willing to accept us as spiritual teachers, or not, when also we were commanded to bless bread and break it with them, and to take wine, bless it, and drink it with them, afterward proceed to ordain each other according to commandment, then call out such men as the Spirit should dictate, and ordain them, and then attend to the laying on of hands for the gift of the Holy Ghost, upon all those whom we had previously baptized; doing all things in the name of the Lord.[27]

Yet, once they eventually did ordain each other, they also made conferring the gift of the Holy Ghost a saving ordinance. Smith's experience in the chamber was not unlike his reception of authority and power to baptize, efficacious only by his divinely received authority.[28]

Ordination and the laying on of hands served as the connective tissue binding the experience in the chamber of Father Whitmer and the institutionalization of Mormonism's saving ordinances. It identified the liturgical element that established Mormonism's developing church government as starkly different from most Protestants' line of authority. One way Smith's church established provenance was by linking it to John the Baptist and other restoration events. Ordination by ordination, priesthood holders could trace their authority back to Smith and Cowdery. The church's authoritative rites demanded that officers perform all clerical ordinations by the laying on of hands in order to demonstrate their line of authority. As discussed earlier, licenses were issued to the early clergy, signed by Smith and Cowdery as the first and second elders of the church, but minutes of early meetings also recorded ordinations by the laying on of hands.[29] The growth of the practice of ordination by the laying on of hands may be why the experience in the chamber of Father Whitmer was lost from early Mormon history. In particular, Christ apparently did not lay hands on Smith in the chamber. This lack of hands-on ordination seems like an aberration in the emerging tradition of laying on of hands, and thus the official narrative would appeal to the chamber experience with less frequency, resulting in its gradual disappearance from the general Mormon historical consciousness.

Such concerns with authority, ordination, and sacrament pointed to the fundamental change that was occurring within Mormonism in the spring of 1830: an unseasoned religious movement was beginning to coalesce as an institutional church. This development was formalized once the Book of Mormon had finally been published and bound on March 26, 1830. Less than two weeks later, on April 6, the Church of Christ was officially established. Its founding ecclesiastical document, the Articles and Covenants of the church, continued the preoccupation with authority and ordination that had concerned Joseph Smith for much of the previous year, directing elders to confirm individuals as members of the church and to confer on them the gift of the Holy Ghost by the laying on of hands.[30] The form of these confirmations extended an implicit authority to male church members by replicating the form of ordination: citizenship in the kingdom of God was given in the same way that authority was accorded to the church's ordained priests, through the laying on of hands.

Yet the historical record also seems to occasionally allow for the vocal authorization that took place in Father Whitmer's chamber. In the Book of Mormon, Christ bestowed the authority to confer the gift of the Holy Ghost through a vocal authorization.[31] The concept of receiving authority from the voice of God, though certainly not the predominant method as the church developed, appears to have been accepted by early members. Parley P. Pratt, for example, wrote in early Mormonism's most influential pamphlet that "all who have no direct revelation from the King of Heaven to themselves, neither by angels, nor by the voice of God, nor by the Spirit of Prophesy: are acting under authority which was given to others, who are dead, and their commission stolen, and their authority usurped." He went on to write, "This manifestation was by the ministering of Angels, and by the voice of Jehovah, speaking from the heavens in plainness, unto men who are now living among you."[32] On March 22, 1839, Smith wrote a letter to Isaac Galland, stating, "We believe that no man can administer salvation through the gospel to the souls of men, in the name of Jesus Christ, except he is authorized from God, by revelation, or by being ordained by someone whom God hath sent by revelation."[33] Even after years of primarily bestowing power through the laying on of hands, Smith acknowledged that God could authorize men to act in his name through spoken revelation. It was not required that all who had authority from God received that authority from a chain of individuals laying their hands on each other, beginning with Christ. The primary requirement was simply authorization from God, though with time the tradition of laying on of hands became for all practical purposes a requirement.

The narrative from the chamber of Father Whitmer had also included a commandment for Smith and Cowdery to ordain each other as elders—another vital step in the creation of a church. Yet it did not happen immediately. While their prayerful request for the power to confer the gift of the Holy Ghost was answered to their "unspeakable satisfaction," they were commanded to wait to ordain each other. The command for Smith and Cowdery to ordain each other was deferred until "such times, as it should be practicable to have our brethren, who had been and who should be baptized, assembled together."[34] This galvanized the authority to confer the gift of the Holy Ghost with the ordination to elder as if the authority to give the Holy Ghost shaped the meaning of that office, which provides a strong indicator that the early ecclesiology of the church was firmly established on the liturgical authority of each office. It was also inseparable from the charismatic nature of communication from the Holy Ghost.

The power to bestow the Holy Ghost was a two-step process: authorization followed by ordination. What Smith and Cowdery possessed in June 1829 was the authority to ordain each other; the actual ordination would come later. Smith's history explains that the commandment in the chamber was not fulfilled immediately, but on April 6, 1830, when the ordinations were performed and the church was established. The sequence of the account in Smith's history, however, emphasizes the significance of the experience in the chamber and thus prioritizes a legitimized authority (potential) over the act of ordination (actualization).

The day Smith's church was established was supposed to be the day of Mormon Pentecost, but the institutionalization of the church became the most important part of the narrative taking shape. Instead of having the Spirit poured out on them, Smith and Cowdery laid hands on each other in ordinations and confirmations. Their charismatic experience was governed by sacramentalism and formalized rituals. Smith described in his history that he followed the commandment received in the chamber of Father Whitmer exactly. (See table 4.2.) He explained that on April 6, 1830, they "opened the meeting by solemn prayer to our Heavenly Father." Second, they "proceeded, (according to previous commandment)" given in the chamber to call on those present to vote on their leadership and the establishment of the church. After the vote, "I then laid my hands upon Oliver Cowdery . . . and ordained him an Elder. . . . he ordained me also to the office of an Elder of said Church." Having fulfilled the commandment to ordain each other, Smith declared, "We then laid our hands on each individual member of the Church present that they might receive the Gift of the Holy Ghost, and be confirmed members of

Table 4.2. Joseph Smith's history "according to previous commandment"

| Commandment | Fulfillment |
|---|---|
| The Chamber of Old Father Whitmer, June 1829, Joseph Smith, History, A-1: 27. | Establishment of the Church, April 6, 1830, Joseph Smith, History, A-1: 37. |
| "commanding us; that I should ordain Oliver Cowdery to be an Elder in the Church of Jesus Christ, and that he also should ordain me to the same office" | "I then laid my hands upon Oliver Cowdery and ordained him an Elder of the Church. . . . He ordained me also to the office of an Elder of said Church." |
| "such times, as it should be practicable to have our brethren, who had been and who should be baptized, assembled together" | "we had received commandment to organize the Church and accordingly we met together for that purpose, at the house of the above mentioned Mr Whitmer [Peter Whitmer Sr.] (being six in number) on Tuesday the sixth day of April, AD One thousand, eight hundred and thirty." |
| "have them decide by vote whether they were willing to accept us as spiritual teachers, or not" | "We proceeded, (according to previous commandment) to call on our brethren to know whether they accepted us as their teachers" |
| "when also we were commanded to bless bread and break it with them, and to take wine, bless it, and drink it with them" | "We then broke bread, blessed it, and brake it with them, also wine, blessed it, and drank it with them." |
| "then attend to the laying on of hands for the gift of the Holy Ghost, upon all those whom we had previously baptized; doing all things in the name of the Lord." | "We then laid our hands on each individual member of the Church present that they might receive the gift of the Holy Ghost, and be confirmed members of the Church of Christ." |

the Church of Christ." Joseph wrote that the ordinations and confirmations were "according to previous commandment."[35] Therefore, Smith understood these ordinations as inseparably connected to the chamber experience, where he and Cowdery had been given permission to confer the gift of the Holy Ghost and commanded to ordain one another to the office of elder.

This interpretation of earlier events sees Smith as explicitly creating an ecclesiology devoid of the chronological precedence of Catholicism and removed from the authority of the priesthood of all believers. In this ecclesiology, he firmly establishes a restoration theology and clergy whose ordinations could be physically traced back to Smith himself. Smith moved deftly between existing models of the institutional expansion of authority and, much in the manner of his prior translation and revelatory projects, established a novel approach that upheld both his own authority as prophet and a structure in which this authority could be shared without diluting the original source.

## Ordaining the Church's Prophet

Joseph Smith was not only ordained as the first elder of the Church of Christ on April 6, 1830, he was also ordained as the prophet of the church. Smith's history is very clear in its description of the ordinations of himself and Cowdery, ordinations that were preceded by a unanimous vote or acceptance of them as "teachers in the things of the Kingdom of God." Smith's history explained that after the vote and ordination, he "received the following commandment."[36] It prophesied that "there Shall a Record be kept among you" and that within that record Smith would be known as a "seer & translator & Prophet an Apostle of Jesus Christ an Elder of the Church." It commanded Cowdery "that he [Joseph] should be ordained by you," the logic being that Cowdery was an apostle and Smith had ordained him as the second elder. This revelation not only validated Cowdery's authority but also called for Smith to be ordained to an additional position aside from first elder of the church. When Cowdery was asked in 1847, "To what did you ordain Joseph on the 6th of April, 1830?" he replied, "I ordained him to be a Prophet, Seer, &c., just as the revelation says."[37] David Whitmer, who also said he was at the meeting, wrote, "Joseph received a revelation that he should be the leader." The revelation, according to Whitmer, also directed Cowdery that Smith "should be ordained by [him] as 'Prophet Seer and Revelator' to the church."[38]

Being ordained as a clergyman with a recognizable institutional title or office, such as elder or even first elder, reflected the common practices of other contemporary Christian churches; the title "prophet," however, was not typical. What did it mean, then, to be ordained as a prophet? Charisma was the power that gave birth to other prophets in the Second Great Awakening who were in some ways similar to Smith, but when he institutionalized his position as the prophet within a church, the role became part of the institution's structure—in fact, this position was so central both institutionally and theologically that it became the defining factor within Mormonism's hierarchical democracy. On April 6, 1830, Smith's own revelation called Cowdery, the presiding elder, to ordain Smith to the position of prophet, revelator, translator, and so on. Smith's revelations guided their behavior and, in this instance, called for an institutional ordination to officially mark Smith as the prophet of God's budding kingdom.

As first elder of the church, Smith ordained clergymen and enacted ordinances; as an ordained prophet he provided revelation. His revelations guided individuals within the church, but they also created the foundation for ecclesiastical, theological, and even practical standards. His unique ordination formed a new kind of church polity in which the ordained priests of the church turned to a single man receiving revelation from God to guide them. Though the governing council of elders did all things by common consent and the lay clergy functioned much like other populist Christians and evangelicals, Mormon priests ultimately found authoritative guidance in the ordained prophet who acted as the oracle of God. Smith's ordained position superseded all the authority of the other elders through his ability to speak authoritatively in the voice of God. Only Smith delivered public revelations at churchwide meetings. Smith continually allowed for a democratic clerical structure that empowered the leaders of the church, but his ordained position as prophet demanded their allegiance to his revelatory guidance.

This was, perhaps, Joseph Smith's most radical doctrine. Unlike other Protestant clergy who adamantly maintained the idea of *sola scriptura*, in Mormonism even the Bible itself was subject to the scrutiny of the prophet of the church. The lay populist leadership of the Mormon church did not turn first to the Bible as the itinerant preachers and evangelicals had done across New York State. Instead, they consulted the modern revelation delivered by their prophet. Placing aside *sola scriptura*, Smith's converts clung to the principle of *sola propheta*, in which the prophet was the supreme authority in all matters of doctrine and practice. Smith's claim to be a prophet whose revelations, as evolving, could modify and even overwrite their predecessors thus insisted that not even the Bible could be fully accepted as God's word. The closest things to creeds within Mormonism were not creedal statements at all—they were declarations in the voice of God through Joseph Smith.[39] When Smith declared policy, governance, or theology, he did so through commandment and in the voice of God. In this sense, he was continually recreating authoritative scriptural text without the guidance or help from the leaders of the church or the Bible.

Smith was not attempting to ignore the Bible or devalue it in any way, at least in his own mind. He produced an extensive literary corpus (the Book of Mormon and the Doctrine and Covenants) that frequently alluded to the Bible, and he also claimed to have prophetic authority to interpret the Bible. A friend of Smith remembered him stating, "After I got through translating the Book of Mormon, I took up the Bible to read with the Urim and Thummim. I read the first Chapter of Genesis and saw the things as they were done. I turned over the next and the next, and the whole passed before me like a grand panorama; and so on chapter after chapter until I read the whole of it. I saw it all!"[40] Almost immediately after the church was established, Smith received a revelation that produced a contemporary conception of prophethood and how he would establish Zion. His act of scripture making was not just perpetuated through the Book of Mormon and his revelations—it was also accomplished through a translation and expansion of the Bible. This act of interpretation proved the importance of his new epistemology more than any other example because if the contemporary prophet had the authority to revise scripture, then clearly the power of prophethood superseded that of scripture. Smith, in fact, expanded verses in Genesis to produce seven chapters of the lost "Book of Moses," and this expansion and revision led him to begin a three-year project in which he made changes throughout the Bible. Though it is unclear how this process specifically functioned, his revisions to the Bible included alterations of around 3,400 verses—changes that suggest Smith's disregard for any Christian theology that valued the text of the Bible as unchangeable. Smith did not see his changes to the Bible as inconsequential. His work on the Bible became his primary stewardship within the church until he finished it in 1833, and it caused numerous theological and structural revelations to be received through him that were later canonized as part of the Doctrine and Covenants.

Smith expanded the Bible and even tried to redefine what it meant to be biblical. Before Smith, to be biblical meant to be authoritative; according to Smith, the scriptures were to be read (and reread) constantly by individuals in an essentially infinite variety of contexts. Thus, to be scriptural for Smith was to be flexible (rather than to maintain the rigidity of absolute authority). When hermeneutic authority and power are transferred to a living prophet, the power of scripture comes into play in its adaptability, its inherent openness, its ability to be read by everyone, and its capacity to have something to say. But significantly, to be scriptural meant to be susceptible to prophetic change and reinterpretation.

Reinterpreting the Bible was not the only task facing the new prophet. Decision making was another. Though the church began with a vocabulary loaded with Methodist predilection for structural equality, including the mandate that all things would be established "by common consent," Smith's institutionalized role as the prophet ensured that the structural instantiation of power would not be purely democratic. As the ordained prophet, Smith's power was in a very real sense absolute: he could delegate it via the properly legitimated institutional channels, but this delegation did not in any way diminish his own right to act for the church as a whole. Other leaders of the movement embraced the democratic zeal of US Christianity to the extent that they challenged Smith's revelations and even attempted to give their own revelations.[41] One of these challenges came from second elder Oliver Cowdery, who had experienced the most intimate and miraculous events of the restoration and who was, aside from Smith, its most respected leader. Just weeks after the first conference of the church on June 8, 1830, Cowdery and Smith taught and baptized believers in Colesville, New York, before Cowdery returned to Fayette, New York, and Smith to his home in Harmony, Pennsylvania. Cowdery soon wrote a letter to Smith challenging a verse in the Articles and Covenants of the church. Likely leaning toward a Calvinist mindset, Cowdery was bothered by the statement that believers must "truly manifest . . . their works" before they were baptized into the church.[42] The Articles and Covenants stated that "Now therefore whosoever repenteth & humbleth himself before me & desireth to be baptized in my name shall ye baptize them." He emphatically wrote, "I command you in the name of God to erase those words, that no priestcraft be amongst us."[43]

Cowdery felt justified in challenging Smith in what he thought was an egregious theological mistake, but his accusation provoked Smith to reestablish his position within the Mormon hierarchy as the ordained prophet. Though Cowdery's assumption of authority is easily understood, because of his previous contributions and experiences establishing Smith's church, he apparently felt he had more authority in the revelatory process than he actually possessed. After some debate, Smith convinced Cowdery and the Whitmers that Cowdery's dispute was in error. Smith recalled that the incident taught all of them "the necessity of Humility, and meekness before the Lord . . . that we might walk in his paths, and live every word which proceedeth forth from his mouth," words that Joseph Smith subsequently delivered.[44]

Soon after Cowdery challenged the contents of the Articles and Covenants, he and the Whitmer family began supporting revelations that his soon-to-be brother-in-law Hiram Page was receiving—a move toward a possible democratization of the revelatory authority within the church. Page was imitating the gifts that made Smith a prophet in the first place. As one member described it, Page "found a smooth stone, upon which there appeared to be writing, which when transcribed upon paper, disappeared from the stone, and another impression appeared in its place. This when copied, vanished as the former had done, and so it continued alternately appearing and disappearing; in the meanwhile, he continued to write, until he had written over considerable paper."[45] Clearly, Page was attempting to write as if he were receiving revelations in the manner that Smith translated the Book of Mormon.

Recognizing the centrality of Zion in the establishment of the church, Page's sense of democratic revelatory power led his own revelations to make declarations about Smith's Zion. His revelation "bore most striking marks of a Mormonite revelation, and was received as an authentic document by most of the Mormonites."[46] Smith's history explained that Page had "got in his possession, a certain stone, by which he had obtained . . . revelations, concerning the upbuilding of Zion, the order of the Church, etc., all of which were entirely at variance with the order of God's house, as laid down in the new Testament, as well as in our late revelations."[47] Newel Knight, who arrived with Smith in Fayette that September, explained that Page "had quite a roll of papers full of these revelations, and many in the church were led astray by them. Even Oliver Cowdery and the Whitmer family had given heed to them."[48] In Page's mind, his actions were in line with Smith's call to establish Zion: Page was fulfilling his part of gathering the nation of Israel and establishing Zion. He had clearly, however, missed Smith's message about the singularity of a guiding prophet. Though Page appeared similar to Smith in terms of his actions prior to the formation of the church, Smith was to be its only ordained prophet.[49]

Both Page and Cowdery attempted to include themselves in receiving and defining the church's revelations, a privilege that Smith insisted was reserved for the prophet of the church. It was not a committee building Zion, nor was it being established by common consent: Zion was being established through the prophetic word. Unknowingly, Page's actions demarcated the line between a charismatic prophet and the kind Smith had become after his ordination on April 6, 1830. At the peak of this early challenge to his prophetic uniqueness, Smith dictated a revelation that defined his position as one that wielded sole authority to receive revelation for the church. It stated, "Thou shalt not command him which is at thy head & at the head of the Church for I have given him the keys of the mysteries of the Revelations which are sealed until I shall appoint unto him another in his stead." Smith had become the only authoritative speaker for the church while simultaneously establishing a church governed by a quasi-democratically distributed organized priesthood.

Smith did not demand complete control, but he did insist that there be only one commanding voice. Smith's revelation declared to Cowdery, "Thou shalt not write by way of commandment . . . thou shall not command him who is at thy head, and at the head of the church." Nonetheless, Cowdery could write according to "wisdom" and was told that "if thou art led at any time by the Comforter to speak or teach . . . thou mayest do it."[50] This relationship between the prophet and the church's leaders exhibits a distinct fluidity, allowing the priesthood to teach and speak authoritatively while simultaneously recognizing the authority of the prophet to be the head of the church. Smith reinforced this pattern, repeating this carefully balanced relationship throughout his ministry. Although Smith was occasionally challenged by others like Cowdery and Page, ultimately the prophet maintained his unique position as the sole recipient of revelation for the whole church.

## From Church to Expanding Priesthood

The tension between Smith, Cowdery, and Page as the church was organized offers a window into how early Mormonism defined the routinization of charisma. Like other charismatic leaders, Smith originally ruled by virtue of his divine power. The Book of Mormon, his revelations, and angelic visits legitimated his leadership to early converts, even the strong-minded Whitmer family. Weber found this kind of leadership to be the least stable and claimed it would naturally develop into more traditional monarchical and bureaucratic models if the movements in question were to survive. The experience in Father Whitmer's chamber demanded that others be empowered, in which the priesthood offered a similar kind of divine power and leadership that functioned alongside Smith's charismatic leadership. The establishment of the church formed a kind of bureaucratization of charisma, making it more religious and less secular, but Smith's ordination as a prophet made the early Mormons' church government a hierarchical democracy. While Cowdery and Page emphasized the democracy aspect, believing they possessed the same kind of revelatory and authoritative voice as Smith within the church, he responded by emphasizing the hierarchical aspect, turning attention to the unique role of the prophet.[51]

Smith created a church that allowed its own priesthood to critically address scripture and receive divine guidance, like other US clergy, yet his position as the ordained prophet created a new perspective on what religious authority could embrace. Smith's claim to be an American prophet was an authoritative revelatory production that, through augmentation and expansion, ultimately shifted the locus of power away from the text and into the personage of the prophet. The prophet's authority, then, superseded that of all previously received revelations, including the Bible itself: *sola scriptura* was translated into *sola propheta*. In the next step of development, Smith expanded his authority by distributing it to the leadership of the church.

# 5
# The Development of Mormon Priesthood

Joseph Smith's charisma was eventually institutionalized within his church, followed by the development of his priesthood order from 1831 to 1835. The fourth restoration point occurred in June 1831 with Smith's ordination to the high priesthood, which initiated a series of authoritative expansions of the priesthood over the next few years. The hierarchical democracy that developed shaped the relationship between the members, the priesthood, and the prophet. Institutionalizing his position as the prophet caused some members and priesthood leaders to compare Smith to a monarch and his critics to complain that he was a "Tyrant! Pope!! King!!"[1] Through the lens of US democracy, the reproaches seemed justified by Mormonism's hierarchical structure. In fact, as the priesthood developed, it was not only hierarchical but primordial; its narrative of authority extended back in time before the garden of Eden and forward in time to Joseph Smith in the last dispensation. The term *priesthood* was hardly functional in Mormonism until Joseph Smith began to connect the dots between the Bible and his new restoration scripture that marked a genealogy of priesthood back to Adam. This was a lineage of power, defined by an authority traced from patriarch to patriarch, presumably preceding apostolic Catholic succession. Just as subjects submit to a monarch because his authority descends through a legitimate kingly lineage, Smith's Bible-believing followers had reason to see him as a kind of king, descended from Adam.[2] With the power of the prophetic voice, Smith recast the Bible and added the book of Moses, the Book of Mormon, and his own revelations to authoritatively define this family tree of prophets leading from Adam to himself.

Yet the Mormon priesthood also benefited from this patriarchal lineage. As the Mormon clergy grew, its priesthood structure grew in tandem, even expanding regionally beyond Smith's direct reach. But the genealogy of the priesthood always ran back through Joseph Smith. Kathleen Flake has carefully carved away the assumptions that Mormonism was populist and antiauthoritarian. She wrote, "Mormonism's ordained priesthood . . . had its privileges over against and duties subordinate to other offices. All offices were attainable, but all officers were accountable."[3] Mormons claimed sacramental power above all, shrugging off the evangelical republicanism and populism of US culture. This chapter will chart the genealogy of Mormon priesthood through Smith's restoration scripture and then describe the institutional priesthood that defined Smith as the president of the high priesthood and ultimate appellate judge within a structure that came to include both a higher and a lower priesthood. Smith became the fountainhead of all things Mormon, distributing and sustaining all authority and power in a well-organized religious system.

## Covenant Theology and the Genealogy of Priesthood in Early Mormon Scripture

Smith did not regard the emerging priesthood order as an innovation but rather a reconnection, at the deepest level, to the past. The priesthood existed to create continuity between God's ancient patriarchs and modern Mormon authority. For Smith, the ancient priesthood and the modern priesthood brought by angels were one and the same thing. Where there was clear historical and biblical discontinuity, as with the old and new covenants, Smith created genealogical continuity. Reinterpreting ancient scripture empowered his understanding of priesthood, and Smith's revelations directed the efforts of those involved. He taught that there was an everlasting covenant and that the Book of Mormon was playing a major role in reestablishing that covenant.[4] The book was an explicit call to gather remnant Israel in America in an attempt to draw two disparate continents together and connect modern Americans to the biblical story.

The narrative within the Book of Mormon shares this theme of continuity. To understand how covenant works in the Book of Mormon, consider one of its later sections, the book of Ether, which, temporally, is significantly displaced from the chronological sequence of the rest of the scripture. Ether contains the history of a people led by God out of destruction more than fifteen hundred years before the main Book of Mormon narrative even began. Moroni, the Book of Mormon's final editor, explained on the title page of the Book of Mormon that the book of Ether was included "to show unto the remnant of the house of Israel what great things the Lord hath done for their fathers; and that they may know the covenants of the Lord, that they are not cast off forever." The book of Ether timeline eventually spans the centuries, and the civilization disintegrates until only one person is left. This person eventually connects with people from the primary Book of Mormon narrative, and he thus establishes a connective link between the book of Ether and the greater project of the Book of Mormon as a whole. In other words, Ether helped to affirm the possibility for continuity within the ancient covenants between pre-Abrahamic people and remnant Israel.[5]

The Book of Mormon's narrative also collapsed distinctions between the Old and New Testaments. Many nineteenth-century Christians emphasized such a division in order to focus on Christ's ministry and thereby privilege the New Testament as superseding the Old. Protestant covenant theology was understood through the radical opposition between the old covenant (found in the Old Testament) and the new covenant (found in the New Testament).[6] But the Book of Mormon blurred that line: prophets such as Lehi and Nephi, who lived approximately six centuries before Jesus's birth, described Christ in their ministry. The Book of Mormon reads as a text in constant battle for the inclusion of prophecy, history, and contemporary issues. It is a book bound to past, present, and future, utterly unconcerned with anachronism. In fact, it seems to glory in its predictive and prophetic nature through its anachronisms—for example, by having ancient characters accept Christianity in a pre-Christian era.

Though the term *priesthood* was absent from the Book of Mormon text after Christ's ministry, the hazy boundary between "old" and "new" covenant theology eventually created a space for an Old Testament priesthood in Smith's modern church. Describing the temporal bridge formed as Smith translated the Bible, one historian declared, "Joseph's attention to the Old Testament text was an aspect of his interest in the entire span of sacred history and his desire to encompass the whole of it within the restored gospel. In his vision of the Gospel kingdom, ancient and modern were to freely intermingle."[7]

Even though Smith did not use the terms *Melchizedek* or *high priesthood* to describe Mormon offices, powers, or authorities before June 1831, the terms were common in Bible commentaries, and they appeared in the Book of Mormon. Both the Bible and the Book of Mormon used the terms generally in reference to the office of high priest.[8] Adam Clarke, who wrote a popular biblical commentary, explained that the chosen among the ancient Israelites in lineal succession held the high priesthood.[9] Many Christians taught that the succession of high priests ended with Christ, the great high priest.[10] These Christians criticized the Freemasons, who used the office of high priest within their ranks, for improperly instituting an order of the priesthood that ended with Christ.[11] Some offered a similar criticism of the Book of Mormon, particularly Smith's use of the office of high priest and claims of covenantal continuity with the Old Testament. It was true. Smith was not perpetuating a supersessionist theology but rather a theology and priesthood that demanded continuity with the distant, holy past.

## The High Priesthood, the Book of Moses, and Melchizedek

As with most of the developments in the nascent church, Smith directed the development of the priesthood through his own revelations and translations, not just the ancient-modern text of the Book of Mormon. Smith's dictation of the book of Moses in early 1831 was the most direct contemporary text describing the bridge connecting the Old Testament priesthood (described in Alma 13 and Hebrews 7) and the Christian era. The book of Moses, now included in the LDS canon as part of the Pearl of Great Price, appears to have been revealed during the time Smith was translating the Bible. As Smith translated, he revealed a passage in the book of Moses that spoke of Adam in the beginning of time. Smith dictated to his scribe that "this same Priesthood [held by Adam], which was in the beginning, shall be in the end of the world also" (Moses 6:7). The same text describes the ordinance of baptism performed and taught by Adam along with his teachings about Jesus Christ (Moses 6:7, 52) as if there were a seamless connection between the Old and New Testament ordinances and priesthood. The Book of Mormon suggested continuity between the ancient and modern remnant Israel; Smith's restoration scripture indicated a link between ancient and modern priesthood.

The book of Moses connected the priesthood to an ancient genealogy, treating priesthood as the binding element that linked all generations of God's people together.[12] This understanding of the priesthood as binding relates to the Book of Mormon and its brief mention of the priesthood of Melchizedek and a prophet who was given an explicit binding power: "I give unto you power, that whatsoever ye shall seal on earth shall be sealed in heaven; and whatsoever ye shall loose on earth shall be loosed in heaven; and thus shall ye have power among this people."[13] Smith's restoration scriptures built on each other, providing a second witness and ancient precedent for modern beliefs and Mormon initiatives. Smith also compared the ancient prophet Melchizedek with Enoch in the book of Moses, connecting Melchizedek to the city of Enoch and to God's covenant people. Smith's translation of Genesis 14 stated that Melchizedek was "approved of God" and "ordained a high Priest after the order of the covenant which God made with Enoch it being after the order of the Son of God."[14]

Once the genealogy of patriarchs leading from Adam to Smith was established through Mormon scripture, it led to further ritual and ordination. Smith's January 1831 revelation promised that the Mormons "would be endowed with power from on high" once they arrived in Ohio, and though the branches of the church did not arrive until the spring of 1831, Smith and a handful of others reached the area in February.[15] Smith declared that once all the elders of the church had gathered from New York—as soon as "they assemble[d] themselves together" for the first general conference in Ohio—the Lord would pour out his spirit.[16] Scheduled for early June 1831, the conference anticipated an outpouring of the spirit and an "endowment from on high."[17] By that time, the early Mormon leadership had worked hard to unite the two groups of Mormons from New York and Ohio and to establish "the Law," which governed Mormons communally as part of a law of consecration. At that first conference after the migration to Ohio, many of the church leaders were ordained to the high priesthood, just as Melchizedek was in Smith's translation of Genesis 14.[18]

Some eyewitness accounts describe the ordinations at the conference as the bestowal of the "Melchizedek priesthood," and others called it the "high priesthood."[19] These terms would be blurred and used synonymously within the next five years, but in the contemporary accounts given about the conference they did not have the same connotations. John Corrill emphatically declared in his history that "the Melchizedek Priesthood was then for the first time introduced, and conferred on several of the elders."[20] Corrill explicitly claimed that this was the first time the priesthood had been introduced.[21] Even Newel Knight explained that "a number were ordained to the Melchizedek Priesthood."[22] Specifically addressing the issue, William Smith, Joseph Smith's younger brother, insinuated that the elders who were ordained at the June 3 conference did not have the Melchizedek priesthood before they were ordained.[23] His late reminiscence, not published until 1883, may have been correct, since the actual minutes of the meeting stated, "it was the privilege of those elders present to be ordained to the high priesthood."[24] If William Smith understood the high priesthood to be the Melchizedek priesthood, his statement is easily justified.[25] Within months of the conference, the church's leaders began conflating "Melchizedek priesthood" and "high priesthood," which affected the memories of those who later reflected on the ordinations and their significance.[26]

To make things even more complicated, even Smith's own 1839 history seems to claim that he ordained the elders to the Melchizedek priesthood at the 1831 conference. One passage in his history originally read, "the authority of the Melchizedek priesthood was manifested and conferred for the first time upon several of the elders." Willard Richards, however, crossed out the passage—which was written by W. W. Phelps—and inserted, "I conferred the high priesthood for the first time upon several of the elders."[27] Who was ultimately responsible for the original statement and who made the decision to make the changes is unknown, but this lack of historical precision seems to demonstrate the difficulty inherent in attempts to make sense of the June 1831 conference and to determine whether the Melchizedek priesthood, identified and understood as such, was itself given. Why did some eyewitnesses use language that claimed that the Melchizedek priesthood was restored in the 1831 conference when other equally reliable sources also claimed that Peter, James, and John had restored the Melchizedek priesthood in either 1829 or 1830? The heart of the issue is how these early church members understood "high priesthood" itself.

Understanding the contemporary use of "high priesthood" is necessary because the term "Melchizedek priesthood" was not used before 1831 and not regularly used in the church until 1835, when it appeared emphatically in the newly published Doctrine and Covenants. The minutes of the 1831 conference, taken by church historian John Whitmer, stated that selected elders "were ordained to the high priesthood under the hand of Brother Joseph Smith, Jr."[28] One of the earliest journal accounts, by Elder Levi Hancock, also recorded that elders were given the "high priesthood."[29] These early accounts did not make an explicit connection between the high priesthood and the Melchizedek priesthood—that connection developed over time.[30] Once the priesthood was split into two orders, higher and lower priesthoods made sense.

The ordinations to the high priesthood were also more than just the bestowal of an ecclesiastical office, a difference that is especially clear when the event is evaluated in the context of Smith's covenant theology and restoration scripture. Smith's translation of the Bible, just months before June 1831, describes high priests of the Old Testament who had the power to move mountains and divide seas.[31] Similarly, the ordination to the high priesthood in June 1831 included powers that elders did not possess before this ordination, such as the power to seal up to life eternal. Such expansion demonstrates how the restoration of priesthood at the conference articulated a significant part of the restoration of authority. Jared Carter, who attended the conference, wrote in his journal that bestowing the high priesthood empowered elders to heal the sick miraculously, implying that the ordination provided more than just an office.[32] Carter wrote that his brother Simeon was ordained "an elder in the high priesthood," which seems to indicate that his brother held the office of elder before the conference and the power of the high priesthood within that office after the conference.[33]

Smith described the high priesthood as a power given to elders "to seal up the saints unto eternal life,"[34] an idea that matched the portrayal of the high priesthood found in the Book of Mormon and the book of Moses. Church leaders already possessed the power to baptize, confer the Holy Ghost, and ordain elders. The high priesthood was an authority beyond those Christian ordinances: its power extended back to the ancient of days and bound God's people together. The leadership's own understanding of what had happened in 1831 was not instantaneous—it involved a process of reflection, pondering, publication of revelation, and a structuring of this kind of priesthood, all of which took place by 1835. Seeing the priesthood restoration in these terms illustrates priesthood as a subject open to ongoing interpretation, in the same way that scripture and theology remained open to Smith's reinterpretation via his prophetic authority. In this particular case, Smith found himself aligning the restoration with the ancient past and providing priesthood power that could bind together covenant Israel.

## President of the High Priesthood

Once the grand order of high priesthood was established, Smith's revelations authoritatively positioned him as its president. Soon after the June 1831 conference and the bestowal of the high priesthood, one of Smith's revelations called him and others to travel to Missouri to establish Zion.[35] As Smith and a handful of missionaries made the month-long trip from Kirtland, Ohio, to Independence, Missouri, discontent arose among the group, most of whom had recently been ordained to the high priesthood.[36] During the trip, newly converted preacher Ezra Booth and the recently called bishop, Edward Partridge, challenged Smith's authority by questioning his decisions about land purchases.[37] This challenge was particularly worrisome to Smith because Bishop Partridge controlled the purse of the church and Booth was likewise an influential convert.[38] Once they returned to Ohio, Booth left the church after being reprimanded for disobedience, but Partridge remained faithful, if distraught.[39]

Though Hiram Page had been reproved personally a year earlier, Smith's revelations revealed a new judicial authority within the high priesthood to discipline Booth. In response to what occurred in Missouri, a few months after returning to Ohio, Smith dictated a revelation that clarified the structural hierarchy of the church. It was addressed to those "in the Land of Zion." The November 11, 1831, revelation commanded Smith to establish an office called "the president of the high priesthood."[40] It explained the position and duties of the president of the high priesthood and the office of bishop. The bishop was described as a "judge in Israel" charged with controlling the temporal affairs of the church. This new high priesthood structure sounded vaguely governmental and used terms like "judge" and "president." A body of elders and the bishop (who controlled the communal economy of the church) would form disciplinary courts within weeks after Booth left the church. The president, meanwhile, was to preside over the courts (as an appellate court) and deal with the most important matters of the church. The revelation also stated that the president would "preside over the whole church & to be like unto Moses," restating the revelation to Page and Cowdery in 1830 and maintaining Smith's ancient authority.

This description not only established a president of the high priesthood; it formulated the church's boundaries that the priesthood controlled, representing a real religious entity. The idea of an unelected president sounded more like monarchy than the representative democracy and separation of powers of US political ideals. It was this model of a president/prophet that finally identified Smith's charisma as authoritative and hierarchical. The combination did not replace Smith's charisma, but instead gave it additional weight.

Smith's institutional position as president also took on restorationist narratives and carried over his genealogical and covenantal authority within those narratives. The office of president of the high priesthood symbolized the authority that Peter apparently held in the New Testament church, according to one of Smith's revelations.[41] Though the revelation only established the office of president and did not specify who would fill that position, Smith would be the first and only person to hold the office during his lifetime. Along with creating the office of president of the high priesthood, the church also began to use the metaphor of "keys" (an idea further elaborated in the next chapter) in conjunction with explanations of official praxis. The president held the keys of administration and had the ability to delegate those keys to other leaders in the church. By October 1831, the keys of the priesthood were described as the same ones held by Peter in the New Testament. This concept had likely been on Smith's mind months earlier when he translated Mathew 16:19 in the New Testament.[42] An October revelation declared, "The keys of the kingdom of God [are] committed unto man on the Earth & from thence shall the Gospel roll forth unto the ends of the Earth."[43] At a conference on January 25, 1832, in Amherst, Ohio, Smith was appointed and ordained as the "Presiding high Priest over the high Priesthood of the Church."[44] By March

1832, Smith had dictated a revelation stating that he had received "keys of the kingdom,"[45] and in the summer of 1832, Smith reported in his history that he had received "kees [*sic*] of the kingdom of God."[46]

By that point, Smith and his revelations had explained that with these keys of the kingdom, he was the only person with both the authority to lead and the ability to delegate responsibility within Christ's church. The keys were used as a metaphor that inevitably reflected the authority claimed by the Catholic pope and the succession of bishops that Episcopalians and Methodists tied to their clerical authority. But, more directly, they represented the authority of the president of the high priesthood to delegate power to the officers, bishops, and regional leaders in the church. By March 1832, another revelation called two counselors, Sidney Rigdon and Jesse Gause, to minister along with Smith.[47] After Gause was excommunicated in December 1832, Smith replaced him with Frederick G. Williams in January 1833.[48] Aided by his councilors, and according to a September 1831 revelation, Smith possessed the keys that unlocked the "mysteries of the kingdom."[49]

Through the development of quorums and councils and the expanding geographical range of the church, keys became an important descriptive analogy for understanding the distribution of authority from the top down. Knowing the importance of the concept of keys, Smith looked back to 1829 and his experiences since then to align them and his prophetic mission with his more institutional position as a prophet and president in 1831. Before this time, his revelations stated that he held the keys of the revelations or the power to connect the ancient past to modern Zion through the processes of translation and revelation. Smith's calling as a prophet (like Moses) and his position as the first elder eventually became the way that he expressed the earliest forms of his presidency, president-prophet. By 1835, Smith explained that the keys of the kingdom had been given to him years before 1832, when he became the president.[50]

## Defining the Aaronic and Melchizedek Priesthoods

Mormons were not the only Christians struggling to form a priesthood order. Smith and particularly Rigdon were both familiar with the debates of the day, especially the ecclesiology of the liturgical traditions and the priesthood of believers that was heavily emphasized by Baptists. Alexander Campbell and the Disciples of Christ provide the most relevant examples here, as Rigdon's congregations, who were connected to the Disciples of Christ, joined the Mormon movement in late 1830. Campbell critically reviewed the Book of Mormon in February 1831 and compared some of its claims to those of the Bible. Campbell's analysis makes it clear that the Mormons had developed doctrines around the Bible's concepts of priesthood and high priesthood by early 1831. Alexander Crawford, a Scottish immigrant who became a significant force in the restorationist movement in the Canadian maritime provinces, influenced Campbell through his belief that there were three priesthoods: "the patriarchal," "the Aaronical," and a priesthood of Jesus Christ. Crawford apparently used priesthood terms in a way that was similar to the way the Mormons would use them, though there is no direct historical connection, and no records indicate that Smith studied Crawford's priesthoods. The claim that Smith utilized Crawford is tenuous because it would require a chain of knowledge from Crawford, to Campbell, to Rigdon, and finally to Smith. The thematic connection between the two conceptions does, however, demonstrate that Smith's contemporaries were taking the orders of priesthoods as described in the Bible seriously. Smith, however, eventually developed a complex order of the priesthood with a specific conceptualization of its power, offices, and ordinances; Smith's version, in this specificity, does not reflect the more general developments by Campbell and Crawford, outside their shared biblical terminology.[51]

With the need to build Smith's authority as president, orders of the priesthood also formed during summer of 1832. These orders would later come to define the local groups or quorums within the church. The introduction of the term "high priesthood" led to usage of the term "Aaronic priesthood," or lesser priesthood. Though no early documents record anyone in the church actively using the term "Aaronic priesthood" until the last third of 1832, the establishment of a higher priesthood in 1831 initiated an implicit division between those who held the high priesthood and those who did not. Hinting at this division, William E. McLellin left one of the few contemporary accounts on October 25, 1831. McLellin wrote in his journal that on "Tuesday night in conference, a number of Elders were ordained to the High-Priesthood of the Holy order of God among whom though I felt unworthy I was ordained and took upon me the high responsibility of that office—A number of others present were ordained to the lesser Priest-Hood."[52] Though McLellin struggled to describe the difference, he clearly identified two kinds of priests: high priests and priests. His simple journal entry showed foresight, though his descriptions of lower and higher priesthood were not used in the minutes and revelations in the fall of 1831.[53]

By September 23, 1832, Smith had dictated a revelation that explicitly traced the lineage of the two priesthoods.[54] The editor of Revelation Book 2 briefly described the revelation in the index as one that "explain[s] the two priest hoods and commission[s] the Apostles to preach the gospel."[55] Smith's September 1832 revelation described the higher and lower priesthoods with more clarity than McLellin had done a year earlier.[56] Smith's revelation drew on biblical precedent by tracing the lineage of those who held both the higher and lower priesthoods to Moses and Aaron, respectively. Those who held the higher priesthood were called "sons of Moses" and those who held the lower priesthood were called "sons of Aaron." The revelation also identified the offices that were associated with the two priesthoods: elders and bishops were appendages to the higher priesthood, and priests, teachers, and deacons were appendages to the lower.[57]

A September 1832 revelation also began to describe a sacred history that bound the Mormons to their ancient ancestors in a line of genealogical authority, something that once again reflected the theme of linear authority found in the book of Moses. The revelation described the distribution of the priesthood from one patriarch to the next, marking an important development in the concept of lines of authority. It claimed that prophets transferred priesthood authority from one prophet to the next, from ancient to modern. The revelation states that

> the sons of Moses according to the holy priesthood which he received under the [hands of his] father in Law Jethro, and Jethro received it under the hand of Caleb. And Caleb received it under the hand of Elihu and Elihu under the hand of Jeremy and Jeremy under the hand of Gad and Gad under the hand of Esaius and Esaius received it under the hand of God, Esaius also lived in the days of Abraham and was blessed of him which Abraham received the Priesthood from Melchesedec who received it through the linage of his fathers even till Noah, from Noah till Enoch, through the linage of thare fathers and from Enoch to abel who was slain by the conspiracy of his brother who received the Priesthood by the commandment of God by the hand of his father Adam.[58]

The revelation explained that the "Priesthood continueth in the church of God in all generations and is without beginning of days or end of years."[59] The priesthood was not just patriarchal, but integral to the church's identity no matter how that identity was realized in any specific cultural context. This same concept was described in Smith's translation of the Bible, which explains that there was a "genealogy of the sons of Adam."[60] Like the bridge that began to take shape in June 1831 with Old Testament priesthood as recounted in the preceding chapter, this revelation described a sacred history that explicitly connected both ancient and modern formulations of authority.

On December 6, 1832, inspired by his translation of the Bible, Smith dictated another revelation that also built on the concept of sacred history and priestly genealogy.[61] Referring to the scattering and gathering of Israel, Smith's revelation reinterprets the parable of the wheat and tares. In millenarian terms, the parable describes the sacred past from the days of Christ's earthly sojourn to the world's end. The parable positions Smith's church as a restoration of the primitive church found in the New Testament and details the passing of the priesthood to the modern church—an essential element for the gathering of Israel in the last days.[62] Speaking as if the saints were literal descendants of Israel, the revelation states, "Thus saith the Lord unto you with whom the priesthood hath continued through the lineage of your fathers. For ye are lawful heirs according to the flesh and have been hid from the world with Christ in God." It continues: "your life, and the Priesthood hath remained and must needs remain through you and your lineage until the restoration of all things spoken by the mouth of all the holy Prophets since the world began."[63] The revelation thus emphasizes the process of transferring the priesthood and begins to focus attention on the narratives of John the Baptist and Peter, James, and John restoring authority, though this connection would not be made explicit for several years.

Because the church would not print many of these germane revelations until 1835, the terms *Aaronic* and *Melchizedek* would not find a home in the saints' vocabulary until a later time. But as these early revelations demonstrate, by the fall of 1832, Smith understood priestly authority in terms that clearly traced a genealogical line back to ancient Israel. The concept of two priesthoods eventually became a material, physical reality in the church's design of the Kirtland temple.[64] The original plat, which included plans for twenty-four temples, was roughly divided into two bodies that have been represented as areas for the Aaronic and Melchizedek priesthoods.[65] Though the Latter-day Saints eventually built only one temple, they "designed [it] with pews in the center of the first and second floors, [while] the east and west side had elevated pulpits for the presiding authorities."[66] On the east side, the presiding authorities of the lower priesthood faced the presiding authorities of the higher priesthood, who were seated above the congregation, spatially demonstrating the distinction between the two priesthoods and their separate leadership roles.[67] By 1836, when the temple was dedicated, the concept of a dual priesthood was well established as a significant part of the Saints' religious practices and was clearly defined within the Doctrine and Covenants.[68]

Though church leaders finalized the design of the Kirtland temple in June 1833, the general membership likely had little knowledge of the layout of the pulpits until the temple was finished in 1836. The original design of the pulpits, however, demonstrates that the designers were not thinking about the priesthood division in terms of an Aaronic and Melchizedek priesthood in 1833; rather, they described them as higher and lower priesthoods.[69] But by September 1835, the Aaronic and Melchizedek priesthoods were mentioned in the first patriarchal blessings and were recorded in Doctrine and Covenants section 107. Within those two priesthoods were officers: the lower, or Aaronic, priesthood was held by deacons, teachers, and priests; while elders and high priests held the higher, or Melchizedek, priesthood. The temple pulpits reflected this division, providing a physical reality to the saints that the priesthood was divided into two orders. Most important for the argument at hand, the pulpits positioned Joseph Smith, as president, elevated above the congregation and the hierarchy of priesthood leaders, who occupied the descending pulpits.

## From Priesthood Executives to Authoritative Narrative

As Joseph Smith translated the Bible and revealed the book of Moses, the idea of authority to perform saving ordinances transformed into a priesthood order that connected God's people back to Adam in an expansive genealogy of the holy order. The priesthood within itself had power to "seal," yet at this point the sealing power was also the priesthood order that went back to Adam. Priesthood ordination functioned as an ordinance that connected ancient and modern Israel. Unlike many other Christians of his day who were anxious to demonstrate the way the "new covenant" superseded the old, Smith used the Book of Mormon's extraordinary collapsing of the Old and New Testaments to show that the seeds of priesthood authority were present in both. This connection was made manifest in Smith's revelation that when individuals undertook the covenant of the priesthood they became "sons of Aaron" and "sons of Moses," with those being the lesser and higher priesthoods, respectively.

The restoration of the high priesthood reinforced Smith's authority and the ongoing influence of his revelations on the creation and development of Mormonism. There was no formal procedural unfolding of the restoration of authority and priesthood. Rather, the restoration was incremental, requiring Smith to reevaluate previous ideas and rebuild them into new initiatives. The bifurcation of the priesthood orders, for example, was a new development once a high priesthood was introduced. It created a natural split and eventually the new office of high priest, which Smith coupled with the office of elder under the high priesthood. With that split, the higher and lower priesthoods could be reconfigured to correspond with biblical priesthood forms. The modern priesthood holders became sons of Aaron and Moses within their respective orders.

The introduction of the high priesthood also gave the prophet a new level of institutional authority. He no longer functioned just as a lawgiver, but as the president—the church's executor and highest appellate judge. Though Smith was ordained as the prophet on April 6, 1830, and his revelations demanded that he act as God's mouthpiece, his position as the president of the high priesthood also allowed him to become the key administrator of the church. Priesthood authority already led back to Smith through successive ordinations, but this position gave him the ecclesiastical authority to govern each of the offices of the priesthood. There was no doubt that Smith also created other authoritative offices, empowering leaders to hold some administrative keys. In fact, the idea of keys played an important role in balancing Smith's hierarchical democracy. The next chapter will engage the relationship that enabled the idea of keys between the restoration narrative of Peter, James, and John and how it created a platform for Smith to maintain his role as the prophet while also offering the same high priesthood to all Mormon males.

# 6

# The Kingdom of God

## The Authority of Peter, James, and John

Joseph Smith's overarching narrative described the archaeology of priesthood power by identifying a continuous chain of authority back to Adam in Mormon scripture. A crucial component of that chain was the idea of administrative keys that developed from the genealogy of Mormon priesthood to link the priestly authority of the New Testament apostles and Joseph Smith's administration. In many ways, that link in the chain became the most important part of the narrative for understanding the administration of power in early Mormonism. This chapter narrows in on how an emerging narrative about Peter, James, and John determined Mormon administration and the ecclesiastical hierarchy.

This apostolic narrative enabled Joseph Smith to empower the Mormon clergy with authority (even authority to become gods, priests, and priestesses) and still maintain his own unique position within the church as its president and prophet. On the one hand, Smith "centralize[d] power in himself," like a monarch over the kingdom of God. He alone held all the keys of full church administration. On the other hand, he empowered regional parallel sites of authority of priests and high priests by distributing some keys freely to others, who also distributed them regionally.[1] This chapter will explore the notion of the Mormon kingdom of God and how the apostolic mythos about Peter, James, and John enabled and maintained a long-lasting Mormon hierarchy. Though Mormonism generally describes the mythos as a decisive event, this chapter will explore it historically as an evolving narrative, to demonstrate how it came to represent the foundations of Mormon authority, what caused Smith and Cowdery to underscore the apostolic narrative in 1835, and how it was reemphasized after Smith's death as the restoration of the Melchizedek priesthood.

## The Mormon Concept of the Kingdom of God in the 1830s

By 1833, there were clear signs that communal Mormonism and its hierarchical leadership structure did not reflect US republicanism, nor would its relationship with politics offer Mormons authority in the antebellum United States as it had for evangelicals. By 1832, the Mormons had established their New Jerusalem in Independence, Missouri, on the borders of the United States and created an economically independent communal system they called the law of consecration.[2] Independence was Mormonism's initial attempt at creating Zion as a community of believers living in equality and harmony, as in the scriptural story of the city of Enoch. But frontier judges and vigilantes in Missouri problematized communal ownership of land and chafed at the exclusionary practices of the Mormon economy.[3] Tensions simmered throughout the 1830s and erupted in 1838 with the expulsion of the Mormons from Missouri. This tumult shifted the geography of revelation to Nauvoo, Illinois, and Smith's revelations began to pick up the pieces and refocus the Mormons' mission.[4] Zion would not fall, however, as long as there was still a prophet to guide the faithful, for the prophet could geographically reconfigure Zion through revelation. It was clear that the stakes (regional groups) of Zion—the gathering of Mormons outside the New Jerusalem—would need to play a more important role to tether the tent of Zion without a center place.[5] To this end, Smith focused on printing and canonizing his revelations and began emphasizing his long-lasting priestly order and delegation of authority through the stakes of Zion. Though they could never replace the New Jerusalem of Independence, the Mormons sacralized the land they moved to in Illinois as Smith continued to receive revelation.[6] The actual location of Zion was temporarily out of reach, but the kingdom of God, in some ways, seemed close.

Joseph Smith built his own kingdom of God, which would serve as a place of refuge from the premillennial destruction that would prepare the earth for Christ's millennial rule. Smith had said that he felt a "deep intrist in the cause of Zion and in the happiness of my brethren of mankind. . . . The time has at last arrived when the God of Abraham of Isaac and of Jacob has set his hand again the second time to recover the remnants of his people." Smith invoked the kind of genealogical authority described in chapter 5 to build his kingdom. As a public warning, he declared, "And now I am prepared to say by the authority of Jesus Christ, that not many years shall pass away before the United States shall present such a scene of bloodshed as has not parallel in the history of our nation hail famine and earthquake will sweep the wicked of this generation from off the face of this Land to open and prepare the way for the return of the lost tribes of Israel."[7] He claimed this plan would culminate under his leadership.

To some degree, Smith's comments were not extraordinary for the time period. Historian Amanda Porterfield has argued that mistrust of partisan politics "enabled the growth of evangelical religion" in the antebellum United States, driving religion's success at the grass roots. She writes, "With increasing regularity, people joined religious groups in much the same voluntary spirit as they favored political parties, choosing the one most representative of their interests." She explains that an interdependent relationship formed between religion and politics.[8] Yet Smith's expressions of frustration went deeper. They were not just a typical religious rant of partisan distrust, but a declaration of immanent authority that implied replacing the government itself—though he clearly felt that the US population would participate and become a major part of the gathering. Smith did not present his movement as just another political choice, but rather as the kingdom of God. Smith's focus on preparing his followers for the return of Christ stemmed directly from the comprehensive premillennial worldview he adopted, a view that was not out of place in the antebellum United States.[9] For radical premillennialists like William Miller, a contemporary of Smith's, Christ's coming was imminent. Miller guided his congregations to abandon all their worldly possessions, clothe themselves in white robes, and seek hilltops to wait for Christ's return. From his zealous calculations from the prophetic literature of the Bible, Miller fixed on a date in 1844 for the Second Coming but also laid the groundwork for the founding of the Seventh-day Adventist Church.[10]

Mormons differed from Miller's group in that they did not set a date for the Second Coming, but they did maintain a strict sense of premillennial beliefs.[11] They were building the kingdom of God on earth in preparation for Christ's return, and their hierarchical priesthood was the superstructure that would usher it in. Sidney Rigdon, who was associated with Alexander Campbell and his postmillennial beliefs before converting to Mormonism, declared that it was "the spur to all the efforts of the religious communities of the present day. . . . The cry Millennium is heard all over the land, and men are required to use all their exertions to usher in the glory of the last days, by converting the world."[12] Rigdon declared, "Unless the scattered remnants of Jacob should be gathered from all countries whither they had been driven, then no such thing as a Millennium could ever exist."[13] Whereas Rigdon's rhetoric is marked by the postmillennialist idea that it is human beings' responsibility to hasten Christ's return through good works—a theological position that gained traction as the nineteenth century wore on—the Mormons' concept of gathering in the New Jerusalem to prepare for Christ's coming marks them as premillennialists.

The priority the Mormons placed on gathering together and building the kingdom of God drove them from New York to Ohio and Missouri. The Book of Mormon declared that a city would be built on the American continent and identified that city as the New Jerusalem.[14] Emphasizing the point, the Book of Mormon never mentions the Second Coming. Instead, the great eschatological event of the last days is depicted as the gathering of Israel; the book indicates that once some Native American groups gather at the New Jerusalem, Christ will return.[15] Smith's revelations also called Mormons to gather in Missouri, near the borders of the United States where Native Americans had been relocated under recent US legislation.[16] Smith's translation of the Bible declared that Enoch and his righteous city had been taken up anciently and would meet Smith's New Jerusalem at the time of Christ's Second Coming, but first the modern Mormons had to be gathered and the kingdom of God established.[17]

Smith's kingdom of God, with its incumbent gathering of Israel, "provide[d] a means of escape from much of the anticipated tribulation of the last days," says historian Grant Underwood. "At the same time, it produced a concentration of Saints who could be properly prepared for the coming of the millennium."[18] In an October 1831 revelation, Smith declared that he had been given authority to establish the kingdom of God on earth, emphasizing that authority by using the concept of his possession of keys of the kingdom, as seen in chapter 5.[19] Smith combined the kingdom of God with an allusion to Peter, James, and John witnessing Christ's transfiguration in another one of his 1831 revelations that stated, "He that endureth in faith and doeth my will, the same shall overcome, and shall receive an inheritance upon the earth when the day of transfiguration shall come; When the earth shall be transfigured, even according to the pattern which was shown unto my apostles upon the mount."[20] In the years after this 1831 revelation, Smith's enlarging narrative about the apostles reinforced his own authority and clarified the focus of what the kingdom would be.

## The Growing Role of Peter, James, and John in Mormonism's Authority Transition

Gathering at the New Jerusalem in Missouri and building the kingdom of God was central to Mormons' efforts from 1830 to the summer of 1833, yet after they lost the New Jerusalem, the geographical emphasis shifted to a broader concept of the kingdom of God that was more inclusive of distant branches of the church. The new structure that developed in 1834 and 1835 distributed Smith's administrative authority to others in far-flung areas. He was able to accomplish this only by drawing on an emerging story of a precedent established by New Testament apostles. Though the idea of the kingdom of God was present even in the Book of Mormon, an evolving narrative about Peter, James, and John helped cement the kingdom as central in Smith's ability to distribute his authority.

Sometime between 1829 and 1830, Peter, James, and John had apparently visited Joseph Smith and Oliver Cowdery on the banks of the Susquehanna River in Pennsylvania. Smith and Cowdery claimed that they both experienced the apostolic visit together in the earliest phases of the church's development, but it is clear that they did not teach their congregations about it until several years later. Cowdery was the first to begin writing about the apostolic restoration narrative after he moved back to Kirtland, Ohio, in 1833. Cowdery was particularly threatened by how the leadership had developed while he was in Missouri. He was not part of the sitting presidency of the church, even though he had originally been its "second elder." It seems pertinent that it was Cowdery who began revealing the miraculous events that he and Smith had kept secret prior to 1834. This act may have been Cowdery's way to build up precedence for his appointment to the presidency of the church once he returned to Kirtland.

It was also more than that, however. Cowdery's disclosure about Peter, James, and John occurred as Smith was creating an order through which he could delegate authority to other Mormon leaders. The context for this was that the church in the mid-1830s was experiencing a transition of authority. The leadership in Kirtland maintained much of the control over the church, even making demands on the saints in Missouri. As discontent developed among the Missouri leadership, which until 1833 included Cowdery, Smith and Rigdon accused them of insubordination and chastened them under their authority within the high priesthood. Smith's decisions as the president of the church bothered leaders like Edward Partridge, W. W. Phelps, and Sidney Gilbert, who felt they were better positioned to make decisions in Missouri.[21] At times, Smith was even making decisions about what land to purchase, though he was not there to survey the land or make an informed decision. One elder, Ezra Booth, left Mormonism, noting that Smith held an "unlimited and despotic sway" over the administration of the church. He specifically took aim at Smith's authoritative voice, claiming that when Smith "says he knows a thing to be so, thus it must stand without controversy," as Smith spoke with the authority of scripture.[22]

Nonetheless, Smith's leadership was one of the few things that kept the bifurcated church together. The geographical division between Missouri and Ohio created a situation in which his authority came into direct conflict with that of other leaders. Smith understood the challenge and began to expand and further develop the Mormon priesthood, not to limit his presidential authority, but to build an infrastructure that would support it. For example, Smith was not the only Ohioan who had the authority to direct affairs in Missouri. Smith also had two counselors, Sidney Rigdon and Frederick G. Williams. A revelation in March 1832 declared that Smith had "authority to preside with the assistence of his councellers over all the Concerns of the church."[23] Then on March 8, 1833, Smith received a revelation that allowed his counselors equal privilege with him "in holding the Keys of the last kingdom." This revelation essentially created three presidents within the church, all of whom lived in Ohio.[24] Their authority was coupled with control over the finances of the church and the law of consecration, an imbalance that Smith's revelations attempted to address with a cooperative called the United Order, but ultimately, the challenge continued to exist.[25]

Like the original revelation that called for a president of the high priesthood in the fall of 1831, Smith delivered a revelation that associated his office with the problems that existed in Missouri.[26] Disputes had been ongoing since the summer of 1831, but in January of 1833, Orson Hyde and Hyrum Smith sent a letter from Kirtland chastising several of the leaders in Missouri, reassuring them that "we have the satisfaction of knowing that the Lord approves of us & has accepted us, & established his name in Kirtland."[27] The letter warned them against "rising up against their prophets and accusing them of seeking after Kingly power" as the Nephites and the children of Israel had done. It explained that though Joseph Smith was acting like a monarch, in doing so he was only magnifying "the high office and calling whereunto he has been called and appointed by the command of God and the united voice of this Church." The letter declared, "We have the best of feelings, and feelings of the greatest anxiety for the welfare of Zion we feel more like weeping over Zion than we do like rejoicing over her. . . . Repent! Awake! Awake!"[28]

Although there are no direct statements that claim the complaints from Missouri caused Smith and Cowdery to begin talking about the visit of Peter, James, and John, it is interesting that it was during this period that the two leaders began to include the narrative in private blessings, histories, and eventually a public revelation in the Doctrine and Covenants. As Smith addressed the concept of keys of authority more often and associated them with the presidency of the high priesthood, his power as president was more firmly established, a fortification that was reinforced still further by the visit of the ancient apostles Peter, James, and John. It has worked as a powerful narrative ever since, enabling Smith and subsequent leaders to maintain the president's authoritative voice while allowing for a strong leadership base that began to coalesce around conferences, quorums, and councils.

## Conferences, Quorums, and Councils

For the first year and a half of its existence, the church gathered at conferences where Smith presided as the first elder over a group of elders and the church. In many ways, this early pattern appeared similar to a Methodist quarterly council of elders, as Kathleen Flake has observed.[29] The public conferences operated in tandem with private councils at which Smith commanded recipients in the voice of God to accomplish major church initiatives. Smith often gave revelations and guided the affairs of the church at the early council meetings: he ordained leaders, settled disputes, called missionaries, and more. The development of the high priesthood and its president created an administrative shift in which the president began forming and governing councils of high priests that had "up to twelve" members.[30] His revelation explained that he could have twelve presidents in his own presidency who would eventually hold all the keys with him. Though he had up to six presidents in the presidency, this number later shrank significantly as the use of councils developed over the next few years.[31] One historian writes, "Joseph thought institutionally more than any other visionary of his time, and the survival of his movement can largely be attributed to this gift," though it made him far from democratic in his approach to church governance.[32]

Though councils were not formally used by the Mormons in 1830, elders of the church had met outside the two conferences on April 6 and September 26. For example, in September John Whitmer and other elders who were reading the newly published Book of Mormon met to ask Smith about the particulars of the book's teachings about Zion.[33] They discussed the text together as leaders, and then Smith dictated a complex apocalyptic revelation to the group.[34] It was authoritative and declarative. In February 1831 another revelation by Smith addressed elders and newly called bishops, instructing them to "Council together & they shall do by the direction of the spirit as it must be necessary."[35] By March 1833, when Smith's counselors Sidney Rigdon and Frederick G. Williams were also given authority and keys over the church, Smith delivered a revelation that instructed them in the importance of councils for the new religion's governance. It stated that it was their "business and mission in all your lives, to preside in council, and set in order all the affairs of this church and kingdom."[36]

Councils developed one step further in 1834 when Smith revealed that they were a central feature in the ancient order of church governance. By February,

Smith declared at a council that he had "never set before this council in all the order in which a Council ought to be conducted."[37] During that meeting he showed them "the order of councils in ancient days as shown to him by vision." His vision apparently allowed him to peer into a council meeting presided over by the New Testament character Peter. He stated, "The apostle, Peter, was the president of the council in ancient days and held the Keys of the Kingdom of God, on the earth was appointed to this office by the voice of the Savior and confirmed acknowledged in it by the voice of the Church. He had two men appointed as counsellors with him, and in case Peter was absent, his counsellors could transact business, or either one of them."[38] In this vision, the keys that Peter held were also accessible to James and John—a model that became more important to Smith in his role as the president of the high priesthood and his formation of councils that governed the church.

The idea of councils, as demonstrated through Smith's vision of Peter delegating in the ancient order of governance, eventually found its way into Mormon scripture. The 1835 Doctrine and Covenants outlined Smith's priesthood structure, which allowed him to entrust priesthood authority throughout the church. Smith's revelation on the topic explained that "Of necessity there are presidents, or presiding officers growing out of or appointed of or from among those who are ordained to the several offices in these to priesthoods."[39] The regional overlap of priesthood leaders functioned through quorums (regional bodies of deacons, teachers, priests, and elders) that were given authority by the president of the high priesthood. Other presidents were later called to receive keys over their own quorums. In an environment where Smith could no longer govern the entire church directly, he delegated authority to the other presidents, along with bishoprics and high councils to assist the presidents in Zion and Kirtland.[40]

Authority was being transformed: it now extended from Smith to the governance of external political and ecclesiastical bodies, without undermining Smith's own prophethood. It was at this point in Mormon history when the delegation of authority was highly necessary that a dialogue was formed around the concept of keys of the kingdom. Smith had to maintain the unique power of *sola propheta* while simultaneously distributing authority. This dispersion of authority externally needed to maintain the force and power of the original authority, but also in its delivery and delegation it could naturally prevent any one individual in the ecclesiastical structure from usurping the rest. The authority had to be divided but not diminished. Once quorums received the keys of the priesthood from the president of the high priesthood, the narrative of Peter, James, and John became very relevant. Since each Mormon leader had the same high priesthood as Smith, keys made their individual positions different and still significant.

## The Restoration Narrative Made Public

Because the apostolic visit supposedly occurred before the church was established in 1830, the way this information was revealed to the Mormon public is important. By 1834, the narrative began to emerge in official documents. Just months after Smith had his vision of the ancient order and Peter, Oliver Cowdery expressed interest in his restored authority and keys. On December 4, 1834, Cowdery was ordained as a president of the high priesthood, wrote about the keys of the priesthood, and may have given the earliest extant account of the Peter, James, and John restoration narrative. Cowdery wrote in his history that his office "held the keys of the kingdom of heaven" and explained why he had not been ordained to the office of president when Smith, Sidney Rigdon, and Jesse Gause (later replaced by Frederick G. Williams) were ordained in 1832, 1833, and 1834, respectively.[41] Cowdery undertook this project to reestablish his own religious authority within the Kirtland administrative structure, which had changed while he was in Missouri assisting W. W. Phelps as a printer for the church until 1833. Once he returned to Ohio and began speaking openly about his role in the Peter, James, and John narrative, he was ordained as the first of three assistant presidents.[42] He justified his appointment by referring to the fact that John the Baptist had told him on May 15, 1829, that he was to be ordained as the second elder of the church in 1830. He wrote, "This promise was made by the angel while in company with President Smith, at the time they received the office of the lesser priesthood."[43] Smith, in his 1839 history, stated, "John, the same that is called John the Baptist in the new Testament, . . . acted under the direction of Peter, James, and John, who held the keys of the priesthood of Melchisedeck, whi[c]h priesthood he said should in due time be conferred on us. *And that I should be called the first Elder of the Church and he the second.*"[44] From Smith's 1839 perspective, Cowdery had received the keys of the priesthood; the office of president, or something similar to it, was given to him in April 1830 when he was ordained as the second elder of the church.[45] Up until that point, Cowdery's accounts of priesthood restoration always centered on John the Baptist but never mentioned keys, terminology that was later associated with the restoration narrative of Peter, James, and John.[46] Cowdery associated his current understanding of keys and delegation with events that took place earlier. To him, those earlier angelic visits justified his position as a member of the presidency and authorized him to hold the keys of the kingdom. Cowdery's narrative was ultimately concerned with reestablishing his own authority.

The year 1835 became a watershed moment in the dissemination of information about the Peter, James, and John narrative. Just as Cowdery's leadership was being reestablished within the presidency, his responsibility to call twelve apostles came to fruition in February 1835, fulfilling a commandment given to Cowdery in June 1829 to call "unto twelve." The presidency chose the twelve apostles and Cowdery set them apart, both as apostles and as a traveling high council. He charged them: "Brethren, you have your duty presented in this revelation. You have been ordained to the Holy Priesthood. You have received it from those who had their power and authority from an angel. You are to preach the gospel to every nation."[47] He empowered them through their possession of the priesthood but reminded them that the priesthood itself was restored by an angel—angelic narratives that he was publicly disclosing to the church. By October 2, 1835, he had apparently become even more overt about his participation in the angelic restorations. The introduction to Cowdery's patriarchal blessing, written in Cowdery's own handwriting, states, "By the hand of the angel in the bush, unto the lesser priesthood, and after received the holy priesthood under the hands of those who had been held in reserve for a long season, even those who received it under the hand of the Messiah while he should dwell in the flesh."[48] Cowdery recorded the blessing, which explained the visit of John the Baptist, followed by this statement: "After this we received the high and holy priesthood: but an account of this will be given elsewhere, or in another place."[49] The blessing is by no means explicit—it does not state the apostles' names—but he wrote it just after the Doctrine and Covenants editorial committee published the Peter, James, and John narrative for the first time in 1835.[50] Underscoring the authority of the presidency, these 1834 and 1835 documents suggest that the apostolic visit was ultimately about the restoration of keys and administrative distribution of authority. The narrative also points to the fact that although there is a clear distribution of authority, it was overseen by a coherent vision and administrative plan by the president of the high priesthood.

Ultimately, the Peter, James, and John narrative was established through scripture that was attributed to Joseph Smith but edited by Cowdery. In 1835, one of Smith's earlier revelations was significantly expanded to include a prophecy about Christ's Second Coming that stated he would partake of the sacramental wine with various prophets and apostles of the Book of Mormon and the Bible.[51] This once again identified the grand and cohesive narrative of priesthood from Adam to Joseph Smith. The additions from this revelation editing committee included the first official public statement about the Peter, James, and John restoration narrative. It declared that Peter, James, and John restored the keys of the kingdom, apostleship, and authority to begin the last dispensation that would usher in Christ's return. Smith's revelation placed the visit within the context of a broad apocalyptic vision that included the restoration of keys by ancient prophets to Smith, but only to indicate how all the ancient patriarchs that delivered the keys to Smith would eventually gather at Christ's Second Coming near the New Jerusalem and give the keys back to Christ.[52] This narrative structure reemphasized the genealogy of the holy order of the priesthood as something that reached back to the ancient patriarchs and placed the kingdom of God in the last dispensation within Mormonism's millennial theology. The crescendo of the narrative was marked by the visit of Peter, James, and John to Joseph Smith.

The 1835 rendition of Smith's revelation emphasized the continuity of prophets from the ancient patriarchs up to Smith himself and represented Mormons' authority to build the kingdom of God before Christ's Second Coming.[53] The accounts given by Smith and the descriptions of the visit in his revelations, however, never specifically mention that Peter, James, and John gave him the Melchizedek priesthood.[54] This was not just a general statement that could have implied the restoration of Melchizedek priesthood; the account was specific. It emphasized the premillennial importance that Peter, James, and John represented by authorizing Smith and Cowdery to open the last dispensation before the Second Coming and granting the keys to administer authority in the church. The only other revelatory account of the Peter, James, and John visit was given seven years later by Joseph Smith and it restated the same points, leaving out the concept of the Melchizedek priesthood. Table 6.1 is a breakdown of the two revelatory accounts about the visit (one in 1835 and one in 1842).

Neither revelation states that Peter, James, and John restored the Melchizedek priesthood, or even the high priesthood, for that matter. These revelations are important because the single nonrevelatory account from Smith that describes how the Melchizedek priesthood was restored, found in his 1839 history, states that it occurred in the chamber of Father Whitmer.[55] The majority of the accounts that explicitly claim that Peter, James, and John restored the Melchizedek priesthood are found in sources created after Joseph Smith's death. The one account recorded during Smith's lifetime that seems to show Smith describing Peter, James, and John restoring the Melchizedek priesthood is third-hand; Willard Richards copied some notes that John Taylor had taken during a sermon Smith gave in 1838. Though Richards seems to have been fairly careful about recording the sermon correctly, the text

Table 6.1. Comparison of D&C 27 and 128

| Revelation circa August 1835 (Doctrine and Covenants 27) | Revelation/Letter September 6, 1842 (Doctrine and Covenants 128:20) |
|---|---|
| 1. "ordained you and confirmed you to be apostles" | |
| 2. "especial witnesses of my name" | |
| 3. "bear the keys of your ministry" | |
| 4. "keys of my kingdom" | "keys of the kingdom" |
| 5. "dispensation of the gospel for the last times" | "dispensation of the fulness of times" |

speaks only of the keys of the priesthood, and like Doctrine and Covenants 27, it cites the visit of Peter, James, and John to explain the restoration of the apostolic keys.

Smith's revelations show an emphasis on restorationism and continuity between God's ancient people and early Mormonism. It is true that the priesthood order Smith had established gave shape to and governance for the kingdom of God, but both the priesthood and the kingdom had been established by several restoration narratives (such as the John the Baptist and Whitmer chamber experience narratives) and molded by dozens of revelations. Looking back, the Peter, James, and John narrative developed the tendency to act as a single reference point for the whole restoration process because it was about the restoration of the keys of the kingdom. Yet the restoration narratives came in addition to Smith's revelations, which gave meaning to each event and provided the details about emerging Mormon ecclesiastical structures. Once the Aaronic and Melchizedek priesthoods were clearly defined after years of development since the events of 1830, accounts of the angelic priesthood restoration visits became increasingly relevant and specific. Smith's revelations about Peter, James, and John never associated their visit with the restoration of priesthood specifically, but it was clear that their visit was the principal event that restored the kingdom of God. Early Mormons' restoration narrative clearly situated their millenarian mindset at the heart of their religious endeavors, with Smith's revelations grounding his own authority in Christ and the twelve New Testament apostles—an emphasis on apostleship that early Mormonism would soon adopt as its own.

## The Twelve Apostles: Reemphasizing Peter, James, and John

The newly called twelve apostles believed they had been given great authority, though the high councils would challenge that authority. The twelve acted "under the direction" of the presidency of the church, but they were ranked above the recently instituted Seventy in terms of authority.[56] Calling the twelve marked the ripening of Smith's religious initiatives and was founded on one of his earliest revelatory commandments. His restoration began with apostles in mind, regardless of the fact that nearly all US denominations agreed that the New Testament apostles could not be reproduced. Out of all of Smith's restoration imperatives, this was one of his most unusual.

Though some historians have minimized the authority and importance of the early apostles—perhaps justifiably in some cases because they did not immediately assume an administrative role in the church upon their ordination in 1835—it is impossible to overestimate their significance in the overarching schema for Smith's restoration. In a nation of restorationists, Mormonism was the only religion that restored the New Testament apostles. Even more remarkable in some ways was Mormonism's claim to restore the original, intact authority of the New Testament apostles in their nineteenth-century counterparts.

The keys of the kingdom described in Smith's revelation that included the Peter, James, and John restoration narrative undoubtedly framed the apostles' mission. Their ordination enabled Smith to tie the loose ends of the priesthood together in an 1835 revelation called "Instruction on Priesthood." The twelve were intended to use the revelation "to travel and preach among the Gentiles until the Lord shall command them to go to the Jews." Smith explained that they held "the keys of this ministry—to unlock the door of the kingdom of heaven unto all nations and preach the Gospel unto every creation."[57]

The apostolic restoration became a predominant narrative in the final years of Smith's life. Once the Mormons moved to Nauvoo, Illinois, in 1839, the apostles became increasingly important to Mormon administration. As Cowdery had in 1834, the Nauvoo apostles reestablished themselves and created a new role within the Mormon administration, and the restoration narrative took on new meaning. Yet, when Smith was murdered in June 1844, there was no clear successor to replace him. The situation became increasingly complicated when members began to recall Smith suggesting several different people to be his successor. Though many aspects of the church's origins in New York had faded from the minds of the general membership as church demographics changed significantly over time, the leadership of Oliver Cowdery, David Whitmer, and Martin Harris in the nascent years of the church was not forgotten.[58] The founding of the presidency of the high priesthood in 1832 also pushed Sidney Rigdon to the front of the conversation, since he was still in the presidency at the time of Smith's death and technically held the keys of the kingdom. Also, William Marks was the senior religious leader of Nauvoo, and he had the support of Emma Smith.[59] Smith had even blessed his son Joseph Smith III in February 1844 to be his successor, leaving the church and its membership to sort out for themselves who would replace the prophet.[60]

The apostles in Nauvoo held the authority of the church in their hands, though their claims did not go unchallenged. The succession crisis ended with the majority of church members following Brigham Young and the twelve, which eventually led to a new first presidency being formed in 1847. The twelve immediately claimed that they possessed the keys of the kingdom in order to argue for their succession. Though they did not possess the same charisma and personality as Joseph Smith, they had become increasingly important to Smith and his administration in the years leading up to the prophet's death.[61] They were participants in Smith's most private councils, including the meetings later known in Nauvoo as the "Quorum of the Anointed," in which the temple rituals were enacted originally. The twelve believed that they possessed the authority to govern the kingdom, and they increasingly framed this authority by reference to the restoration of the keys by Peter, James, and John.[62] Significantly altered from Smith's 1835 revelation describing the apostolic restoration, the apostles' new narrative claimed that Peter, James, and John restored the keys and the Melchizedek priesthood.[63] The succession crisis caused the twelve to describe Smith's priesthood restoration as an individual event rather than a process of angelic visits, progressive revelations, and ongoing struggles. The crisis required a definitive response, and its strength was located within specific historical events rather than the more nebulous narratives of process.

The Nauvoo apostles believed that all the keys of the priesthood had been given to them during their participation in the quorum of the anointed and early temple rituals, which will be addressed in more detail in chapter 7. Leaders like William Marks and William Law had not been part of that group, and Rigdon was only a junior member. Therefore, these men had not received the "fullness of the priesthood" that was included in the rituals.[64] Speaking specifically about the authority of those who had participated in the rituals, Brigham Young declared, "if . . . he is a king and Priest, let him go and build up a kingdom."[65] Young's logic depended on the power and authority shared as part of the temple rituals: if people had not participated in them, Young questioned how they could claim a specific endowment of power over the church.

The apostles who were intimately involved in the later temple rituals that Smith implemented chose to represent their own authority as having been passed to them through Peter, James, and John. In early December 1845, more than a year after Smith's death, it appears that they added a ritual to the endowment that included actors who played Peter, James, and John as the intercessors between temple-goers and God. This framing took on a particular significance within the temple rituals once they were performed by the church at large, in part because of the role of Peter, James, and John within the ritual: they are referred to in terms that reinforce their power and priesthood, and they serve as a legitimating body authorized by Christ himself. On December 12, 1845, William Clayton recorded the various individuals who participated in the endowments. For each of the first few ceremonies, he recorded who played the roles of Elohim, Jehovah, Michael, and Lucifer with some detail, but Peter, James, and John were yet to be included in the drama.[66] Reflections on earlier endowments show Smith had administered the endowment to the recipients himself. Yet, by the night of December 12, Clayton documented that "an arrangement was made establishing better order in conducting the endowment." He explained,

> Under this order it is the province of Eloheem, Jehovah and Michael to create the world, plant the Garden and create the man and give his help meet. Eloheem give the charge to Adam in the Garden and thrusts them into the telestial kingdom or the world. Then Peter assisted by James and John conducts them through the Telestial and Terrestial kingdom administering the charges and tokens in each and conducts them to the vail where they are received by the Eloheem and after . . . admitted by him into the Celestial kingdom.[67]

Thus, the authority of the Nauvoo-era apostles was emphasized in the temple through saving rituals that referred to the roles of Peter, James, and John in ways that reinforced the apostolic restoration narrative as central to questions of authority. The guiding role that Joseph Smith once played was now represented by Peter, James, and John in the endowment. The control that the twelve held over the temple rituals marked their distinct power and authority in the church, which they emphasized by adding Peter, James, and John as the guides through the endowment ritual. Once the rituals were expanded to members of the church outside Smith's chosen circle, the endowment emphasized the central role of Peter, James, and John as the apostles who restored the keys of the kingdom.[68]

The consolidation of power in the hands of the twelve apostles meant that any church leaders outside that quorum were in a somewhat awkward position after Joseph Smith's death. That included Oliver Cowdery, who had once been at the epicenter of Mormon revelation. Cowdery had left the church in 1838 after suffering economic difficulties and disapproval from church members.[69] After Smith's death, the twelve apostles stressed the importance of keys and authority, focusing especially on those keys that were restored by the ancient apostles. This was in some ways of benefit to Cowdery, who had been present for those early apostolic visitations and now reasserted their importance. As Cowdery inched his way back to the church, he encouraged the apostolic emphasis in a letter to Phineas Young in 1846. Cowdery wrote, "I have been sensitive on this subject, I admit; but I ought to be so," explaining to Young that he wanted to set the record straight, "for the sake of the truth, but might not blush for the private character of the man [Joseph] who bore that testimony." Cowdery felt compelled to emphasize his testimony because he had "stood in the presence of John, with our departed brother Joseph, to receive the Lesser Priesthood—and in the presence of Peter, to receive the Greater, and look down through time, and witness the effects these two must produce."[70]

Cowdery began an open dialogue with the twelve apostles, and he eventually rejoined the church in 1848. Reuben Miller recorded in his journal that Cowdery delivered a sermon at Council Bluff on October 21, 1848, that once again championed the visit of Peter, James, and John and the importance of the keys of the priesthood. Miller remembered Cowdery stating, "I was . . . present with Joseph when the Melchesideck priesthood was conferred by the holy angels of god." Yet Cowdery apparently also stated that the priesthood was conferred on them "in order that by which we then confirmed on each other by the will and commandment of god."[71] The apostolic visit, in which the ancient apostles who ordained Smith and Cowdery restored the keys of the priesthood, was inseparably connected with the keys and authority that the apostles held after Smith's death. Thus, Brigham Young and the apostles emphatically stressed the visit of Peter, James, and John in their missionary work and sermons after 1844. In the case of the apostles and Cowdery, the Peter, James, and John narrative served as a mark of their authority, even though Cowdery had to accept a diminished role in order to prioritize the authority of the apostles.

## From the Apostolic Narrative to Elijah, Moses, and Elias

A clear development of official interpretations eventually linked the restoration of the Melchizedek priesthood to Peter, James, and John and subsequently to the modern Mormon apostleship. There are three main historical milestones for this development: 1829 (when the three ancient apostles apparently came), 1835 (when twelve modern apostles were chosen), and the

1839–46 Nauvoo period (which culminated with the modern apostles becoming the official administrators for the whole church). The first period, dealt with in chapter 3, is known for the Book of Mormon's claim that Christ called twelve disciples in the United States. Later narratives located these events in 1829 in order to identify when Peter, James, and John appeared to Smith and Cowdery. The second period developed around an expanding network of priesthood leadership in the mid-1830s in the form of quorums, councils, and presidencies, which marked the need for a delegation of authority and thus framed authority in terms of receiving the keys of the kingdom. The events of 1835 are the first period in which the narrative of Peter, James, and John emerges in the historical record, its arrival marking Smith's ability to transfer authority without weakening his own role. At this time, the apostolic visit was explained as the occasion when Smith and Cowdery received the keys of the kingdom and the authority to open the last dispensation. This narrative was then reinterpreted again during the last period as the Nauvoo apostles began to administer church affairs as a whole. They became Smith's trusted confidants and part of the Quorum of the Anointed in Nauvoo. Once Smith died, their authority was associated with the visit of Peter, James, and John, which was emphasized more heavily than during any previous period and associated with the restoration of the Melchizedek priesthood.

These developments occurred at crucial times in the church, times when authority was being threatened or needed some sort of clarification. Understanding the development of the Peter, James, and John narrative is central to major theological and governance issues within the church, including the formation of Zion, the building of the kingdom of God, the last dispensation, the governance of the church, and the restoration of authoritative power via the Melchizedek priesthood. The Peter, James, and John restoration narrative did not emerge immediately or even as a cohesive whole, but it has had the longest-lasting effect of all of Smith's restoration narratives. In fact, for some, it has become the quintessential demonstration of authority and even democratic hierarchy.[72]

The narrative also defined authority in a political sense, something that Brigham Young and the Nauvoo apostles emphasized. The authority of governance, which is implicit in possessing the keys of the kingdom, was apparently operating in administrative dimensions of the priesthood that took shape between 1833 and 1835. This priesthood reign was delegatory, offering leaders keys from which they too could govern, but not without upholding the presidency. As the president of the church with authority to command in the name of God, Smith had power, but the continual exertion of that power unilaterally caused some to see his authority as dictatorial. It was hierarchical, but the theological purpose of the keys and distribution of authority to lay members of the church allowed Smith to exert his power over the church by delivering up his own authority to regional leaders. He used the analogy of keys to literally share his religious authority with the other presidents, and each regional leader held all the keys for his specific region. Therefore, Smith's exertion of power became the delivery of authority to others, who then, in turn, exerted their power by delivering authority to others democratically, all the while forming an even stronger hierarchy. As a result, Smith freed up space for charismatic revelation throughout the church. The keys analogy allowed Smith's commandments and revelations to remain absolute and definitive, all the while deflecting charges of a dictatorial reign. In the end, it appeared the only way Smith could exert power was by giving it away or transferring his authority to others. In the next step, as Smith continued his central role, he moved even one step further toward hierarchical democracy by enabling the lay membership to become kings and queens of the kingdom of God. This was soon enabled by a restoration account about the Old Testament prophets Elijah, Moses, and Elias.

# 7

# Calculating Salvation

## Priesthood Practice and Mormon Ritual

Though Mormonism initially coalesced around Smith's charisma and authoritative voice, its longevity was due to the fact that he created a theology that offered the same authority and charisma to his priesthood orders. In fact, Smith sought to secure salvation for the church's membership before his death. To him, his high-ranking position was only valuable insofar as it offered the saints the ability to find certainty of their own salvation. On the one hand, Smith created the Mormon law (Doctrine and Covenants [D&C] 20 and 42) and formed a hierarchical priesthood structure to govern the kingdom of God, yet he also received the law charismatically through revelation, restored his church through angelic visits and theophany, and expected his parishioners to have their own revelations and to see God for themselves (D&C 88:1).

In this sense, Smith tried to reconcile the tension between following the law (even his own revelatory commandments), empowering a hierarchy of priests, and being assured salvation through physical rites. This chapter charts the beginning of new Mormon ritual efforts to re-create its members as prophets/prophetesses, priests/priestesses, and kings/queens, *all while maintaining Smith's central role.*[1] Smith developed rituals that endowed the Mormon membership with authority and connected them to the ancient order of Melchizedek, leading to Christ's Second Coming. Their participation in rites such as solemn assemblies, anointings, and the School of the Prophets assured them of their salvation and their role in the kingdom, but it also allowed for a hierarchical ecclesiology that upheld Smith's authority. His new liturgies, particularly those featured in the new House of the Lord (later termed temple) in Kirtland, offered members kingly and prophetic authority without threatening the hierarchical structure of the priesthood.

This chapter will examine the emergence of several new rituals in the Kirtland period before turning attention to Smith's 1836 priesthood restoration narrative about Elijah, the Old Testament prophet, who reportedly visited Smith on April 3, 1836. The idea of Elijah returning to usher in the Second Coming was commonly preached by antebellum Protestants who accentuated the fourth chapter of Malachi.[2] Beyond this shared interest in Malachi, Smith also drew deeply from other parts of the Old Testament: he began studying Hebrew and inevitably ran into the ancient Passover tradition that required Jews to leave a cup of wine for Elijah in anticipation of his return.[3] The restoration of priesthood by Elijah was seen as the pinnacle of major developments within the Mormon priesthood that would endow the Mormons with power from on high. This restoration narrative proved to be a significant turn of events in which a new religious ritual would bind humankind together in eternity.

## The School of the Prophets

In the early 1830s, Smith established a short-lived group for the Mormon clergy called the School of the Prophets, which on the surface appeared to be a theological seminary similar to the early clerical education provided by Yale or Harvard.[4] In December 1832, Smith dictated a revelation that commanded the formation of this group, which began to formalize and practice new religious rituals that would help Mormon men experience God's revelation for themselves. Smith called for theophany among the priesthood holders: the goal of the school was acquiring the ability to see the face of God as part of God's holy order. His revelation commanded "as all have not faith, seek ye diligently and teach one another words of wisdom; yea, seek ye out of the best books words of wisdom; seek learning, even by study and also by faith."[5]

In this ecstatic hope, early Mormons were not alone. Restorationists believed that signs would follow the restoration of the New Testament church, and an emphasis on personal religious experience had attended the influential Second Great Awakening. Groups such as the Shakers would eventually identify part of the 1830s as an era of manifestations because of the remarkable charismatic outpouring of the period. Smith's experiential rationalism tempered such uncontrolled ecstatic experiences, yet he did call for them, guiding the priesthood toward the experience of theophany. The call for education and experience that accompanied the new school was inextricably connected to a commandment to build a house of the Lord in Kirtland, Ohio.[6] It was intended to be "a house of learning" as well as a "house of glory" and was conceptualized as a place where sacred work could be done and where the school could meet.[7]

The former Baptist minister, Sidney Rigdon, even wrote and delivered the earliest formal Mormon theological curriculum for the school. The lectures on faith, as they were called, were eventually canonized in 1835 as part of the Doctrine and Covenants: the doctrine was identified as these lectures, and the covenants referred to Smith's revelations and commandments. The school also eventually taught English and composition, along with Hebrew, Greek, and German, and printer W. W. Phelps intended to publish textbooks and other educational materials for common education.[8] Smith was not overzealous for the religious enthusiasm that characterized other new movements. His sense of liturgy and grounded educational disposition tamed unfettered expressions of religious devotion. The average Latter-day Saint was encouraged to attend Hebrew classes. Smith's revelation demanded that they should read from "the best books" and "seek learning" by both formal education and by faith.[9]

As part of his intentions to cleanse the priesthood holders who attended the school, Smith introduced rites that were familiar to most Christians because they had their origin in the Bible. One was the washing of feet as Christ had done for his apostles in the New Testament.[10] This emphasis on foot washing may have stemmed from Rigdon, whose previous ministry had a profound impact on the development of Mormonism in Ohio, especially in the school.[11] Smith's revelation declared, "ye shall not receive any among you into this school save he is clean from the blood of this generation," and those who were permitted to participate "shall be received by the ordinance of the washing of feet, for unto this end was the ordinance of the washing of feet instituted."[12] Commanding Smith to wash the feet of all the participants, the revelation commanded, "the ordinance of washing feet is to be administered by the president, or presiding elder of the church" after prayer and the Lord's Supper as directed and in the "pattern given in the thirteenth chapter of John's testimony."[13] Though most churches in the antebellum United States did not practice foot washing, the rite was occasionally performed, and it functioned much like the initiation of baptism. Smith, on the other hand, was initiating members of the school into something more than just church membership or priesthood ordination, both of which they already possessed. Foot washing launched them into their ecclesiastical duty to build God's kingdom on earth, binding humankind to God. It was preparatory to their taking the gospel to the world.

Early Mormon men performed this rite in "token or remembrance of the everlasting covenant."[14] Smith opened each meeting of the school on his knees, as if at an altar, before formally greeting the priesthood, stating, "Art thou a brother or brethren? I salute you in the name of the Lord Jesus Christ, in token or remembrance of the everlasting covenant, in which covenant I receive you to fellowship, in a determination that is fixed, immovable, and unchangeable, to be your friend and brother through the grace of God in the bonds of love, to walk in all the commandments of God blameless, in thanksgiving, forever and ever."[15] Smith's revelation declared, "let the teacher arise, and, with uplifted hands to heaven, yeah, even directly, salute his brother or brethren."[16] The fraternal language was part of Smith's revelation on the School of the Prophets and reinforced the concept that the high priesthood was the holy order of God that could be traced back to the ancient patriarchs. This ritual practice, delivered by revelation, empowered the participants while also upholding Smith's hierarchical position as the president of the high priesthood and as the one who presided over the meetings.

The school helped prepare the elders for their ministry, though it met only for a short time, from its organization on January 23, 1833, until it was adjourned in April.[17] In 1834 the School of the Elders was established in its stead.[18] The change of name for the new institution may at first make it seem that he was reserving the title "prophet" for himself, in his own journal he still referred to it as the "school of the prophets."[19] There is no record of the church using the formal greeting and performing the ordinance of washing the feet in the school of the elders. Washing and anointing quickly became associated with the Kirtland temple and later the Nauvoo temple also.

By revelation, Smith commanded the Mormons to build a temple where the school could meet.[20] Smith's revelations charged his followers to build the House of the Lord, which would serve as a place of instruction, including religious services and even secular learning. But what is most important was that the House of the Lord would be a place where God would reveal himself and endow Latter-day Saints with "power from on high."[21] Smith had originally received the power to confer the gift of the Holy Ghost in the chamber of father Whitmer, which was followed by a Pentecostal-type experience on April 6, 1830, and then another endowment of power upon being ordained to the priesthood in June 1831.[22] Then, in the School of the Prophets of 1833 in Kirtland,

> while engaged in silent prayer, kneeling, with our hands uplifted each one praying in silence, no one whispered above his breath, a personage walked through the room from east to west, and Joseph asked if we saw him. I saw him and suppose the others did, and Joseph answered that is Jesus, the Son of God, our elder brother. Afterwards Joseph told us to resume our former position in prayer; which we did. Another person came through; He was surrounded as with a flame of fire. He (Bro. C[oltrin]) experianced a sensation that it might destroy the tabernacle as it was of consuming fire of great brightness. The Prophet Joseph said this was the Father of our Lord Jesus Christ. I saw Him.[23]

The participants in the school recorded these experiences in terms that connected their experiences of divine power with Smith's educational initiatives. Though Smith clearly operates as the person in charge of the situation in this passage, he does so in order to disseminate the experiential spirituality that characterized his own early prophethood. In other words, the school provides another example of the ways Smith nimbly negotiated power, continually reinforcing his position as the head of the LDS church while simultaneously enacting a hierarchical democracy grounded in the idea that such authority could be shared. The building of the Mormon temple brought even more endowments of such power.

## Preparing for the House of the Lord

Promising a Pentecostal experience, Smith preached of the day when the House of the Lord would be finished. He promised his followers that there would be an endowment of power, evoking language that he first used in a December 1830 revelation that commanded Mormons to move from New York.[24] (By *endowment*, Smith seems to have meant an outpouring of charismatic gifts, rather than the endowment ceremony that was inaugurated in the 1840s in Nauvoo.) As the Mormons labored to finish the temple, he encouraged them to prepare themselves for the solemn assembly that would take place once it was completed.[25] Smith told the twelve apostles that they would soon function under new ordinances.[26] His journal records that "we are even entitled to greater blessings than they [the ancient New Testament church] were, because they had the person Christ with them, to instruct them in the great plan of salvation, his personal presence we have not, therefore we need great faith on account of our peculiar circumstances."[27]

As preparations for the temple continued, Smith became fixated on the order of the priesthood. The Mormon government had allowed Smith to delegate responsibilities to the various presidents and regional leaders; he also instituted ceremony into many of the priesthood meetings. The ceremonies demonstrated and ritually identified and represented the church's hierarchical structure and its democratic procedures. Decisions made by Smith and revelations from him were deliberated through a complex voting system that started with the presidency of the high priesthood and moved its way through the twelve apostles, the seventy, and the high councils of Missouri and Kirtland. Before 1835, Smith's presidency and the Kirtland high council made the administrative decisions, but once the twelve apostles were called, the revelation that instructed them to establish congregations outside Zion created order beyond Kirtland.[28]

By August 1835, an assembly of leaders met in a Grand Council to sustain the recently published, but yet to be bound, Doctrine and Covenants. The leading representatives of ten priesthood quorums rose individually to cast their sustaining votes, one by one. Once the senior officials had cast their votes, the congregation in attendance sustained the new Mormon scripture. Voting was unanimous and set a precedent for the ceremonial procedure to sustain the priesthood of the church. The practice continued through most of 1836, which offered the church a sense of democracy while firmly establishing a pragmatic hierarchy. The Grand Council demonstrated how Smith's Zion saw eye to eye, something scripturally prophesied in the Book of Mormon.[29] Even though the priesthood leadership functioned democratically, the kingdom of God was dictatorial. Smith eventually taught that councils were an intricate part of how the primitive church was governed.[30]

In promoting such ceremonies of hierarchical democracy, Smith taught his followers to live his idea of a heavenly order. Though the rite of foot washing had not been done regularly for almost two years, Smith began performing it again in November 1835 as the temple neared completion.[31] He prepared the elders for a solemn assembly conceived as an endowment of power. A revelation commanded, "O my people; sanctify yourselves; gather ye together, O ye people of my church. . . . Be ye clean that bear the vessels of the Lord."[32] On January 17, 1836, in council, "the Lord poured out his spirit upon us, and the brethren began to confess their faults one to the other and the congregation were soon overwhelmed in tears . . . the gift of tongues, come upon us also like the rushing of a might wind."[33] By January 1836, Smith and a group of elders began a series of washings, anointings, and blessings anticipating the coming endowment of power.[34]

In January 1836, they also began washing their whole bodies, as priests in the Old Testament had once done. At one of the meetings, Smith and John Corrill gathered and prepared water to wash their bodies. Along with the water, they bathed themselves with "whiskey, perfumed with cinnamon." Smith recorded in his journal that "we attended the ordinance of washing our bodies in pure water, we also perfumed our bodies and our heads, in the name of the Lord."[35] Oliver Cowdery recorded the extent of the Mormon effort to prepare for the endowment. After days of meetings with quorums of the church, he wrote, "O may we be prepared for the endowment—being sanctified and cleansed from all sin." Cowdery described these washings as "purification" and compared them to "how the priests anciently used to wash always before ministering before the Lord." He explained, "this we did that we might be clean before the Lord for the Sabbath, confessing our sins and covenanting to be faithful to God."[36] Smith also anointed them after they were clean. He wrote, "I took the oil in my left hand, father smith being seated before me and the rest of the presidency encircled him round about,—we then stretched our right hands to heaven and blessed the oil and consecrated it in the name of Jesus Christ."[37]

The events that followed that winter and early spring became known as the endowment of power that had been promised since 1831.[38] Starting with their anointing on January 21, 1836, Smith recorded several remarkable visions and experiences in his journal. He wrote that he saw God and the celestial kingdom. This experience apparently happened soon after the School of the Prophets was dismissed as the sun began to set in Kirtland. After a group of leaders associated with the school were washed, they were anointed. These two ceremonies launched Smith into his vision of God and the cosmos of heaven.[39]

Smith's experience that day provided an archetype for later temple rituals, though this can be seen only retrospectively. Nonetheless, on January 21, 1836, Smith began the ritual as the saints in Nauvoo would later, explaining that they "attended to the ordinance of washing [their] bodies in pure water, [they] also perfumed [their] bodies and [their] heads, in the name of the Lord." With the potent smells representing ancient Israel radiating from their bodies, they then met with the presidency individually. In adjoining rooms, the high councils of Zion and Kirtland met, waiting "in prayer while [the presidency] attended to the ordinance." They waited patiently for their turn to be anointed but did not attend the first meeting of the presidency. The presidency first circled around Joseph Smith Sr. and stretched their "right hands to heaven" to bless and consecrate the oil. They then laid their hands on his head individually, anointing him and blessing him. Joseph Smith Sr., the patriarch, then anointed the presidency and each member of the presidency confirmed the others.[40]

As at the Nauvoo endowment years later, in which recipients would symbolically enter the celestial kingdom after their washing and anointing, Smith claimed in his journal that he saw a grand vision after his blessing from the patriarch. He writes, "father anointed my head, and sealed upon me, the blessings, of Moses, to lead Israel in the latter days, even as Moses led him days of old—also blessing of Abraham Isaac and Jacob." Then, quoting Paul, Joseph declared, "let us come to visions and revelations." In 2 Corinthians, chapter 12, Paul explained, "I knew a man in Christ above fourteen years ago, (whether in the body, I cannot tell; or whether out of the body, I cannot tell: God knoweth;) such an one caught up to the third heaven" (KJV). Drawing on that passage, Smith declared, "The heavens were opened upon us and I beheld the celestial kingdom of God, and the glory thereof, whether in the body or out I cannot tell." He saw God the Father and Christ sitting on their throne in heaven and "Beautiful streets of that kingdom, which had the appearance of being paved with gold."

Smith's vision also revealed some of the ideas that would later be elaborated as part of the Nauvoo endowment. As the presidency circled him and anointed his head, Smith claimed that he "saw the transcendent beauty of the gate through which the heirs of the kingdom will enter" and "the blazing throne of God, whereon was seated the Father and the Son."[41] The vision proceeded atemporally, as if it were a prophecy of the heavenly future in which Smith saw Adam, Abraham, and his deceased brother Alvin, as well as his mother and father who had yet to die. Within this expansive vision of God and ancient prophets, Smith focused on how his brother could have been in heaven when he had "not been baptized for the remission of sins."[42] Alvin had died in 1823, years before the restoration and with no opportunity of being baptized into the new church. Partially in explanation of this occurrence, Smith was told by revelation that "all who have died without a knowledge of this gospel, who would have received it, if they had been permitted to tarry, shall be heirs of the celestial kingdom of God."[43] Therefore, Alvin and others who had passed away before having an opportunity to receive the gospel would still be heirs in eternity. Over time, it became clearer how this might be accomplished. By 1841, Smith began revealing the concept of vicarious rituals for the dead, which would become a primary component of temple work for future generations of Mormons. The seeds for Smith's eventual understanding of his power and authority as functionally sealing—that is, able to affect heaven via earthly ordinances—were sown in this 1836 vision of the celestial kingdom.

Accompanying the vision of the celestial kingdom, Smith saw the ministry and progress of the recently called twelve apostles. In a panoramic vision reminiscent of John the Revelator, he explained, "I saw the 12 apostles of the Lamb, who are now upon the earth who hold the keys of this last ministry." He witnessed portions of their ministry in foreign lands and "in desert places" preaching and gathering Israel. He also apparently saw the twelve "in the celestial kingdom of God." Though they, like his parents, were still on earth, he saw a future state in which they were saved.

After the entry in Smith's journal describing this experience, Warren Parrish, his scribe, and Smith explained that the other leaders of the church had the same experience: washing, anointing, and the theophany of celestial vision, in that order. Parrish wrote for Smith, "Many of my brethren who received this ordinance with me, saw glorious visions also."[44] Those waiting outside filed into the presidency's room by rank and received their anointing—first the bishoprics of Zion and Kirtland and then the presidencies of the high councils. The bishops and presidents of the high council received their anointing first, and then anointed the other councilors. Smith recorded this in his journal: "The vision of heaven was opened to these also, some of them saw the face of the Saviour, and others were ministered unto by holy angels, and the spirit of prophesy and revelation was poured out in mighty power, and loud hosannas and glory to the God in the highest, saluted the heavens for we all communed with the heavenly host's,—and I saw in my vision all of the presidency in the celestial kingdom of God, and many others who were present."[45] The next morning, they met together again and "spent the time in rehearsing to each other the glorious scenes that transpired the preceding evening."[46]

The outcome of their anointing was a vision of heaven, though the recipients do not appear to have had identical visions. Still, all of them were offered a glimpse into the celestial kingdom once they were anointed. They saw the course of human history and the celestial kingdom of God. Like Smith's, the leaders' experiences included both past, present, and future panoramic visions of events, including the future state of ancient patriarchs and their families in the celestial kingdom of God. Though Smith did not officially identify the endowment of power as occurring until a solemn assembly was held and the keys of the temple ordinances were given by Elijah in April, it is clear that in this January experience the participants "communed with the heavenly hosts" and were given "mighty power" through the spirit of prophecy and revelation. And though Smith may have never intended to shape the Nauvoo temple endowment around this earlier experience of washing, anointing, and celestial vision, the two have distinct structural similarities. In Nauvoo, the washing and anointing would be followed by a ritualized experience of God's plan for humankind as each recipient passed through a veil to enter a room representing the celestial kingdom.[47]

As usual, Smith was given revelations about issues that extended beyond the leadership of the church. His prophetic voice was understood as leading his followers "unto the door of the tabernacle" much like Aaron and his priests in the Old Testament.[48] Writing about that day of washing and anointing, Oliver Cowdery explained that they "were anointed with the same kind of oil and in the manner that were Moses and Aaron, and those who stood before the Lord in ancient days."[49] In other words, Smith was introducing the washing and anointing of ancient Old Testament priests to the leadership of the church. As Richard Bushman has written on the significance of these ceremonies, "in an era when many Christians were sloughing off the Hebrew Bible and taking their Gospel solely from the New Testament, Joseph drew upon ceremonies in Exodus."[50]

Like the order of voting in the Grand Council, early Mormon rituals worked their way through the hierarchical structure of the priesthood, anointing each member of the Mormon leadership. Smith wrote, "The president of each quorum then anointed the heads of his colleagues, each in his turn beginning, at the eldest."[51] In this way, the ceremonies simultaneously provided a shared democratic experience (all priesthood leaders were invited to receive divine visions) and reinforced the structural hierarchy. Within the next week, they continued to wash, anoint, and seal all the priesthood leaders. This experience was followed by weeks of instruction and anointing, which continued until the end of February 1836.

This massive cleansing and anointing pointed the Mormons toward a far more inclusive and liturgical approach to religious authority than ever before. This holy season reinforced their priestly authority. Smith introduced powerful rituals that repeated the hierarchical structure of the priesthood in a cadence that could be captured only in the mindset and action inherent in the repetition of religious rites. Bushman observes, "They were washed, anointed, and blessed—ministered to, rather than upbraided—a more liturgical than evangelical method."[52] The anointed were soon gathered and their blessings were "sealed." "The Kirtland rituals amounted to another form of revelation," writes Bushman, "comparable in importance to the visitations of angels, the voice of the Spirit speaking for God, the translation of historical texts, and the organization of the Church councils by precedent and experience."[53]

The hierarchy was reified not only by the orderly procedure through the chain of command in the priesthood, but by the exclusion of women. In the cultural milieu of the antebellum United States that excluded women from priesthood leadership more generally, their exclusion is not a surprise. The patriarchal grand narrative that united the Mormon ritual system and priestly hierarchy did not naturally yield a way to women to lead the church. Nevertheless, early stages of Joseph Smith's ministry showed signs of departure from the strict patriarchy of his time that took root early on and would blossom in its final phases. For example, one of Smith's revelations to his wife, Emma, gave her the responsibility to teach, expound, and interpret the scriptures within Mormonism. Though she was not a priest, she could perform some priestly duties. Like the leading ministers in Methodism, she was also given the duty to compile a selection of sacred hymns, which became a primary pedagogical tool in Mormonism to teach its doctrine internally.[54] Women would eventually play a more liturgical role in Mormonism as priestesses, but in 1836 they at least participated in the endowment and solemn assembly.

## Solemn Assembly

When the Mormons gathered to dedicate the temple in March 1836, the building's architecture was itself a grand display of the priesthood order. On each end of the House of the Lord, multitiered altars were built high above the floor where the congregation sat in box pews like those found in the Church of England. Each altar had three tiers to hold the presidents of the quorums and councils, layered from the presidency of the high priesthood on the highest tier to Smith's scribes at the bottom. Every quorum and council was accounted for in order of precedence.

Amid this display of grandeur and order, more than one thousand people attended the dedication of the Kirtland temple on March 27, 1836. After Smith delivered a dedicatory prayer that he had prepared according to a revelation, miracles apparently abounded and the ritual continued. Smith's journal declared, "I then bore testimony of the administering of angels.—Presdt Williams also arose and testified that while Presdt Rigdon was making his first prayer an angel entered the window and took his seat between father Smith, and himself."[55] In Methodist fashion, they sealed the meeting by "shouting hosanah to God" repeated three times and finishing with "Amen, Amen, and Amen."[56]

On March 30, 1836, three days after the dedication, the long-awaited endowment was given as part of the solemn assembly of the elders of the church, which came alongside a series of ritual practices. Elders received the ritual washing of feet, various individuals made prophecies, and blessings were given.[57] The Mormons intended to have similar assemblies once a year in the Kirtland temple, but they were driven from Kirtland by 1838 and forced to leave the temple and its assemblies behind.[58] In the Grand Council at the solemn assemblies, Smith created a kingdom of priests. In tedious repetition, the entire priesthood hierarchy was sustained by the Grand Council's vote. The massive assembly sustained each individual leader by standing and sitting, raising their hands. Like a wave of ritual actions, the congregation proceeded to uphold Smith's kingdom of priests, who would take their message to the world. Though Mormonism seemed to rest on the revelatory shoulders of its sole prophet, Joseph Smith, the foundation of priests acted as a sturdy platform to support his declarations to the world.

Therefore, in the early Mormon understanding, the priestly hierarchy became inseverably connected with the notion of the endowment of power from God. Smith stated, "I had now completed the organization of the church and we had passed through all the necessary ceremonies, that I had given them all the instruction they needed and that they now were at liberty after obtaining their licenses to go forth and build the kingdom of God."[59] In November of the previous year, Smith had promised that all who would prepare themselves would see Christ at the endowment.[60] Almost disappointed, though the spiritual manifestations were abundantly described, Smith stated, "the Saviour made his appearance to some, while an angel ministered unto others, and it was a penticost and enduement indeed." Though not everyone had the promised experience, it was an impressive display of priesthood and ritual that positioned the Mormons to believe the heavens were open to them. Smith was satisfied.

## The Coming of Elijah

The restoration of the priesthood was not complete, however, until after the solemn assemblies. Four days later, on April 3, near the commemoration of the establishment of the church, the veils that subdivided the four levels of the temple's pulpit were dropped and Smith and Cowdery joined one another in prayer on the top level. As members of the presidency of the high priesthood, they met to pray in a symbolic spot reserved for the presidency of the church. Encompassed by the veils, they bowed their heads to seek the Lord's guidance, according to Smith's journal.[61] A series of visions ensued, beginning with Christ, who stood on the breastwork of the pulpits. Then Moses, Elias, and Elijah appeared before them and offered their keys and dispensations. Moses gave them the keys of the gathering of Israel, Elias contributed the gospel of Abraham, and—as Smith explained later—Elijah furnished them with all the keys to carry out God's ordinances on the earth.[62]

As in the process that occurred when Smith perceived the vision of Alvin Smith, this shared vision with Cowdery was the culmination of revelation and Smithian prophecy. Smith understood this experience and the keys he received to be within the framework of a genealogical priestly authority that stretched back to Adam. Describing the patriarchal priesthood, Smith's revelation to the twelve in the spring of 1835 stated, "The order of this priesthood was confirmed to be handed down from father to son, and rightly belongs to the literal descendants of the chosen seed, to whom the promises were made."

Elijah's role was of particular importance and had something of a back story in early Mormonism. From 1830, Smith's restoration was uniquely tied to the gathering of Israel. As ardent premillennialists, early Mormons believed that God's people could be preserved and prepared for the Second Coming together as the kingdom of God on earth. In 1839, Smith claimed that the angel Moroni, who visited him from 1823 to 1827 and delivered the gold plates to him, quoted a passage from the book of Malachi in the Old Testament to demonstrate the purpose of priesthood restoration and its relationship to the

Second Coming. Smith declared that Moroni "first quoted part of the third chapter of Malachi and he quoted also the fourth or last chapter." Likely only realizing this later, he stated that Moroni changed a portion of the biblical passage.[63] The changes were extremely important for Smith's concepts of restoration and salvation. Quoting Malachi, Moroni stated that the wicked would burn "as stubble." But Moroni changed chapter 4 verse 5, which in its King James version claimed only that Elijah would be sent "before the coming of the great and dreadful day of the Lord," declaring that God would "reveal unto you the Priesthood by the hand of Elijah" before that day.

Smith's 1839 history emphasized Elijah's purpose without describing the April 3, 1836, visitation. His history revealed that Smith had been told by Moroni in 1823 that Elijah would eventually restore the priesthood. In October 1840, Smith addressed the Malachi passage again by asking the question "Why send Elijah?" He answered, "Because he holds the Keys of the Authority to administer in all the ordinances of the priesthood and without the authority is given the ordinances could not be administered in righteousness."[64] Analogously, Smith explained that the gathering of Israel (restored through Moses) was like hewing bricks from the side of a mountain. The bricks were then gathered in Zion where they were cemented together by the sealing power of Elijah and formed with the solidarity of a temple structure. Smith explained that Elias committed the gospel of Abraham, or the assurance "that in us and our seed all generations after us should be blessed."[65]

Elijah, then, served as the connective tissue that brought the power of the priesthood to bear on the vexing problem of preparing the saints for the coming of the Lord. Though Mormons would later emphasize the restoration visits of Peter, James, and John and John the Baptist to describe Smith's restoration narrative of the priesthood, Smith remembered in 1839 that Moroni claimed the priesthood would be restored by Elijah. Smith taught that Moroni described this restoration in the context of the Second Coming and the importance of building the kingdom of God before Christ's reign—setting the restoration within a premillennial worldview.

The Elijah narrative had another important function, which was to unite disparate generations, past and present, ancient and modern. Moroni made an additional change that reflected this overarching purpose for Smith's restoration. The Book of Malachi states that Elijah "shall turn the heart of the fathers to the children, and the hearts of the children to their fathers, lest I come and smite the earth with a curse."[66] Yet Smith declared that Elijah would restore the priesthood, which would "plant in the hearts of the Children the promises made to the fathers, and hearts of the children shall turn to their fathers."[67] Moroni's statement was different in the sense that it called out Smith's generation to become cognizant of their forefathers. The change made by Moroni seemed to personalize the passage to focus on Smith and his generation, rather than the interdependent role of the children and fathers. Scholar Samuel Brown explains, "This Mormon Elijah provided the cement to unite the society of heaven, an extension of sealing power that secured election for the Saints both individually and corporately."[68] Instead of falling to the will of a sovereign Calvinist God or being threatened by the doctrine of backsliding in Methodism, Smith wanted to bind and seal an eternal relationship with the dead and the living through the priesthood that Elijah bestowed on him.[69]

Smith made this point even more clearly in 1842, as this relationship between the dead and the living began to take shape in Mormon ritual. Having first changed the Elijah narrative in 1839, he wrote a letter to the Mormons in Nauvoo that addressed the meaning of the Malachi passage directly. Once the Mormons had begun baptizing the dead in Nauvoo, Smith declared, "It may seem to some to be a very bold doctrine that we talk of—a power which records or binds on earth and binds in heaven."[70] Quoting Matthew 16, which states, "whatsoever thou shalt bind on earth shall be bound in heaven," he explained that to those who have authority on earth, like those with the keys of the kingdom and the Mormon priesthood, "it became a law on earth and in heaven" once they performed the ordinances. He wrote, "Now the great and grand secret of the whole matter, and the summum bonum of the whole subject that is lying before us, consists in obtaining the powers of the Holy Priesthood. For him to whom these keys are given there is no difficulty in obtaining a knowledge of facts in relation to the salvation of the children of men, both as well for the dead as for the living."[71]

He argued that the dead and the living needed to be bound together because "their salvation is necessary and essential to our own salvation." In this, Smith claimed to possess the power and authority of the priesthood on earth, but this authority reached beyond temporal constraints and could affect the salvation of all God's children, both living and dead. Addressing the Malachi passage, after years of contemplation and development within his priesthood order, Smith wrote, "it is necessary in the ushering in of the dispensation of the fulness of times . . . that a whole and complete and perfect union, and welding together of dispensations, and keys, and powers, and glories should take place, and be revealed from the days of Adam even to the present time."[72] The Elijah narrative gave Smith the ability to bind all generations of time and all eternity together, not just the holy order of the priesthood. The keys and priesthood that Elijah offered Smith in the last dispensation would create a perfect union with all the other dispensations on earth.

## On to Nauvoo

In many ways, Smith's experience in the Kirtland temple marks the *foundation* of the Mormon priesthood. Mormon authority had been established theologically and ecclesiastically, founded on the metaphor of keys, so all that was left to do was to turn the key and open the door. Like Mormonism's authoritative discourse that flowed from the mouth of the prophet, the institutional administration also derived from the prophet with whom all the keys rested. Mormonism's ongoing openness to revelation overlapped with its distribution of priesthood keys. The priesthood functioned much like Mormonism's open canon and was subject to continual revelation and change.

Smith's vision in the Kirtland temple reinforced his authority while broadening the opportunities of others. Through the religious and educational initiative known as the School of the Prophets, early Mormon men had an authorized vehicle through which to seek their own ecstatic experiences of God. Through temple rituals such as washing and anointing, the resounding final message was clear. Elijah declared, "The keys of this dispensation are commited into your [Smith's] hands." This was not an ordination, nor was it an ordinance, but rather, Elijah's message was that with all the keys in Smith's hands, the saints could focus on "the great and dreadful day of the Lord," which was "near, even at the doors."[73] First, this passage declared that the Second Coming was predicated on the delivery of the keys to the prophet. His revelation explained that he was visited by Moses, who officially gave him the keys of "the gathering of Israel from the four parts of the earth." It was that ancient patriarch, who Smith believed empowered him to gather modern-day Israel, who marked the official commencement of the gathering to the temple. Thus Mormonism always turned to the prophet for authority, yet, as in this case, the saints were given equal opportunity to speak with God. If they gathered Israel from around the world to the temple, they would all see God.

Furthermore, they would mark a future generation who would benefit from the blessings of Abraham. Elias declared in Smith's revelation, "that in us and our seed all generations after us should be blessed." Looking backward toward Israel and forward toward future generations of Israel, Smith's leadership would "turn the hearts of the fathers to the children, and the children to the fathers."[74] Smith drew on the promise in the Book of Malachi about Elijah to stop the "utter destruction" of the earth by ritually binding all the dispensations together through secret temple rituals. The grand order from Adam to Smith could be delivered to the membership through these rituals, which would naturally balance the authoritative voice of the prophet with the power delivered to the saints.

# Epilogue

## The Fullness of the Priesthood

This is a book about the foundations of Mormon authority, but it's only the beginning of a long saga detailing the captivating story of Mormon priesthood. It has focused on what has traditionally been called the restoration of Mormon priesthood, which expanded further in the final years of Joseph Smith's life. Stretching this volume a little beyond its intended scope, this epilogue will briefly open the door to the next phase of authority in Mormon history, tracing the development of Mormon liturgy in five key areas.

First, Smith's concern for the fate of those who died before baptism, as seen in his January 1836 vision of the ancient patriarchs and his brother Alvin in the celestial kingdom, inspired a new Mormon ritual in 1840. On August 15 of the latter year, Smith taught the practice of baptisms for the dead in a funeral sermon.[1] Just weeks later, the Mormons performed the first baptisms for the dead on the banks of the Mississippi River near Nauvoo, Illinois. In December 1840, Smith elaborated on the rite to the twelve apostles who were then serving in England, providing for them the biblical precedent from which the rite emerged: "This was certainly practiced by the ancient churches and St. Paul endeavours to prove the doctrine of the resurrection from the same, and says, 'else what shall they do which are baptized for the dead.'"[2] Smith further expanded the doctrinal practice of this new ritual by explaining that "The Saints have the privilege of being baptized for those of their relatives who are dead, who they feel to believe would have embraced the gospel if they had been privileged with hearing it, and who have received the gospel in the spirit through the instrumentality of those who may have been commissioned to preach to them while in prison" (a state before the judgment of the wicked).[3] Although these comments do not allude directly to Joseph's 1836 revelation on his brother, they use a terminology similar to what Joseph recorded in his journal for January 21, 1836, which describes his vision of Alvin and was later canonized as section 137 of the Doctrine and Covenants. The parallels stand as evidence that the rite of baptism for the dead initially began its development years before its actual performance.

Just as ordinary baptism offered citizenship within the kingdom of God on earth, baptism for the dead parlayed the option of such citizenship in heaven. Smith's visions had blurred the lines between earth and heaven, especially in his 1836 vision, in which time and space did not operate according to the usual logic: he saw Abraham from the ancient past, Alvin from his recent past, and his parents, who were still living. All of them were in a state of salvation in the future celestial kingdom. The vision was a clear demonstration of the patriarchal order and Smith's interpretation of Malachi's prophecy. Baptisms for the dead were the first step in binding the parents to the children and the children to the parents and, by doing so, they expanded the saints' understanding about who could experience the blessings of salvation.[4] Smith was connecting all previous dispensations of time to the current dispensation of the fullness of time. As baptisms for the dead were first being performed, Smith wrote in his journal that "a whole, and complete and perfect union, and welding together of dispensations and keys, and powers and glories should take place, and be revealed, from the days of Adam even to the present time."[5] He wanted the practice to move from the Mississippi River to the new temple the saints were to build in Nauvoo, the cornerstones of which were laid on a hill in the spring of 1841.[6]

Second, Smith's goal of binding the human family did not stop at baptism for the dead but extended to eternal marriages and sealings. The idea of sealing families together back to Abraham placed a significant emphasis on marriage. In fact, it caused Smith to radically reinterpret the idea of marriage. Under the new understanding, men and women were sealed together in a ritual as salvific in nature as baptism, which enabled relationships to last for eternity after death. Controversy famously flowered under Smith's unique system of "celestial" marital relations: plural marriage.

Joseph Smith may have considered plural marriage soon after his church was established, for there were references to it in the Book of Mormon, and he certainly broached the topic as he translated the Bible from 1830 to 1833.[7] The Book of Mormon argues that plural marriage was abhorrent in the sight of God, but Smith's later Nauvoo revelation explained that the ancient patriarchs had practiced plural marriage because God commanded them to.[8] Smith's restoration of all things also came with a command from God to practice plural marriage in the dispensation of the fullness of times. He married a second wife in the mid-1830s but established the practice secretly in the early 1840s in association with temple rituals, eventually marrying around thirty women. By 1852, the Mormons were openly and publicly practicing plural marriage, which continued until nearly the end of the nineteenth century.[9] As Smith's revelation explained, plural marriage bound spouses together and exponentially expanded the line of Abraham through birth, as individuals were ritually adopted into the family of Israel and God's heavenly kingdom. Nineteenth-century plural marriage was practiced by most of the church leadership, including the high priests, who understood their actions in terms of an extension of the kingdom of God, which occurred prominently through their posterity. Eventually, with the suspension of polygamy, vicarious sealings of the dead were regularly practiced in the Mormon temples, and such sealings became the primary means of binding the human family together. Once plural marriage ended, vicarious sealings and temple work were heavily emphasized within Mormon temple rituals.[10]

Third, Smith expanded the priesthood through the exploration of Freemasonry in Nauvoo. In a January 1841 revelation, Smith promised that he would reveal additional knowledge to the saints in secret: "I deign to reveal unto my church things which have been kept hid from before the foundation of the world, things that pertain to the dispensation of the fulness of times."[11] There was always a tension between the public and private sphere and the authority that each provided the Mormons. Smith originally excluded most of his highest rituals from public practice, which created a sense of private knowledge and power that exhibited itself only in its secrecy.

With a flair for esotericism, Smith's rituals emerged alongside the Mormon interest in Freemasonry. Soon after the temple was dedicated and under construction, the church took the required steps to establish a Freemasons' lodge in Nauvoo. By March 15, 1842, Smith and Sydney Rigdon were initiated into the fraternity in Smith's Red Brick Store. Interest in Masonry quickly made the Nauvoo lodge the most populous in the state, boasting more than five hundred members. To Smith, the rituals in the Masonic rites reflected an ancient past, though they were an eighteenth-century creation framed with a narrative that claimed they derived from Solomon's temple.[12] Smith's green thumb for religion once again cultivated a new and unique ritual, this time from the well-known seed of Masonry. The day after Smith was initiated, his close friend and associate Willard Richards stated, "Masonry had its origin in the Priesthood."[13] Though Masonry offered a framework for understanding how temple worship could be informed by perceived ancient practices, it was clear that Smith's most insightful theologies and revelations had found a comfortable home where members of his church could experience them in a temple ritual.

Just weeks later, Smith established an elite priesthood order, referred to as the Quorum of the Anointed, in the Red Brick Store. Beginning with only nine male members, by the spring of 1843 it included sixty men and women, primarily married men and women who had been chosen to practice polygamy. The quorum's meetings were distinguished in the Nauvoo records and journals by their peculiar prayer ritual.[14] As in both Protestant revivals and Masonic practice, prayer circles engaged the members in communal prayer while participants stood around the altar performing the necessary ritual signs and tokens. But for Smith, such prayers weren't simply rote practice: they were to be the primary mechanism by which the Mormon leadership could obtain divine revelation and truth within their priestly order. Through united prayer, he believed others could experience divine manifestations similar to his own.[15]

This sharing of divine manifestations had apparently been a long-time goal of Smith's. The Kirtland endowment was his deliberate attempt to open the heavens in ritual fashion. In a similar way, Smith met with the members of the Quorum of the Anointed sometimes biweekly in ritual prayer to access God's vast knowledge of the past, present, and future through ritual. Brigham Young was explicit about the fact that the true order of prayer was formed around rituals that represented a panoptic view of eternity.[16] Young taught that devout petitioners should "offer up before the Father, in the name of Jesus, the signs of the holy Priesthood, and then ask God to give a revelation concerning that doctrine, and they have a right to receive it."[17] Similarly, reflecting on the ritual process, Heber C. Kimball explained that once an individual performed the ritual, "you enquire concerning things past, present & future."[18]

Fourth, and related to the Quorum of the Anointed's panoptic prayer, Smith created Mormonism's most extensive ritual—the endowment—during the Nauvoo period. Richard Bushman explained, "In early revelations, the word 'endowment' referred to seeing God, a bequest of Pentecostal spiritual light. The use of the word 'endowment' in Nauvoo implied the goal of coming into God's presence would be realized now through ritual rather than transcendent vision. This transition gave Mormonism's search for direct access to God an enduring form."[19] This new endowment ceremony went beyond a Pentecostal experience of seeing God. Smith intended this new ritual to fix the Mormon priesthood more firmly within the heavenly kingdom, stating that the endowment would "give [them] a comprehensive view of [their] condition and true relation to God."[20] In 1843, Smith explained that "knowledge of these things can only be obtained by experience through the ordinances of God set forth for that purpose."[21] Like his new order of prayer, Smith hoped to open the heavens and offer participants a panoptic view of the past, present, and future.

The endowment was the culmination of Smith's most innovative and enlightening doctrinal revelations. Samuel Brown writes, "To his baptisms for the dead, his ritual washings and anointings, his celestial sealings of men to women he added new rites that incorporated sacred translations of Masonic rituals alongside dramatic narratives from Latter-day Saint scriptures."[22] As in the Book of Mormon's narrative about the brother of Jared, who was taken up to the heights of a mountain to commune with God, Smith ritualized individual ascension through the presentation of a grand narrative that highlighted the most distinctive events in the history of the priesthood, beginning with the creation. Central to that narrative was that each initiate acted as either Adam or Eve as the heavenly plan was revealed through the holy priesthood of God. The endowment emphasized the central role of the priesthood on earth to communicate with God. Initiates coupled various signs of the priesthood alongside covenants to build the kingdom of God. After communing with God, the initiates then passed through to the celestial kingdom, its glory emulating that in Smith's original panoptic vision. The grand ritual drama that the endowment captured was portrayed by actors and originally delivered to the holy quorum. In Nauvoo, at the first endowment ceremony, Smith gathered potted trees to re-create the garden of Eden on the second floor of the Red Brick Store.[23] Once this practice was moved to the temple, the saints prepared rooms that represented each stage of the endowment; W. W. Phelps remembered that they even sang "Adam-ondi-Ahman," a song he had written for the hymnal.[24]

Though men were the only individuals who originally obtained their endowment, the ritual depended on women.[25] Initiates communed with God in a marriage relationship with men acting as Adam and women acting as Eve. This association was central to the endowment and closely connected to other family relationships, which extended both back in time to a rich network of ancestors and forward toward potential descendants. Brown argues, "Through this liturgy Smith familialized the afterlife. Ancestral connectedness proved central to the temple cultus in a way that Masonic hermeticism never quite achieved."[26]

Women also received holy power in another way in Nauvoo. In 1842, Smith created a Female Relief Society. At its creation, he called for women to organize like a priesthood quorum and act with authority, though they would not be ordained to the priesthood. Using distinct priesthood terms like *key*, *ordain*, and *preside* in reference to their responsibilities, Smith declared, "I now turn the key to you in the name of God and this Society shall rejoice and knowledge and intelligence shall flow down from this time." He professed to the Society that "Those ordain'd to lead the Society, are authoriz'd to appoint to different offices as the circumstances shall require."[27] By September 1842, Emma Smith was the first woman to receive her endowment, though Smith had already been sealing women to himself for some time. The endowment represented the centrality of men and women who had been sealed together as an "order of the priesthood."[28]

Once women were also participating in the ceremony and receiving their own endowment, Smith introduced the fifth innovation, which he termed the fullness of the priesthood: the notion of human deification.[29] Smith's Nauvoo temple rituals had developed around his evolving theology on the nature of God.[30] His materialism was permanently situated within ritual practice and supported by his assiduous efforts to endow God with a physical body as real as humankind's. He eventually taught that humans and God were ontologically the same and that God wanted his children to become like him. By the summer of 1843, Smith revealed, in association with celestial and plural marriage, that human inheritance went far beyond simply returning to God's presence: "Shall they be gods, because they have no end . . . [in addition to] a continuation of the seeds forever and ever."[31] As children of God, humankind would, following Smith's logic, grow up and receive godhood, their natural inheritance.

In April 1843, Smith preached that people needed to know their true relationship with God, which was fully understood through the temple rituals, in order to obtain "exaltation." (*Exaltation* signified obtaining all that God the Father possessed, including a resurrected body and salvation in the celestial kingdom.) In his most provocative doctrine, Smith was recorded as claiming that God "was once as one of us" and that God's plan was to enable humankind to become exalted like him. Smith preached that if human beings were to comprehend their true relationship with God, they would understand that they needed to learn "how to be a god."[32] This learning for Smith often occurred in the context of the temple ordinances, which framed mortal existence as an ongoing, educative process.

In keeping with this emphasis on human deification, Smith introduced a "second anointing" ceremony in the temple that was intended to actualize the formation of kingdoms in heaven that would last for eternity. These kingdoms were in addition to the restoration's overall project to build up the kingdom of God on earth. The second anointing ratified the election of the individual's royal and priestly status before God. The new Nauvoo rites offered Mormons control over their own eternal fate, and the rituals assured them that they would reign within heavenly kingdoms.

Joseph and Emma Smith were anointed to this fullness of the priesthood on September 28, 1843. Smith's journal references to the event explain that they were "anointed & ordd [ordained] to the highest and holiest order of the priesthood."[33] Wilford Woodruff remembered that "by common consent Joseph Smith the Prophet Received his second Anointing of the Highest & Holiest order."[34] Together the Smiths were anointed as king and priest, queen and priestess, in the kingdom of God. Their second anointing was eventually followed by the second anointing of the other leaders in the holy quorum, especially the twelve apostles, who were anointed to reign over the kingdoms of heaven in the next life.[35] After Smith's death, Brigham Young explained the culminating significance of this second anointing, "Every man that gets his endowments . . . [and is] ordained to the Melchisedeck Priesthood, which is the highest order of the Priesthood . . . [and those who have] received their washing & anointing will be ordained Kings & Priests, and will then have received the fulness of the Priesthood, all that can be given on earth, for Brother Joseph said he had given us all that could be given to man on the earth."[36] The promises associated with this second anointing were expansive in scope, but significantly they also expressed a culmination of power and authority within Mormonism—nothing greater, according to Smith, could be given or received on earth. In this sense, in sharing the anointing with the holy quorum, Smith, for the final time, walked that peculiar line within Mormonism in which his prophetic role allowed him to share the highest form of power through these temple ordinances while maintaining his own authority as the prophet of the restoration. He had officially solidified his hierarchical democracy.

In this way, all five of the temple rites he initiated—baptism for the dead, sealings, the order of prayer within the Quorum of the Anointed, the endowment, and the second anointing—became steps on the path to learning godliness. Each ritual grew from the earlier foundations of priesthood he had established in the Kirtland period a decade before. The rituals he was introducing in the early 1840s eventually crowned initiates as kings and queens in heavenly kingdoms above. The sealing rites enacted through temple rituals were understood in terms of a saving grace so powerful that they could and would claim salvation not only for the believer but anyone covenantally bound to the believer through sealing. This possibility of a salvation that was secured on earth rather than bestowed in heaven reflected the paramount importance of both Smith's leadership and the Melchizedek priesthood.

The concept of Melchizedek priesthood thus became incredibly, and creatively, potent. It was this priesthood that allowed individuals to rule in the eternities, providing the Mormons kingly power. It likewise became the power to ensure one's own salvation. On April 27, 1843, Smith preached about humankind's heavenly glory as "joint heirs with Jesus Christ . . . by one having the same power & authority of Melchisedec." Determined in his premillennial beliefs, Smith declared that the council in heaven had already decreed that he would build the kingdom of God in the last dispensation. Franklin D. Richards remembered Smith teaching that the Melchizedek priesthood was "not the power of a prophet nor apostles nor Patriarch only but of King & Priest to God to open the windows of Heaven and pour out the peace & Law of endless life to man."[37] Smith's new emphasis on the Melchizedek priesthood was so profound that it was burned into the minds of the twelve apostles and became central to their own understanding of authority once Smith died.[38]

This book has pushed Smith to the pinnacle of Mormon authority. It has tempered the idea that populist and democratic influences were most important in early Mormonism and instead highlighted the hierarchical structure of Mormon governance. Yet it cannot be overstated that this structure was built on the prophetic words that fell from Smith's lips and the priesthood that upheld them. The narratives, commandments, and translations did the heavy lifting of the Mormon construction project. The solidarity of scripture and God's words moved people to action and built the Mormon kingdom as Smith reacted to the pressures and tensions of the antebellum United States and religious authority.

Throughout this book, we have seen that Smith's restoration narratives emerged alongside his concerns for religious authority. Being a religious minority created tensions that Smith reacted against and even sometimes exacerbated. Through stories of the opening of the heavens, yearly meetings with an angel, and gold plates, Smith emphasized the uniqueness of his prophetic calling. Mormon restorationism was not only a reaction to Protestant biblicism, but a distinct expression that amalgamated the effects of the Enlightenment and the religious excesses of revival. Smith's prophetic voice and scripture represented religious authority, feeding on the discursive power of the Bible while also challenging the centuries-old devotion to *sola scriptura*.

Ensconced within antebellum US culture, Smith struggled to find a balance between kingly authority and kingdom building on the one hand and democratic and antinomian realities within Mormonism on the other. The religious practices that emerged from the tensions of being a minority religion spawned religious narratives that empowered the Mormons with strong governance and devotion to the Mormon kingdom. In nearly every case, these narratives built Mormon ecclesiastical structures and shaped rites and ceremonies for the future. John the Baptist initiated the sacrament of baptism and underscored the need for ecclesiastical authority; Jesus demanded the physical, hands-on ordination of elders; Peter, James, and John instituted the development of various kinds of priesthood bodies; Elijah laid the foundation for an elaborate temple endowment ritual.

From the beginning, Smith's governance depended on and was established by his prophetic voice, leaving a long-lasting effect on Mormonism that resounds into the twenty-first century. The restoration of priesthood authority is embodied within continuing revelation and a prophetic mantle. Smith's priesthood order allowed for both malleability and the rigidity of strict devotion to one individual. This prophetic mantle still reigns within Mormonism, and the priesthood structure has maintained, albeit in a bureaucratized form, the structure that was revealed by 1835.[39] Nevertheless, that original structure also allowed for change. The shaping and reshaping of Mormon authority arrived through the prophet and marked the essence of Mormonism and the Mormon priesthood restoration. The rituals, the restoration narratives, the radical doctrines, the idea of Zion and the gathering of remnant Israel, the priesthood, the religious initiatives, and the restoration scripture—all were formed through Smith's authoritative revelations and prophetic voice. These precedents facilitated the rise of Mormonism and provided its long-lasting effect as a US-born religion.

# Notes

## Introduction

1. "Mitt Romney Pledges to Serve No One Religion in Faith Speech," *Fox News*, last updated January 13, 2015, http://www.foxnews.com/story/2007/12/06/mitt-romney-pledges-to-serve-no-one-religion-in-faith-speech.html.

2. Hewitt, *Mormon in the White House?* 16–17.

3. Romney, "Faith."

4. See S. Harper, "Dictated by Christ." "The cultural work done by Smith's revelations explains his appeal—and the hostility against him. Democratization meant devaluation of direct, 'dialogic' revelation. Smith's followers objected to the process of transferring sovereignty from God to the people. His revelations assert an authoritative, sovereign, biblical God, even as they locate agency in individuals. . . . Smith's revelation created the dynamics for both loyalty and hostility. They gave him political power" (Haws, *Mormon Image*, 234–35).

5. For secular authority, see Grasso, "Religious and Secular," 365: The "relation of power to the establishment of religious and secular domains" is an inseparable component of antebellum American scholarship, which includes that on Mormonism. Rivett, *Science of the Soul*; Schmidt, *Hearing Things*; Delbourgo, *Most Amazing Scene*; Hatch, *Democratization*. For the concept of "fostering doubt," see Porterfield, *Conceived in Doubt*, 114.

6. "With allegiance to a divine monarchy a means of managing mixed feelings about political independence, religious activists rose up to extinguish the blaze of critical thinking about religion that Paine's *Age of Reason* had popularized. . . . With more aggressive organization than before, religious institutions kept pace with population growth in cities, towns, and throughout the West, filling voids of moral authority, easing fears of social ruin, and working to discredit any intellectual inquiry or political philosophy that did not begin and end with biblical revelation" (Porterfield, *Conceived in Doubt*, 114).

7. For an example of the reception of prophetic authority in long-standing Anglo-American prophetic tradition, see Juster, *Doomsayers*.

8. Hatch does portray the development of Mormonism as a regression from democratized clergy to a single prophet, accepting the paradox of authority and democratization, while using Mormonism's appeal to the common man and woman as an ideal example of his thesis. Hatch, *Democratization*, 120–22 and 134–35.

9. Flake, "Ordering Antinomy," 142.

10. See Bushman, *Joseph Smith: Rough Stone Rolling*, 251.

11. Porterfield, *Conceived in Doubt*, 12.

12. Porterfield, *Conceived in Doubt*, 13; Glenn, "Troubled Manhood," 90; Wuthnow, "Democratic Renewal," 365.

13. Porterfield, *Conceived in Doubt*, 13.

14. Fluhman, *Peculiar People*, 23–24.

15. See Ashurst-McGee et al., *Joseph Smith Papers*, xix–xxvii.

16. Sehat, *Myth*, 284.

17. Fluhman, *Peculiar People*, 9.

## Chapter 1. Prophetic Authority: The Prophet of the Burned-Over District

1. See Grow et al., *Joseph Smith Papers* [hereafter, *JSP*], *Administrative Records*, 85.

2. Givens, *By the Hand of Mormon*.

3. Flake, "Ordering Antinomy," 142.

4. Fluhman, *Peculiar People*, 21–48. See Green, *Second Disestablishment*; Hamburger, *Separation of Church and State*; and Sehat, *Myth*.

5. See Juster, *Doomsayers*.

6. Porterfield, *Conceived in Doubt*, 11, 114, 177.

7. Bushman, "Visionary World," 11; Rakestraw, *Extraordinary Instances*.

8. Young, "Discourse," 239–40.

9. Porterfield, *Conceived in Doubt*, 6, 114–46.

10. Hatch, *Democratization*, 67–122. For the Baptist and Methodist denominations, see Heyrman, *Southern Cross*.

11. Bushman, *Joseph Smith: Rough Stone Rolling*, 275–78; Johnson and Wilentz, *Kingdom of Matthias*.

12. Phelps, "Letter No. 6," 97.

13. Phelps, "Letter No. 6," 97; Jonathan Hadley, "Golden Bible," *Palmyra Freeman*, August 11, 1829. Hadley wrote in August 1829, "It appears not a little strange . . . that a person like this Smith (very illiterate) should have been gifted by inspiration to find and interpret [the gold plates]."

14. Givens, *By the Hand of Mormon*, 80; Bakhtin, "Discourse," 42. Mario S. De Pillis hyperbolically argues that "Smith alone clearly saw the need for authority and this might have made Mormonism a unique solution even if his new, heterodox

scriptures had not been published" De Pillis, "Quest for Religious Authority," 82. The production of the Book of Mormon and its relationship to Joseph Smith established the earliest form of Mormon authority, contrary to De Pillis's argument.

15. E. Brooks Holifield (*God's Ambassadors*) argues that 1830s US clergy derived their authority primarily from either their education as professional clergy or from populist ideals driven by an internal sense of calling. As Hatch points out, Smith's vision is "intensely populist in its rejection" of those religious conventions (*Democratization*, 120).

16. MacKay et al., *JSP*, *Documents*, 1: 121. See also Davidson et al., *JSP*, *Histories*, 1: 220–22.

17. Writing of the significance of other early events, like the "First Vision," Jan Shipps states that "it obscures the centrality of the story of the appearances of Moroni and the coming forth of the Book of Mormon and, as a result, also obscures the extent to which Mormonism, through its demonstration that divinity had not ceased direct intercourse with humanity at the end of the apostolic age, responded to the concerns of the inhabitants of the biblical culture out of which it emerged" (*Mormonism*, 33).

18. Hadley, "Golden Bible," 3. Since Moroni was known in the narrative to have been the angel who told him where the plates were hidden, it is assumed the "spirit of the Almighty" was Moroni.

19. Hadley, "Golden Bible."

20. The angel explained to Joseph that he "must have no other object in view in getting the plates but to glorify God, and must not be influenced by any other motive but that of building his kingdom, otherwise [he] could not get them" (Davidson et al., *JSP*, *Histories*, 1: 230).

21. Davidson et al., *JSP*, *Histories*, 1: 222.

22. Bushman, "Visionary World," 185.

23. Davidson et al., *JSP*, *Histories*, 1: 232.

24. Stephanson, *Manifest Destiny*, 5. American providentialism has been addressed more recently in the work of Guyatt, *Providence*; and McBride, *Pulpit and Nation*.

25. See Enders, "Snug Log House"; Bushman, *Joseph Smith: Rough Stone Rolling*, 31–35; and L. Smith, *History, 1844–1845*, bk. 4: 1–2: "In the course of our evening conversations Joseph would give us some of the most amusing recitals which could be imagined he would describe the ancient inhabitants of this continent their dress their manner of traveling the animals which they rode The cities that were built by them the structure of their building with every particular of their mode of warfare their religious worship."

26. Huddleston, *Origins*; Vogel, *Indian Origins*. Reverend Ethan Smith, for example, wrote *View of the Hebrews* (1825), which further popularized this idea during Joseph Smith's lifetime.

27. See Bennett, "Nation Now Extinct"; MacKay, "Git Them Translated"; Hadley, "Golden Bible."

28. Jonathan Hadley, "Golden Bible," *Palmyra (NY) Freeman*, August 11, 1829, 3.

29. MacKay and Frederick, *Joseph Smith's Seer Stones*, 5–28; Bushman, *Joseph Smith and the Beginnings*, 64–76; Walker, "Persisting Idea"; R. L. Anderson, "Mature Joseph Smith."

30. Davidson et al., *JSP, Histories*, 1: 220–36; "Letter IV," *Messenger and Advocate*, February 5, 1835, 79. For the beginning of the translation, see Briggs, "Visit to Nauvoo," 454. Smith's wife Emma explained that she and Smith worked hour after hour, day after day before Martin Harris served as scribe; Joseph Smith III, "Last Testimony of Sister Emma," *Saints' Herald*, October 1, 1879, 289–90. Harris began in mid-April. He stated, "Joseph knew not the contents of the Book of Mormon until it was translated"; Kirtland Council Minute Book, February 12, 1834. Harris stated that he wrote "about one third of the first part of the translation of the plates as [Joseph] interpreted them by the Urim and Thummim" (*Saints' Herald*, May 24, 1884, 324).

31. Joseph Smith III, "Last Testimony of Sister Emma," 289–90; Whitmer, *Address*, 12. For a careful examination of the process of translation, see MacKay et al., *JSP, Documents*, 1: xxix–xxxii.

32. See MacKay et al., *JSP, Documents*, 1: 58, 171.

33. Oliver Cowder, "Dear Brother [Letter 1]," *Messenger and Advocate* 1, no. 1 (October 1834) 14.

34. Janiece L. Johnson, ""The Scriptures Is a Fulfilling": Sally Parker's Weave," *BYU Studies Quarterly* 44, no. 2 (2005): 115–19; David B. Dille, September 15, 1853, "Additional Testimony of Martin Harris (One of the Three Witnesses) to the Coming Forth of the Book of Mormon," *Millennial Star* 21, no. 34 (August 20, 1859): 545–55; "Mormonism—No. II," *Tiffany's Monthly* 5, no. 4 (August 1859): 163–70; Howe, *Mormonism Unvailed* (Painesville, OH: by author), 232–37, 240–49; "A Journal of Mary A. Noble," 2–3, Joseph B. Noble reminiscences, 1836–1866, Reminiscences, circa 1836, Church History Library, Salt Lake City [hereafter, CHL]; Emer Harris, Utah Stake General Minutes, L. R. 9629, Series 11, 10: 268–70, April 6, 1856, CHL; W. H. McIntosh, *History of Ontario Co. New York* (Philadelphia: Everts, Ensign and Everts, 1876), 42–43.

35. Taves, *Revelatory Events*, 60.

36. Book of Mormon, Mosiah 8:16.

37. Book of Mormon, Mosiah 8:15.

38. Doctrine and Covenants [hereafter, D&C], 17.

39. Book of Mormon, 2 Nephi 3:17.

40. Holland, *Sacred Borders*, 156–57.

41. Holland, *Sacred Borders*, 17. Hatch, *Democratization*, 113–22; Porterfield, *Conceived in Doubt*, 11.

42. Nevin, "Early Christianity," 255.

43. Davidson et al., *JSP, Histories*, 1: 210.

44. Holland, *Sacred Borders*, 24, 29.

45. Abner Cole, "Selected Items," *Reflector*, September 2, 1829, 1.

46. Contextualizing Smith's unique doctrine on revelation, Terryl L. Givens explains, "While countless Christians believe that God is mighty to answer prayers, instill comfort, and guide the seeker, theology has to some extent abandoned the

idea that God issues specific, content-laden (propositional) responses to individual, prayerful queries" (*Wrestling the Angel*, 75).

47. Hadley, "Golden Bible," 3.

48. Holifield, *Theology in America*, 332.

49. Whereas, as Richard Bushman observes, the Mormon community emphasizes the immediacy and authority of the revelations: "To the believers, [Smith's] revelations sounded like scripture. They were immediately treated like the Bible, a status that no other contemporary visionary writings achieved" (*Joseph Smith: Rough Stone Rolling*, 128).

50. MacKay et al., *JSP*, *Documents*, 1: 13nn50, 52.

51. MacKay et al., *JSP*, *Documents*, 1: 9–11.

52. D&C 4:3–4.

53. L. Smith, *History, 1844–1845*, bk. 7, 12.

54. MacKay et al., *JSP*, *Documents*, 1: 393–94.

55. MacKay et al., *JSP*, *Documents*, 1: 394.

56. See MacKay and Dirkmaat, *From Darkness*, 105–18.

57. Ole A. Jensen, "Testimony of Martin Harris," Ole Anderson Jensen Collection, 1838–1922, MS 5569, MS 7814, CHL, 2–3.

58. MacKay et al., *JSP*, *Documents*, 1: 13–19; D&C 5:2–3.

59. See Outram, *Georges Cuvier*; Coleman, *Georges Cuvier*.

60. Moore, *Knife Man*, 465–74.

61. MacKay et al., *JSP*, *Documents*, 1: 85–92, 378–85; S. Harper, "Evaluating," 37–49; MacKay and Dirkmaat, *From Darkness*, 141–62.

62. MacKay et al., *JSP*, *Documents*, 1: 6–9.

63. Davidson et al., *JSP*, *Histories*, 1: 252–62. See also L. Smith, *History, 1844–1845*, 127; D&C 10; Preface to the Book of Mormon, 1830 ed., iii.

64. Joseph Smith's 1839 history explained that by mid-July the plates and the interpreters were given back to him, but after the revelation, "both the plates and the Urim and Thummin were taken . . . again." Then, "after a few days," they were returned (*JSP*, *Histories*, 1: 252).

65. He added parenthetically, "for it had been taken from me in consequence of my having wearied the Lord in asking for the privilege of letting Martin Harris take the writings which he lost by transgression" (MacKay et al., *JSP*, *Documents*, 1: 6–7).

66. Compare pages 8 and 10 of Davidson et al., *JSP*, *Histories*, 1: 252–62.

67. See MacKay et al., *JSP*, *Documents*, 1: 6–9; *JSP*, *Histories*, 1: 252; and Davidson et al., *JSP*, *Histories*, 1: 246, draft two.

68. Schmidt confirms that "the laity remained all too ready to demand an account of such a legitimating experience from their preachers" (*Hearing Things*, 48).

## Chapter 2. Authority, Baptism, and Angelic Restoration

1. See Givens, *Feeding the Flock*, ch. 4.

2. Hughes, *Reviving*, 113–14; Campbell, *Debate on Christian Baptism*, 177–219, 242, 308; Randolph, "We Speak," 101; Leonard, *Baptist*, 144.

3. See Ralston, *Review of a Debate*; Campbell, *Christian Baptism*.

4. Luke Johnson, "The History of Luke Johnson (by Himself)," *Millennial Star* 21, no. 53 (1864): 26.

5. Godfrey et al., *Joseph Smith Papers* [hereafter, *JSP*], *Documents* 2: 59–62, 143–45, 148, 155; Rowley, "Ezra Booth Letters."

6. Ezra Booth, "Mormonism No. II," *Painesville Telegraph*, November 1, 1831.

7. MacKay et al., *JSP*, *Documents* 1: 137–38.

8. "The Articles and Covenants of the Church of Christ," *Evening and Morning Star*, June 1832, 1–2; Thomas Campbell, "The Mormon Challenge," *Painesville Telegraph*, February 15, 1831; "The Golden Bible," *Painesville Telegraph*, November 16, 1830, 3.

9. Pratt, "Discourse," 293.

10. For example, elders can ordain; elders and priests can baptize; priests cannot ordain elders. Teachers and deacons cannot perform baptisms (Book of Mormon, Moroni 3–5; Doctrine and Covenants [hereafter, D&C] 20).

11. See Duffy, *Stripping of the Altars*; Thomas, *Religion*.

12. Davidson et al., *JSP*, *Histories*, 1: 230–34; Oliver Cowdery, "Dear Brother [Letter I]," *Messenger and Advocate* 1, no. 1 (October 1834): 14.

13. Book of Mormon, Mosiah 18:8–10.

14. One passage stated, "And they began to establish the church more fully; yea, and they were baptized in the waters of Sidon and were joined to the church of God; yea, they were baptized by the hand of Alma, who had been consecrated the high priest over the people of the church, by the hand of his father Alma" (Book of Mormon, Alma 4:4).

15. Book of Mormon, Alma 6:2.

16. Book of Mormon, 3 Nephi 7:25.

17. Cowdery to Phelps.

18. Alma 4:4; 5:3, 62; 6:2; 7:14; 8:5, 10; 9:27; 15:13; 19:35; 32:16; 48:19; 49:30; 62:45; Helaman 3:24, 26; 5:17, 19; 16:1–5; 3 Nephi 1:23; 7:24–26.

19. Book of Mormon, 1830 ed., 192.

20. Book of Mormon, 3 Nephi 11:21–22.

21. Though William E. McLellin claimed that the power to baptize was given to them by revelation, which he deduced from the fact that neither Smith nor Cowdery talked about John the Baptist until 1834, both Smith and Cowdery emphatically claimed this early period was not defined just by Smith's prophetic revelations, but that it was also a time when angelic visitations occurred.

22. K. Davidson, et al., *JSP*, *Histories*, 1: 48.

23. D&C 128:18.

24. For a broader discussion of Mormon liturgy, see Stapley, "Last Rites."

25. The earliest newspaper accounts, in 1829, mention the angel that Smith retrieved the plates from but not the angel who gave Joseph the authority to baptize. See, for example, Jonathan Hadley, "Golden Bible," *Palmyra Freeman*, August 11, 1829, 2.

26. Bushman, *Joseph Smith and the Beginnings*, 61–65.

27. Warren Isham, "Mormonism," *Observer and Telegraph*, February 24, 1831.

28. "The Golden Bible," *Painesville Telegraph*, November 16, 1830.

29. *Painesville Telegraph*, December 7, 1830.

30. "The conference minutes and record book of Christ's Church of Latter Day Saints [Kirtland High Council, Minutes]," February 12, 1834, CR 100 403, Church History Library, Salt Lake City [hereafter, CHL].

31. Kirtland High Council, Minutes, April 21, 1834.

32. Oliver Cowdery, "The Following Communication," *Messenger and Advocate* 1, no. 1 (October 1834): 16. See also Oliver Cowdery, "Copy of a Letter," *Times and Seasons* (November 1, 1840): 200–202.

33. Patriarchal Blessings, Book 1, 8–9, CHL. This blessing was likely not taken from a record of the early 1833 blessing because it used 1835 church terminology. Furthermore, Cowdery wrote at the bottom of the blessing, "recorded September 1835."

34. It is interesting that Oliver Cowdery wrote at the bottom of the blessing, "These blessings were given by vision and the spirit of prophecy, on the 18th of December, 1833, and written by my own hand at the time." Unfortunately, his early record is not extant and the 1835 blessing was clearly written with 1835 terminology in mind. This likely indicates that his later blessing was not copied word for word from the 1833 record.

35. Emma Smith, *Collection of Sacred Hymns*, 33. Pratt wrote a poem, "The Millennium," which stated, "Again an angel did appear, As witnesses do record bear. Restored the priesthood, long since lost, In truth and power, as at the first; Thus commissioned from on high, Came forth and did repentance cry" (P. Pratt, "The Millennium," 38).

36. MacKay et al., *JSP*, *Documents* 1: 289–303; D&C 84.

37. See Givens, *Feeding the Flock*, chs. 3 and 4.

38. D&C 13.

39. Book of Mormon, Alma 13.

## Chapter 3. Apostleship and the Authority of Change

1. Esplin, "Joseph, Brigham"; Esplin, "Emergence of Brigham"; Walker, "Six Days"; Blythe, "Recreating Religion"; Quinn, *Mormon Hierarchy: Origins*, 105–264.

2. Shaw, *Catholic Apostolic Church*; Flegg, *Gathered*.

3. Underwood, *Millenarian World*, 42, 134–36.

4. Shaw, *Catholic Apostolic Church*, 70.

5. Holifield, *God's Ambassadors*, 13.

6. Outler, "Biblical Primitivism," 134–37.

7. Noll, *Rise of Evangelicalism*; Worthen, *Apostles of Reason*.

8. Handy, "Biblical Primitivism," 145.

9. Vogel, *Religious Seekers*.

10. Acts 1.

11. See Prince, *Power*, 56–62.

12. See Acts 14:4 and 14.

13. Clarke, *New Testament*, 736–37.

14. MacKay et al., *Joseph Smith Papers* [hereafter, *JSP*], *Documents* 1: 69–73; Doctrine and Covenants [hereafter, D&C] 18:9; Vogel, *Religious Seekers*, 145; Quinn, *Mormon Hierarchy: Origins*, 10.

15. Relying heavily on newspaper sources, Gregory Prince argues that twelve apostles were chosen by 1830 (Prince, *Power*, 56–62). The *Cleveland Herald*, on November 25, 1830, wrote that the church had "sent out twelve Apostles to promulgate its doctrines." One year later, Ezra Booth also described a few of the church leaders as apostles (*Painesville Telegraph*, December 6, 1831). In the first instance, the first missionaries were sent throughout Ohio to preach the gospel, but it was not twelve missionaries who were called (see MacKay et al., *JSP*, *Documents*, 1: 202–5). As for the second instance, Booth may have been referring to the concept of apostle as an elder or missionary.

16. For an in-depth description of Smith's creation of both these documents, see MacKay et al., *JSP*, *Documents*, 1: 116–25, 368–77.

17. Vogel, *Religious Seekers*, 145; Quinn, *Mormon Hierarchy: Origins*, 10.

18. Book of Mormon, 1 Nephi 12:9.

19. See Petrey, "Purity."

20. At the June 9, 1830, conference, "The following persons were then seated respectively & received their licenses. . . . Elders of this Church. David Whitmer John Whitmer Peter Whitmer Ziba Peterson Samuel H. Smith" (Kirtland High Council Minutes, June 9, 1830), CR 100 403, Church History Library, Salt Lake City [hereafter, CHL].

21. *Apostle* was crossed out in graphite and the insertion "who is an Apostle of our Lord" appears to be written in the same iron gall ink Cowdery was using for the other licenses.

22. See MacKay et al., *JSP*, *Documents* 1: 368–77. Cowdery likely wrote the Articles in the second half of June, probably soon after he had finished Nephi's account.

23. There seemed to be a difference between Smith and Cowdery and the others as early as 1830. The minutes of church conferences, for example, did not list anyone as an apostle, although Smith and Cowdery officially signed the priesthood certificates as "apostles of the Lord." John Whitmer himself kept much of this record as the first church historian, and he wrote *The Book of John Whitmer* and kept a journal after 1832. Within these writings, he never once mentioned that he was an apostle. On the contrary, within the extant records, he gave himself other titles. Just after he was given his priesthood certificate, acting as a minister of the Church of Christ, he signed the certificates of Newel Knight as an elder (in the summer of 1830) and William Smith as a teacher (on October 5, 1830). Knight's certificate specified that Whitmer was an elder and William Smith's was signed "John Whitmer, Joseph Smith, Leaders" (MacKay and Hartley, *Rise of the Latter-day Saints*, 82; and W. Smith, *William Smith on Mormonism*, 18).

24. *Reflector* (Palmyra, NY), September 23, 1829, 14.

25. *Reflector* (Palmyra, NY), June 1, 1830, 28.

26. "Mr. Editor," *Reflector* (Palmyra, NY), April 19, 1830, 1.

27. Marks, *Life*, 340.

28. Quote is in *Ashtabula Journal*, December 4, 1830; see also *Cleveland Herald*, November 25, 1830; *Western Reserve Chronicle*, December 9, 1830.

29. "We are however credibly informed, that at a disorderly meeting on Sunday evening at the *MARKET* one of Jo's greatest apostles, gave decided token of entire approbation." "We have been informed that a 'Gold Bible' apostle lately undertook to anathematize an infidel!!!" *Reflector* (Palmyra, NY), September 23, 1829, 14. See also "Mr. Editor," *Reflector* (Palmyra, NY), April 19, 1830; *Reflector* (Palmyra, NY), June 1, 1830, 28; *Reflector* (Palmyra, NY), June 22, 1830.

30. Marquardt, "Ezra Booth."

31. Ezra Booth, "Mormonism," *Ohio Star* (Ravenna), November 24, 1831.

32. Davidson et al., *JSP*, *Histories* 2: 44–45; MacKay and Hartley, *Rise of the Latter-Day Saints*, 35.

33. Ezra Booth, "Mormonism," *Ohio Star* (Ravenna), November 17, 1831.

34. Soon after the dedication, Smith dictated the revelation that suspended Ziba Peterson's authority, which Booth claimed was a loss of his office as an elder and apostle (Godfrey et al., *JSP*, *Documents* 2: 3–5, 12–21).

35. "Dear Brethren, previously to delivering the charge I shall read a part of a revelation. It is known to you that previous to the organizing of this church in 1830 The Lord gave revelations or the Church could not have been organized. . . . The Lord gave us a revelation, that in process of time there should be Twelve chosen to preach his gospel to Jew & Gentile. Our minds have been on a constant stretch to find who these Twelve were" (Kirtland High Council Minutes, February 21, 1835, CR 100 403, CHL).

36. MacKay et al., *JSP*, *Documents*, 1: 69–73.

37. MacKay et al., *JSP*, *Documents*, 1: 70. "Revelation to Joseph Smith Jr, Oliver Cowdery, and David Whitmer." The association with apostleship in that revelation, however, may have been realized only months and even years later.

38. Cannon, "Seventy Contemporaneous Priesthood Restoration Documents," 256.

39. The Quorum of the Twelve Apostles was formed on February 14–15, 1835 (Godfrey et al., *JSP*, *Documents* 4: 219–33).

40. Pratt, "Experience in Missionary Labors."

41. Mackay and Hartley, *Rise of the Latter-day Saints*, 25.

42. With that in mind, Jared Carter declared in his journal that he was an apostle. In his case, however, he likely used the term to refer to his missionary work and his newly ordained office of high priest. On September 22, 1831, Carter wrote that, just before his eastern mission, he "had been to Kirtland, where I received the authority of an apostle." Referring to his ordination, he wrote, "the power of the ordinance wherewith I had been ordained, which was to the high privilege of administering in the name of Jesus Christ, even to seal on earth, to build up the Church of Christ

and to work miracles in the name of Christ" (Jared Carter, manuscript journal, MS 1441, 6, 9, CHL). Parley P. Pratt later wrote in his autobiography that "a judge who boasted of his intention to thrust us into prison, for the purpose of testing the powers of our apostleship, as he called it, although I was only an elder in the church" (Pratt, *Autobiography*, 51).

## Chapter 4. Church: Materializing Authority and Ordaining the Prophet

1. Porter, "Restoration of Aaronic."

2. Scholars have not realized the connection between these three events in Joseph Smith's history (i.e., John the Baptist, the chamber of Father Whitmer, and the establishment of the church on April 6, 1830). His history demands that they be examined as the same narrative and that the history exclude a narrative about Peter, James, and John. The John the Baptist narrative is always associated with Peter, James, and John, though they are not clearly associated together. Smith's history gives Smith and Cowdery the power to baptize through John, then John states, "this Aaronic priesthood had not the power of laying on of hands, for the gift of the Holy Ghost, but that this should be conferred on us hereafter." The narrative then explains that John was acting under the authority of Peter, James, and John, "who held the keys of the priesthood of Melchisedek." Because the apostles were mentioned, most historians have assumed that Peter, James, and John would give them that priesthood and the power to confer the gift of the Holy Ghost. But John never identifies Peter, James, and John as the messengers that would give Smith the priesthood. The history states that the "priesthood . . . should in due time be conferred" on them, but also that they would be called as "elders." Smith's history also does not turn to the narrative about Peter, James, and John but instead picks up the same story line in the "chamber of Father Whitmer." Smith wrote, "We now became anxious to have that promise realized to us, which the Angel that conferred upon us the Aaronick Priesthood had given us, viz: that provided we continued faithful; we should also have the Melchesidec Priesthood, which holds the authority of the laying on of hands for the gift of the Holy Ghost." It is indisputable that it was in the chamber of Father Whitmer that they asked for (1) the power to give the gift of the Holy Ghost and (2) the Melchizedek priesthood. Then to their "unspeakable satisfaction did we realize the truth of the Saviour's promise; 'Ask, and you shall recieve, seek, and you shall find, knock and it shall be opened unto you.'" Still in the "chamber," the Lord then commanded them to give the gift of the Holy Ghost and ordain each other elders, once they established the church, on April 6, 1830. Then the third event in his history, picked up "according to previous commandment" on April 6, 1830, when they did all that was commanded them in the chamber of Father Whitmer. Thus, these events are inseparable and part of the same narrative, according to Joseph Smith (MacKay et al., *Joseph Smith Papers* [hereafter, *JSP*], *Documents*, 1: xxxviii; Davidson et al., *JSP*, *Histories* 1: 294–96 and 326–28).

3. Doctrine and Covenants [hereafter, D&C] 6:6; emphasis added.

4. D&C 11:6 and 12:6.

5. D&C 4:1.

6. D&C 14:6.

7. D&C 14:10; 1 Nephi 13:34, 14:5, 15:17, 22:9.

8. The dating of this event is difficult to pinpoint, but it had to have occurred before Cowdery wrote the Articles of the Church (see MacKay et al., *JSP, Documents,* 1: 368–77). The ordinance of giving the gift of the Holy Ghost and ordaining elders or the first and second elders are left out of the articles just as the Lord commanded in the chamber of Father Whitmer. (A later section of this chapter gives further descriptions of this event.) It also likely came after Doctrine and Covenants 18 was given in the first several days of June 1829 (see MacKay et al., *JSP, Documents*, 1: 69). With the negotiations with local printers in mind and the efforts to procure a copyright for the Book of Mormon within the first two weeks of June, the experience in the chamber likely occurred in the second half of June (see MacKay et al., *JSP, Documents*, 1: 58–91, esp. 63–65).

9. Though their experience with the voice of the Lord is not found in priesthood restoration accounts once Smith died, it did feature prominently among Smith's few accounts of the restoration (Doctrine and Covenants 20 does not mention the chamber experience, but it does emphasize the ordination of elders on April 6, 1830, which was an important part of the experience. "Joseph Smith, jun. who was called of God and ordained an apostle of Jesus Christ, an elder of the church, and also to Oliver Cowdery, who was also called of God an apostle of Jesus Christ, an elder of the church, and ordained under his hand" (MacKay et al., *JSP, Documents*, 1: 116–25). The 1835 Doctrine and Covenants does not mention the chamber experience (MacKay et al., *JSP, Documents*, 1: 164–66; D&C 27). Nonetheless, Joseph Smith's 1839 history (Davidson et al., *JSP, Histories* 1: 326–28) includes the primary account of the experience in the chamber, which will be reproduced throughout this chapter. In an 1842 letter that has not survived, he also included an account of the chamber experience along with visits from Michael, Gabriel, Peter, James, John, and others (D&C 128:20–21; Joseph Smith, "Letter from Joseph," *Times and Seasons*, October 1, 1842, 935–36).

10. D&C 128:12.

11. Davidson et al., *JSP, Histories* 1: 326.

12. D&C 76:15 states, "For while we were doing the work of translation, which the Lord had appointed unto us, we came to the twenty-ninth verse of the first chapter of John, which was given unto us as follows." Then verse 30 states, "for thus came the voice of the Lord unto us," whereas verse 40 states, "And this is the gospel, the glad tidings, which the voice out of the heavens bore record unto us." This wording is also similar to Smith's summation of restoration theophany in D&C 128:19–21, in which he mentions the "chamber of Father Whitmer" in verse 21.

13. Smith, "Letter from Joseph"; D&C 128:11.

14. MacKay and Dirkmaat, *From Darkness*, ch. 8.

15. David Whitmer was excommunicated on April 13, 1838, at Far West (Minute Book 2, April 13, 1838; R. L. Anderson, *Investigating*, 69; Cook, *Revelations*, 25; "Whitmer, David," in Jenson, ed., *Latter-day Saint Biographical Encyclopedia* 1: 265). William E. McLellin was excommunicated in 1838 (J. Smith, Journal, May 11, 1838; Jessee, *JSP*, *Journals* 1: 268n141; Cook, *Revelations*, 107).

16. After his excommunication in 1838 and Smith's death in 1844, Whitmer joined together with William E. McLellin to form another church. He was ordained by McLellin to preside over the church in 1847, though he later rejected McLellin's church and eventually formed yet another breakoff group of his own in 1875 (Porter, "Odyssey," 343; H. Smith, "Biography of David Whitmer," 303–4; R. L. Anderson, *Investigating*, 69).

17. Zenas H. Gurley, "Interview of Davide Whitmer," January 14, 1885, Gurley Collection, CCLA.

18. William E. McLellin, who joined the church in 1831 and later became an apostle, had also been told about the experience, yet he too used knowledge of the experience only years after he had left the church and only to discredit Smith's claims about the angelic restoration of the priesthood. Like many of the events in 1829 and 1830 as the Church of Christ was developing, there are very few records describing what occurred, and most of the records are reminiscent accounts. Accounts like Oliver Cowdery's letters to W. W. Phelps describing the early history of the church published in the *Messenger and Advocate* in 1834 left out any reference to the experience (vol. 1, no. 1, 5–8; vol. 1, no. 2, 8–14; vol. 1, no. 3, 15–17; vol. 1, no. 5, 17–19; vol. 1, no. 6, 21–24; vol. 1, no. 7, 25–31; vol. 1, no. 10, 31–37).

19. Davidson et al., *JSP*, *Histories*, 1: 294.

20. His history stated, "We now became anxious to have that promise realized to us, which the Angel that conferred upon us the Aaronick Priesthood had given us" (Davidson et al., *JSP*, *Histories* 1: 294–96).

21. Porter, "Restoration of Aaronic." Porter claims that the chamber experience was in response to the visit with Peter, James, and John, which contradicts what Joseph Smith included in his history. That history states, "We now became anxious to have that promise realized to us, which the angel that conferred upon us the Aaronic priesthood had given us" (Davidson et al., *JSP*, *Histories* 1: 326).

22. Book of Mormon, 3 Nephi 18:36–37, 1830 ed., 493; emphasis added.

23. Book of Mormon, Moroni 2:1.

24. MacKay et al., *JSP*, *Documents*, 1: 69–73.

25. MacKay et al., *JSP*, *Documents*, 1: 66–68.

26. Davidson et al., *JSP*, *Histories* 1: 366.

27. Davidson et al., *JSP*, *Histories* 1: 326–28.

28. Givens, *Feeding the Flock*, iv.

29. MacKay et al., *JSP*, *Documents*, 1: 139–41, 190–92.

30. Articles and Covenants, ca. summer 1829, in Book of Commandments 24:34 [D&C 20:43].

31. Book of Mormon, Moroni 2–3.

32. P. Pratt, *Voice of Warning*, 113.

33. Joseph Smith, "Copy of the a Letter from J. Smith Jr. to Mr. Galland," *Times and Seasons* 1 (February 4, 1840): 51–56.

34. Davidson et al., *JSP*, *Histories* 1: 326–28.

35. Davidson et al., *JSP*, *Histories* 1: 326–28 and 365–66.

36. MacKay et al., *JSP*, *Documents*, 1: 129.

37. William E. McLellin, "The Successor of Joseph, the Seer," *Ensign of Liberty*, December 1847, 42.

38. See McLellin, "Successor of Joseph," 42; Whitmer, *Address to All Believers in the Book of Mormon*, 33. A broader discussion of this topic is in MacKay, *Sacred Space*.

39. MacKay et al., *JSP*, *Documents*, 1: 116–26.

40. See Matthews, "*Plainer Translation*," 25–26n13.

41. Challenges like these also occurred throughout Smith's ministry; for example, Laura Hubble, Black Peter, the Brewsterites, and David Whitmer. The two examples here are just the earliest to demonstrate the concept immediately after the Church of Christ was organized.

42. MacKay et al., *JSP*, *Documents* 1: 116–25.

43. Davidson et al., *JSP*, *Histories* 1: 426.

44. Davidson et al., *JSP*, *Histories* 1: 426–28.

45. MacKay and Hartley, *Rise of the Latter-day Saints*, 20–21.

46. Ezra Booth, "Mormonism—Nos. VIII–IX," *Ohio Star* (Ravenna), December 8, 1831, 1.

47. Davidson et al., *JSP*, *Histories* 1: 436.

48. MacKay and Hartley, *Rise of the Latter-day Saints*, 22.

49. For the Page incident, see also David Whitmer and John Whitmer, "Letters from David and John C. Whitmer," *Saints' Herald*, February 5, 1887, 90; G. A. Smith, "Historical Discourse"; Provo, Utah, Central Stake General Minutes, April 6, 1856, vol. 10, 273, LR 9629 11, Church History Library, Salt Lake City.

50. MacKay et al., *JSP*, *Documents* 1: 185.

51. Bushman, "Joseph Smith and Power."

## Chapter 5. The Development of Mormon Priesthood

1. Godfrey et al., *Joseph Smith Papers* [hereafter, *JSP*], *Documents*, 4: 104.

2. See Weber, *Theory of Social and Economic Organization*, 358–59.

3. Flake, "Ordering Antinomy," 150. See also Godfrey, "Seeking after Monarchal Power."

4. Levi Richards Journal, cited in Jessee, "Earliest Documented Accounts," 24.

5. See Givens, *Feeding the Flock*, 14–44.

6. See Givens, *Feeding the Flock*, ch. 2.

7. Bushman, *Joseph Smith and the Beginnings*, 185.

8. Alma 13:6–10: Some were called to "this High Priesthood being after the order of his Son, which order was from the foundation of the world; or in other words,

being without beginning of days or end or years, being prepared from eternity to all eternity, according to his foreknowledge of all things. Now they were ordained after this manner: Being called with a holy calling, and ordained with a holy ordinance, and taking upon them the High Priesthood of the holy order, which calling, and ordinance, and High Priesthood, is without beginning or end." Speaking of the many generations that have past, it states that "many . . . were ordained and became High Priests of God."

9. Clark, *New Testament*, 573–74.

10. MacKay et al., *JSP*, *Documents*, 1: 321.

11. See MacKay et al., *JSP*, *Documents*, 1: 321nn425, 426.

12. Moses 6.

13. Book of Mormon, Alma 13 and Helaman 10:7.

14. Faulring, Jackson, and Matthews, *Joseph Smith's New Translation*, 127.

15. MacKay et al., *JSP, Documents*, 1: 232.

16. MacKay et al., *JSP*, *Documents*, 1: 260–61.

17. See "The Conference minutes, and Record Book of Christ's Church of Latter Day Saints. Belonging to the High Council of said Church, or their successors in office, of Caldwell County Missouri; Far West: April 6, 1838" [hereafter, Minute Book 2], LDS Church History Library, Salt Lake City [hereafter, CHL], April 9, 1831; Levi Ward Hancock, "The Life of Levi Hancock (1803–1836)," unpublished typescript, MS 570, folder 1, HBLL, 24; "Mormonism II," *Ohio Star* (Ravenna), October 22, 1831. John Corrill wrote, "Previous to this there was a revelation received, requiring the prophet to call the elders together, that they might receive an endowment. This was done, and the meeting took place some time in June. About fifty elders met, which was about all the elders that then belonged to the church" (Corrill, *Brief History*, 18).

18. Hancock autobiography, 24.

19. Joseph Smith's translation of Genesis 14 states that Melchizedek was "a high Priest after the order of the covenant which God made with Enock it being after the order of the Son of God." His translation of Hebrews 7:3 also stated that "Melchisedec was ordained a priest after the order of the Son of God" (Faulring, Jackson, and Matthews, *Joseph Smith's New Translation*, 539 and 139–40). Doctrine and Covenants 76 states that those who are granted the celestial kingdom in the next life will be "priests of the Most High, after the order of Melchizedek, which was after the order of Enoch, which was after the order of . . . the Only Begotten Son" (Doctrine and Covenants [hereafter, D&C] 76:57). Doctrine and Covenants 84 eventually explained that the offices of bishop and elder were appendages to the high priesthood, like teachers and deacons were appendages to the lower priesthood (Minute Book 2, October 25, 1831; D&C 72:1).

20. Corrill, *Brief History*, 18.

21. See Hill, *Quest*, 25; Quinn, *Mormon Hierarchy: Origins*, 29. Demonstrating this point, Brigham Young wrote in 1877 that he had "never been ordained to the high priesthood" (*Deseret Evening News*, May 25, 1877).

22. MacKay and Hartley, *Rise of the Latter-day Saints*, 33: "The Elders, from vari-

ous parts of the country where they had been laboring, came in, and the power of the Lord was displayed in our midst. A number were ordained to the Melchizedek Priesthood, and the hearts of the Saints rejoiced in the rich blessings bestowed upon them."

23. W. Smith, *William Smith*, 20.

24. Godfrey et al., *JSP, Documents,* 2: 81.

25. Godfrey et al., *JSP, Documents,* 2: 81.

26. John Whitmer stated that some were "ordained to the high priesthood under the hand of Brother Joseph Smith, Jr" (MacKay et al., *JSP Documents*, 1: 236). Ezra Booth wrote, "Many of them have been ordained to the high priesthood, or the order of Melchizedek, and profess to be endowed with the same power as the ancient apostles" (Booth, "Mormonism," *Ohio Star* (Ravenna), October 10, 1831, and November 3, 1831). See also Howe, *Mormonism Unvailed*, 180, 188. Because of the conflation, many historians have speculated that the high priesthood was the restoration of the Melchizedek priesthood, while others have claimed that it was simply an office in an already established priesthood order (Quinn, *Mormon Hierarchy: Origins*, 25–26; Prince, *Power*, 21–35 and 70–71; and Hartley, *My Fellow Servants*).

27. MacKay et al., *JSP*, *Documents*, 1: 336–37.

28. MacKay et al., *JSP*, *Documents*, 1: 324–27.

29. Hancock autobiography, 48–49.

30. See Book of Mormon, Alma 13; Old Testament Revision 1, 33–34 (Faulring et al., *Joseph Smith New Translation*, Genesis 14:27, 30–31). Furthermore, Joseph Smith's translation of the Bible, in early 1831, referenced Melchizedek by stating "he was ordained a high Priest after the order of the covenant which God made with Enock." See also Jared Carter, Journal, 1832, Carter Papers, MS 1441, 10, CHL. Even by January 1832, there may have been some confusion about the priesthood. For example, Levi Hancock and Lyman Wight "had some conversation on the priesthood and neither of us understood what it was" (Hancock autobiography, 43). William McLellin also claimed not to know the duties of the high priest in the fall of 1831 (W. E. McLellan to Davis H. Bays, May 24, 1870, in Larson and Passey, *William E. McLellin Papers*, 458).

31. The passage explained that "every one being ordained after this order and calling should have power by faith to break Mountains to divide the seas to dry up watters to turn them out of their course to put at defience the armies of nations to divide the earth to break every band to stand in the preasence of God to do all things according to his will" (Faulring et al., *Joseph Smith's New Translation,* 33–34).

32. Carter journal, 10.

33. By April 1832, ten months after the June priesthood ordinations, church leadership had made more sense of what happened at the conference and how it would be described ecclesiastically (Godfrey et al., *JSP Documents* 2: 231). In the Minute Book, kept at each meeting, those ordained at the June 1831 conference were listed as "elders" who had been ordained to the "high priesthood" (MacKay et al., *JSP, Documents* 1: 325–26). By April 1832, those ordained to the high priesthood were listed as

"high priests" (Godfrey et al., *JSP Documents* 2: 231). Though neither John Whitmer nor Joseph Smith explained this change, extant records between June 1831 and April 1832 give some indication for what occurred. The records make it clear that those ordained to the high priesthood were given additional power that they did not possess as elders before the conference. By October 1831, John Whitmer began listing those ordained to the high priesthood separately from elders and other officers, as if they composed a new office of the church (they were listed as "elders" and "elders with the high priesthood," respectively; Godfrey et al., *JSP, Documents* 2: 77). By December 4, 1831, regardless of whether there had been confusion in the past, Smith had received a revelation that explained that those who had been ordained to the high priesthood were considered high priests. The revelation addresses the office and its officers directly: "O ye who have called yourselves together who are the High Priests of my Church" (Godfrey et al., *JSP, Documents* 2: 150–53).

34. Godfrey et al., *JSP, Documents,* 2, 82.

35. See MacKay et al., *JSP, Documents,* 1: 327–32; D&C 52.

36. See Godfrey et al., *JSP, Documents,* 2: 12–14, 22–23, 24–29.

37. Ezra Booth, "Mormonism—No. VII," *Ohio Star* (Ravenna), November 24, 1831, 1; Minute Book 2, March 10, 1832. Partridge apparently told Joseph Smith to stop "tell[ing] us any more, that you know [things] by the spirit when you do not" (Godfrey et al., *JSP, Documents,* 2: 12–21; D&C 58).

38. "License for Edward Partridge," in Godfrey et al., *JSP, Documents,* 2: 24–29; Marquardt, "Ezra Booth."

39. See Minute Book 1, September 6, 1831; Godfrey et al., *JSP, Documents,* 2: 59–61. At the September 6, 1831, conference in Nelson County, Ohio, Booth was prohibited from "preaching as an Elder in this Church." The elders voted to silence Booth.

40. Godfrey et al., *JSP, Documents,* 4: 308–21; D&C 107:91–92; Godfrey et al., *JSP, Documents,* 2: 132–36.

41. Godfrey et al., *JSP, Documents,* 2: 308–21; D&C 107:66, 91.

42. Faulring, Jackson, and Matthews, *Joseph Smith's New Translation,* 64–67.

43. See Matthew 16:19 and compare Davidson et al., *JSP, Histories,* 1: 10–11.

44. No minutes survived, but what happened at the meeting is mentioned in the minutes of another day (Godfrey, *JSP, Documents,* 2: 78–86).

45. See the minutes of April 26, 1832, for the meeting when all the high priests sustained Joseph as the president (Godfrey et al., *JSP, Documents,* 4: 308–21; D&C 107:65). For Bible references that describe Peter's authority, see Isaiah 22:20–23; Matthew 10:3, 16, 18–19; Luke 22:32; John 21:17; Acts 2:14, 10:46; and Galatians 1:18.

46. Smith, History, ca. Summer 1832, 1; See also Godfrey et al., *JSP, Documents,* 2, 216–18; MacKay and Hartley, *Rise of the Latter-day Saints,* 30.

47. Revelation Book 2, 10–11, and Minute Book 2, April 1832, 26–27, both in Godfrey et al., *JSP, Documents* 2: 229–33.

48. See Jessee et al., *JSP, Journals,* 2: 10.

49. Godfrey et al., *JSP, Documents,* 2: 92–93 (September 11, 1831); D&C 65:4.

50. D&C 27:12–13.

51. See Staker, *Hearken*, 148–62; Campbell, *Delusions*, 11.

52. William E. McLellin, Journal, 1831, July 18–November 20, October 25, MS 13538, William E. McLellin Papers, CHL.

53. See also David Pettegrew, "A History of David Pettegrew," typed transcript, MS 473, 12, L. Tom Perry Special Collections, Harold B. Lee Library, Brigham Young University.

54. See D&C 84.

55. Esplin, Bushman, and Jessee, *Joseph Smith Papers, Revelations and Translations*, 1: 413.

56. Godfrey et al., *JSP*, *Documents*, 2: 289–303; D&C 84.

57. Godfrey et al., *JSP*, *Documents*, 2: 289–304.

58. D&C, 84.

59. Godfrey et al., *JSP*, *Documents*, 2: 294–95.

60. Moses 6:22.

61. See D&C 86.

62. Godfrey et al., *JSP*, *Documents*, 2: 325.

63. Godfrey et al., *JSP*, *Documents*, 2: 327. Building Zion was a reality to the saints, and it inspired their temporal and daily labors along with their spiritual struggles and hopes. Because of their ongoing efforts to build Zion, they viewed the December revelation as addressing how the priesthood would help them carry out that project and bring forth God's millennial reign.

64. John Corrill wrote, "In each of the [assembly halls] were built two pulpits, one in each end. Each pulpit consisted of four different apartments. . . . Each of these apartments was just large enough, and rightly calculated to receive three persons, and the breast-work in front of each . . . was constituted of three semi-circles, joining each other, and finished in good style" (Corrill, *Brief History*, 21–22).

65. Dirkmaat et al., eds., *JSP*, *Documents*, 3: 91–101, 121–31, 131–46.

66. Ibid., 121–30.

67. Dirkmaat et al., *JSP*, *Documents*, 3: 141–43.

68. See D&C 107.

69. For an example to demonstrate that even by 1835 Joseph Smith referred to higher and lower priesthoods, see Marquardt, *Early Patriarchal Blessings*, 12.

## Chapter 6. The Kingdom of God: The Authority of Peter, James, and John

1. Godfrey, "Seeking after Monarchal Power," 31. See also Flake, "Ordering Antinomy," 142. Flake has convincingly argued that "the practical effect of these overlapping power structures was to ensure no individual had ultimate authority in every circumstance."

2. Book of Mormon, 3 Nephi 21:23–25; Godfrey et al., *Joseph Smith Papers* [hereafter, *JSP*], *Documents*, 2: 5–11, 114–20; Doctrine and Covenants [hereafter, D&C] 57:1–3, 133:56.

3. See Staker, *Hearken, O Ye People*, 393–548.

4. See Spencer, *For Zion*, chs. 10–11.

5. Godfrey et al., *JSP*, *Documents*, 2: 114–20, 233–36; D&C 133:9, 82:13–14.

6. Kenney, *Wilford Woodruff s Journal*, 2: 374–82, 4: 435, 5: 474–78.

7. Godfrey et al., *JSP*, *Documents*, 2: 355.

8. Porterfield, *Conceived in Doubt*, 48 and 76.

9. Underwood, *Millenarian World*.

10. Rowe, *God's Strange Work*.

11. For a definition and summary of some of the early literature about pre- and postmillennialism, see Underwood, *Millenarian World*, ch. 1, and Moorhead, "Between Progress and Apocalypse."

12. "Latter-day Glory," *Messenger and Advocate* 3, no. 2 (November 1836): 401–4.

13. *Evening and Morning Star* 2 (January 1834): 126.

14. Book of Mormon, 3 Nephi 21:23–25; Ether 13:4, 6–8.

15. Book of Mormon, 3 Nephi 21: 23–25.

16. MacKay et al., *JSP*, *Documents*, 1: 245–55; D&C 42:9, 35, 62, 45:65–67, 84:2, 4.

17. Moses 7:63.

18. Underwood, *Millenarian World*, 29.

19. D&C 65:2; Matthew 16:19.

20. Godfrey et al., *JSP*, *Documents* 2: 51; D&C 63.

21. Godfrey, "Seeking after Monarchal Power," 27n74.

22. Ezra Booth, "For the Ohio Star," *Ohio Star* (Ravenna), October 13, 1831.

23. Godfrey et al., *JSP*, *Documents* 2: 201–3.

24. Dirkmaat et al., *JSP*, *Documents*, 3: 24–30.

25. See Parkin, "Joseph Smith."

26. Godfrey et al., *JSP*, *Documents* 2: 132–35.

27. Godfrey et al., *JSP*, *Documents* 2: 367.

28. Godfrey et al., *JSP*, *Documents* 2: 374.

29. Flake, "From Conferences to Councils."

30. D&C 64:36–43.

31. See Jessee et al., *JSP*, *Journals*, 1: 452–53; MacKay et al., *JSP*, *Documents*, 1: 124, 282; Godfrey et al., *JSP*, *Documents* 2: 75–76, 80–87.

32. Bushman, *Joseph Smith: Rough Stone Rolling*, 252.

33. MacKay et al., *JSP*, *Documents* 1, 177–79.

34. MacKay et al., *JSP*, *Documents*, 1: 177–83.

35. MacKay et al., *JSP*, *Documents*, 1: 245–55.

36. Dirkmaat et al., *JSP*, *Documents*, 3: 24–31; D&C 90:16.

37. Dirkmaat et al., *JSP*, *Documents*, 4: 429.

38. Minute Book 1, February 12, 1834 (Dirkmaat et al., *JSP*, *Documents* 4: 228–31).

39. Godfrey et al., *JSP*, *Documents*, 4: 308–21; D&C 107:21.

40. See the work of Darowski, "Seeking after the Ancient Order."

41. Joseph Smith had been designated as the president of the high priesthood in November 1831 and was ordained to that position by January 25, 1832 (Godfrey et

al., *JSP, Documents*, 2: 132–35). Frederick G. Williams was appointed in March 1833 (Dirkmaat et al., *JSP, Documents*, 3: 43–45). In addition to Cowdery's ordination, the next day (December 6, 1834), Joseph Smith Sr. and Hyrum Smith were ordained as presidents of the high priesthood (Davidson et al., *JSP, Histories*, 1: 37).

42. Davidson et al., *JSP*, *Histories*, 1: 32.

43. Joseph Smith's history would later recount that he and Cowdery received the lesser priesthood from John the Baptist on May 15, 1829. The history would also convey the angel's instruction that Cowdery would be second elder, next to Joseph Smith as first elder, in the church that was yet to be organized. Joseph Smith and Cowdery were acknowledged in these positions at the organization of the church (Davidson et al., *JSP*, *Histories*, 1: 292–94; Revelation, April 10, 1830, in Doctrine and Covenants [1835] 2:1 [D&C 20:2–3]).

44. Davidson et al., *JSP, Histories*, 1: 294, italics added. This statement about Smith and Cowdery being the first and second elders, respectively, was later crossed out.

45. MacKay et al., *JSP*, *Documents*, 1: 126–29; D&C 21; Davidson et al., *JSP Histories* 1: 326.

46. "The Golden Bible," *Painesville Telegraph*, November 16, 1830, and December 7, 1830. The *Painesville Telegraph* reported about Cowdery and his claims soon after he and the Lamanite missionaries taught Sidney Rigdon's congregation. Though they are not directly from Cowdery, they do mention that he conversed with "angels" in the plural. One article wrote, "He proclaims destruction upon the world within a few years,—holds for that the ordinances of the gospel, have not been regularly administered since the days of the Apostles . . . who pretends to have a divine mission, and to have seen and conversed with Angels, is Cowdray [*sic*]."

47. Kirtland High Council Minutes, February 21, 1835, 159 (Godfrey et al., *JSP*, *Documents* 4: 243).

48. Marquardt, *Early Patriarchal Blessings*, 8–9.

49. Godfrey et al., *JSP*, *Documents*, 4: 246. See also Marquardt, *Early Patriarchal Blessings*, 3.

50. D&C 27:11–12.

51. Compare Godfrey et al., *JSP*, *Documents*, 4: 409.

52. MacKay et al., *JSP*, *Documents*, 1: 164–66; D&C 27; Godfrey et al., *JSP*, *Documents*, 2: 197–99; D&C 78:15–16, 107:53; Jessee et al., *JSP*, *Journals*, 1: May 19, 1838, 270–72.

53. D&C 27.

54. MacKay et al., *JSP*, *Documents*, 1: 164–66. D&C 27, for example, states that they "ordained you and confirmed you to be apostles, and especial witnesses of my name, and bear the keys of your ministry and of the same things which I revealed unto them; Unto whom I have committed the keys of my kingdom, and a dispensation of the gospel for the last times." From at least 1835, the restoration of the Melchizedek priesthood has been associated with Peter, James, and John. One historian demonstrates that the written record "repeatedly testif[ied] that Peter, James, and John had appeared to them and restored this high priesthood authority" (Brian Cannon,

"Seventy Contemporaneous Priesthood Restoration Documents," 218). Cannon wrote the commentary about this collection of documents and it was in his introduction that he makes this assessment.

55. See Davidson et al., *JSP, Histories*, 1: 326–28; Willard Richards, Pocket Companion, MS 1490, 65, Willard Richards Journals and Papers, 1821–1854, Church History Library, Salt Lake City [hereafter, CHL]; Ehat and Cook, *Words of Joseph Smith*, 9.

56. Godfrey et al., *JSP, Documents*, 4: xxviii, 312–13, 314, 315, 318.

57. Godfrey et al., *JSP, Documents*, 4: 251–54.

58. MacKay et al., *JSP, Documents*, 1: 116–26.

59. Dirkmaat et al., *JSP, Documents*, 3: 435–39; Godfrey et al., *JSP, Documents*, 4: 88–90.

60. Quinn, "Mormon Succession Crisis"; R. Harper, "Mantle of Joseph."

61. Smith declared, "God placed in the church first apostles, secondarily prophets" in the spring of 1842 (Editor, "Try the Spirits," *Times and Seasons* 3 [April 1842]: 746). See Lively, "Catholic Apostolic Church."

62. O. Pratt, *Divine Authority*, 4–5, 7; P. Pratt, *Proclamation*, 1–2; Kenney, *Woodruff Journal*, 3: 257.

63. See B. Cannon, "Seventy Contemporaneous."

64. Heber C. Kimball explained that Sidney Rigdon "has no authority only what he receives from the church, if he was one with us, why was he not in our councils? He was not in the council pertaining to the High Priesthood until just before he started for Pittsburgh. Brother Phelps was the means of bringing him in, but he has not got the same authority as others; there are more than thirty men who have got higher authority than he has" ("Continuation of Elder Rigdon's Trial," *Times and Seasons*, October 1, 1844, 664).

65. Kenney, *Woodruff Journal*, 2: 437.

66. D. Anderson and Bergera, "Friday, December 12, 1845," in *Nauvoo Endowment*, 11–15; multiple entries in the minutes demonstrate who was administrating the endowment on December 12, 1845, but none of them is Peter, James, or John, 11–15.

67. William Clayton, "Diary, kept for Heber C. Kimball" (minutes for December 13, 1845), in D. Anderson and Bergera, *Nauvoo Endowment*, 21.

68. Polygamy also focused the Mormon sense of religious authority in the hands of the twelve apostles. The private group Smith chose to receive their temple rituals included those who were handpicked to begin the practice of polygamy. The twelve apostles were central to the dynastic practices that polygamy perpetuated in the years after Smith's death, in which members of the church were sealed and married into a line of Israel leading back to the ancient patriarchs and Adam. Because vicarious works were performed only occasionally for decades after the Mormons left Nauvoo, polygamy and ritual sealings (men sealed to the prophets, or the twelve apostles as adopted sons) emphasized the role of the twelve apostles and Brigham Young in building the kingdom of God and sealing members of the church to the ancient patriarchs and tribe of Israel. The only way to obtain entrance into the kingdom was

through the temple rituals, and polygamy connected the members to Israel dynastically through the twelve and the prophets.

69. See S. Harper, "Oliver Cowdery."

70. "28. Oliver Cowdery (March 23, 1846)," in Welch, *Opening the Heavens*, 244: "Had you stood in the presence of John, with our departed brother joseph, to receive the Lesser Priesthood—and in the presence of Peter, to receive the Greater" (255); "66. Reuben Miller (1847)," in Welch, *Opening the Heavens*, 255: "An a short time after, the Melchisedek priesthood from Peter, James, and John, the ancient Apostles." His use of the term *Melchizedek priesthood* therefore might be better rephrased as the "keys of the Melchizedek priesthood" because the keys allowed them to later ordain each other to the office of elder, as they were commanded to do in the chamber of Father Whitmer (Davidson et al., *JSP*, *Documents* 1, 326–28). Otherwise, they were ordained twice, once by the apostles and once by each other. Cowdery wrote from Kirtland, Ohio, to W. W. Phelps in Independence, Missouri, that John the Baptist restored the priesthood: "We received under [the angel's] hand the holy priesthood, as he said, 'upon you my fellow servants, in the name of Messiah I confer this priesthood and this authority, which shall remain upon the earth, that the sons of Levi may yet offer an offering unto the Lord in righteousness!'" (Oliver Cowdery to W. W. Phelps, September 7, 1834, in *Messenger and Advocate* 1, no. 1 [October 1834]: 14–16).

71. Cowdery to Young, March 23, 1846; "66. Reuben Miller (1847)," in Welch, *Opening the Heavens*, 255.

72. Young, "Temple Corner Stones," 134.

## Chapter 7. Calculating Salvation: Priesthood Practice and Mormon Ritual

1. See Flake, "Ordering Antinomy"; Wacker, "Holy Spirit"; T. Smith, "Righteousness and Hope."

2. See S. Brown, "Prophet Elias Puzzle"; J. Brown, *Dictionary of the Holy Bible*, 448–49; Wood, *Dictionary of the Holy Bible*, 401–2; Horne, *Introduction*, 1: 627.

3. Ricks, "Appearance of Elijah and Moses," 483–86; Adams, "15th of Nisan"; Zeitlin, "Liturgy."

4. See Darowski, "School of the Prophets."

5. Doctrine and Covenants [hereafter, D&C] 88:118.

6. Dirkmaat et al., *Joseph Smith Papers* [hereafter, *JSP*], *Documents* 4: 91–103. See also Robinson, *First Mormon Temple*; Andrew, *Early Temples*.

7. Godfrey, *JSP*, *Documents*, 2: 237.

8. See Givens, *Wrestling the Angel*, 94; Fluhman, "Authority"; Roberts, Van Wagoner, and Walker, "Lectures on Faith."

9. Godfrey, *JSP Documents*, 2: 237–38.

10. See John 13.

11. Staker, *Hearken, O Ye People*, 40.

12. See Godfrey et al., *JSP, Documents*, 2: 334–36; D&C 88.

13. D&C 88:141.

14. D&C 88:131.

15. Godfrey et al., *JSP, Documents*, 2: 334–47; D&C 88:130–33.

16. Godfrey et al., *JSP, Documents*, 2: 334–47; D&C 88:132.

17. Godfrey et al., *JSP, Documents*, 2: 334–47; D&C 88:78–80.

18. J. Smith, History, B-1: 557–62.

19. J. Smith, Journal, October 5, 1835.

20. Dirkmaat et al., *JSP, Documents*, 3: 104–7; D&C 95:17.

21. Quote is from MacKay et al., *JSP, Documents* 1: 232. See also Dirkmaat et al., *JSP, Documents*, 3: 104–7; Godfrey et al., *JSP, Documents*, 2: 334–35; D&C 95:8, 88:117–26.

22. MacKay et al., *JSP, Documents*, 1: 317–26.

23. Zebedee Coltrin, Minutes, Salt Lake City School of the Prophets, October 3, 1883, CR 390 5, Church History Library, Salt Lake City [hereafter, CHL].

24. D&C 18:32.

25. S. Harper, "Pentecost."

26. Godfrey et al., *JSP, Documents*, 2: 114–20; D&C 133:4–7.

27. Jessee et al., *JSP, Journals*, 1: 97.

28. Godfrey et al., *JSP, Documents*, 4: 308–21. See D&C 107.

29. 3 Nephi 20:32.

30. "Conference Minutes," *Times and Seasons*, August 15, 1844, 614.

31. Jessee et al., *JSP, Journals*, 1: 97–98.

32. Godfrey et al., *JSP, Documents*, 2: 114–20; D&C 133:4–7.

33. Jessee et al., *JSP, Journals*, 1: 160.

34. Jessee et al., *JSP, Journals*, 1: 68, 83–84, 166–72, 174–75, 178, 180–82.

35. Jessee et al., *JSP, Journals*, 1: 167.

36. Arrington, "Oliver Cowdery's Kirtland, Ohio, 'Sketchbook,'" 416.

37. Jessee et al., *JSP, Journals*, 1: 167.

38. MacKay et al., *JSP, Documents*, 1: 229–32.

39. Jessee et al., *JSP, Journals*, 1: 167.

40. Jessee et al., *JSP, Journals*, 1: 166–67.

41. D&C 137:2–3.

42. Jessee et al., *JSP, Journals*, 1: 168.

43. Jessee et al., *JSP, Journals*, 1: 168–71.

44. Jessee et al., *JSP, Journals*, 1: 170–71.

45. Jessee et al., *JSP, Journals*, 1: 170. See also Oliver Cowdery Diary 1836, January–March, January 21, 1836, MS 2737, box 85, FD 1, CHL; Edward Partridge, Journal, January 1835–July 1836, January 21, 1836, Partridge Papers, CHL.

46. Jessee et al., *JSP, Journals*, 1: 171.

47. See L. Brown, "Sacred Departments," 369, which is a model of William Clayton, Nauvoo Temple layout, produced on December 11, 1845.

48. Oliver Cowdery, Diary, January 22, 1836.

49. Oliver Cowdery, Diary, January 22, 1836. See also Partridge, Journal, January 22, 1836.

50. Bushman, *Joseph Smith: Rough Stone Rolling*, 312.

51. Jessee et al., *JSP*, *Journals*, 1: 170.

52. Bushman, *Joseph Smith: Rough Stone Rolling*, 314.

53. Bushman, *Joseph Smith: Rough Stone Rolling*, 315.

54. D&C 25.

55. Jessee et al., *JSP*, *Journals*, 1: 211; G. A. Smith, "Historical Discourse," 10.

56. "Minutes," *Messenger and Advocate* 2, no. 6 (March 1836): 281. This ritual was drawn from Matthew 21, which reads, "the multitudes that went before, and that followed, cried, saying Hosanna to the Son of David: Blessed is he that cometh in the name of the Lord; Hosanna in the highest." This exclamation of praise and deliverance was also used in ancient worship, according to 3 Nephi in the Book of Mormon, which describes the reaction of the people when Christ came to America: "Hosanna! Blessed be the name of the Most High God! And they did fell down at the feet of Jesus, and did worship him."

57. Jessee et al., *JSP*, *Journals*, 1: March 30, 1836; Partridge Journal, March 30, 1836; Stephen Post Journals, 1835–1879, March 30, 1836, MS 1304, Post Papers, CHL.

58. Bushman, *Joseph Smith: Rough Stone Rolling*, 316.

59. Jessee et al., *JSP*, *Journals*, 1: 215.

60. See J. Smith, Journal, November 12, 1835. For the experiences in the second assembly, see Partridge, Journal, March 31, 1836; George Post, Journal, March 31, 1836; W. W. Phelps to Sally Phelps, April 1836, W. W. Phelps Papers, L. Tom Perry Special Collections, Harold B. Lee Library, Brigham Young University, Provo, Utah.

61. This portion of Smith's journal was in the handwriting of Warren Cowdery (J. Smith, Journal, September 1835 to April 1836, 192–93; and Jessee et al., *JSP*, *Journals*, 1: 218–22). See also Stephen Post, Journal, April 3, 1836, and W. W. Phelps to Sally Phelps, April 1836.

62. The revelation, D&C 110, was documented by Warren Cowdery in Smith's journal (Jessee et al., *JSP Journals*, 1, 219). Robert B. Thompson recorded Smith's claim that Elijah gave him the keys to carry out all the earthly ordinances (Robert B. Thompson, sermon notes, October 5, 1840, MS 155, box 7, fond 2, CHL). See also Wilford Woodruff, Journal, March 10, 1844.

63. As will be shown in what follows, the changes made to the passages in Malachi were written down in 1839 in Smith's history and in 1842 in D&C 128. The preoccupation with the difference seems to have arisen after 1836 because the Book of Mormon quotes Malachi without the change.

64. Thompson, sermon notes, October 5, 1840.

65. D&C 110:12.

66. Malachi 4:6.

67. D&C 2:2.

68. S. Brown, *In Heaven*, 165.

69. Ehat and Cook, *Words of Joseph Smith*, 366–67; S. Brown, "Prophet Elias Puzzle."

70. D&C 121:9.

71. D&C 128:11.

72. J. Smith, Journal, September 11, 1842, 199.

73. D&C 110:16.

74. D&C 110:15.

## Epilogue

1. Simon Baker, "15 Aug. 1840 Minutes of Recollection of Joseph Smith's Sermon," MS 155, Joseph Smith Collection, Church History Library [hereafter, CHL].

2. Joseph Smith to the Quorum of the Twelve, Letter Book 1, December 15, 1840, MS 155, Joseph Smith Collection, CHL, 6.

3. Joseph Smith to Quorum of the Twelve, December 15, 1840, 6.

4. See Gregory Prince, *Power*, 142–46; Bushman, *Joseph Smith: Rough Stone Rolling*, 422.

5. Doctrine and Covenants [hereafter, D&C] 128:18.

6. Baugh, "For This Ordinance Belongeth"; Baugh, "Practice of Baptism."

7. See Jenson, "Plural Marriage"; "Report of Elders Orson Pratt and Joseph F. Smith," *Millennial Star* 40 (December 16, 1878): 788; Bachman, "New Light."

8. D&C 132. For an apologetic approach to this topic, see Hales, "Continuation of the Seeds."

9. See Daynes, *More Wives Than One*; Compton, *In Sacred Loneliness*; Kern, *Ordered Love*; Foster, *Women, Family, and Utopia*; Hardy, *Doing the Works*; Bringhurst, Foster, and Hardy, *Persistence of Polygamy*; Van Wagoner, *Mormon Polygamy*; Hales, *Joseph Smith's Polygamy*; M. Smith, *Revelation*.

10. Bennett, "Line upon Line."

11. D&C 124:41.

12. Homer, "'Similarity of Priesthood."

13. Willard Richards to Levi Richards, March 7–25, 1842, in Stevenson, *Richards Family History*, 3: 90.

14. Anderson and Bergera, *Joseph Smith's Quorum*.

15. Quinn, "Latter-day Saint Prayer Circles"; Parry, "Temple Worship"; Nibley, "Early Christian Prayer Circle."

16. On December 28, 1845, Brigham Young was recorded using the concept of past, present, and future or a panoptic reality to describe the purpose of the endowment and the conceptual framework for using a "new name," ritual signs, and tokens in the Nauvoo temple. See Anderson and Bergera, *Nauvoo Endowment Companies*, 204, 211–13.

17. Young, "Priesthood," 90.

18. Anderson and Bergera, *Nauvoo Endowment Companies*, 204.

19. Bushman, *Joseph Smith: Rough Stone Rolling*, 451.

20. Joseph Smith, "Monday, 2o'clock, P. M," *Times and Seasons*, September 15, 1843, 331.

21. J. Smith, "Monday, 2o'clock."

22. S. Brown, *In Heaven*, 183.

23. G. D. Smith, *Intimate Chronicle*, 205.

24. Anderson and Bergera, *Nauvoo Endowment*, 29; Emma Smith, *Collection of Sacred Hymns*, 29–30.

25. See Quinn, "Mormon Women."

26. S. Brown, *In Heaven*, 188.

27. Derr et al., *First Fifty Years*, 59.

28. D&C 131:1–4.

29. See J. F. Smith, "Fulness of the Priesthood."

30. See Givens, *Wrestling the Angel*, section "The Divine"; LDS Gospel Topics Essays, "Becoming like God," accessed July 8, 2019, https://www.lds.org/topics/becoming-like-god?lang=eng#38.

31. D&C 132.

32. See Joseph Smith, "Discourse," *Times and Seasons*, April 7, 1844, 614; Hedges et al., *Joseph Smith Papers*, Church History Library, Salt Lake City [hereafter, *JSP*], *Journals*, 3, 216–22.

33. Hedges et al., *JSP*, *Journals* 3: 104.

34. Hedges et al., *JSP*, *Journals*, 3: 104n482.

35. Anderson and Bergera, eds., *Joseph's Quorum*, xxxix–xliii.

36. Kimball, Journal, December 26, 1845.

37. Ehat and Cook, *Words of Joseph Smith*, 245.

38. See Ehat, "Joseph Smith's Introduction."

39. See D&C 107.

# Bibliography


Adams, William James Jr. "Discovery: The 15th of Nisan." Ensign 7, no. 1 (January 1977): 46.

Anderson, Devery S., and Gary James Bergera, eds. *Joseph Smith's Quorum of the Anointed, 1842–1845: A Documentary History*. Salt Lake City: Signature, 2005.

———, eds. *The Nauvoo Endowment Companies*. Salt Lake City: Signature, 2005.

Anderson, Rex A. *Investigating the Book of Mormon Witnesses*. Salt Lake City: Deseret, 1981.

———. "The Mature Joseph Smith and Treasure Searching." *BYU Studies* 24, no. 4 (October 1984): 489–560.

Andrew, Laurel. *The Early Temples of the Mormons: The Architecture of the Millennial Kingdom in the American West*. Albany: State University of New York Press, 1978.

Arrington, Leonard J., ed. "Oliver Cowdery's Kirtland, Ohio, 'Sketchbook.'" *BYU Studies* 12, no. 4 (July 1974): 410–26.

Ashurst-McGee, Mark. "A One-Sided View of Mormon Origins." *Farms Review of Books* 15, no. 2 (June 2003): 309–64.

Ashurst-McGee, Mark, David W. Grua, Elizabeth A. Kuehn, Alexander L. Baugh, and Brenden W. Rensink, eds. *The Joseph Smith Papers, Documents*. Vol. 6, *February 1838–August 1839*. Salt Lake City: Church Historian's Press, 2017.

Bachman, Daniel W. "New Light on an Old Hypothesis: The Ohio Origins of the Revelation on Eternal Marriage." *Journal of Mormon History* 5 (1978): 19–32.

Bakhtin, Mikhail. "Discourse in the Novel." In *The Dialogic Imagination: Four Essays*. Edited by Michael Holquist, 258–425. Austin: University of Texas Press, 1981.

Baugh, Alexander L. "'For This Ordnance Belongeth to My House': The Practice of Baptism for the Dead Outside the Nauvoo Temple." *Mormon Historical Studies* 3, no. 1 (Spring 2002): 47–58.

———. "The Practice of Baptism for the Dead Outside of Temples." *Religious Studies Center Newsletter* 13, no. 1 (1998): 3–6.

Bennett, Richard E. "'Line upon Line, Precept upon Precept': Reflections on the 1877 Commencement of the Performance of Endowments and Sealings of the Dead." *BYU Studies* 44, no. 3 (June 2005): 38–77.

———. "A Nation Now Extinct, American Indian Origin Theories as of 1820: Samuel L. Mitchill, Martin Harris, and the New York Theory." *Journal of the Book of Mormon Studies* 20, no. 2 (2011): 30–51.

Blythe, Christopher J. "Recreating Religion: The Response to Joseph Smith's Innovations in the Second Prophetic Generation of Mormonism." MA thesis, Utah State University, 2001.

Briggs, Edmund C. "A Visit to Nauvoo in 1856." *Journal of History* 9 (October 1916): 446–62.

Bringhurst, Newell G., Craig L. Foster, and Carmon B. Hardy, eds. *The Persistence of Polygamy: From Joseph Smith's Martyrdom to the First Manifesto, 1844–1890*. Independence, MO: John Whitmer, 2013.

Brown, John. *A Dictionary of the Holy Bible*. Pittsburgh, PA: Zadok Cramer, 1807.

Brown, Lisle G. "The Sacred Departments for Temple Work in Nauvoo: The Assembly Room and the Council Chamber." *BYU Studies* 19, no. 3 (July 1979): 361–74.

Brown, Samuel. "Early Mormon Adoption Theology and the Mechanics of Salvation." *Journal of Mormon History* 37, no. 3 (Summer 2011): 3–52.

———. *In Heaven as It Is on Earth: Joseph Smith and the Early Mormon Conquest of Death*. New York: Oxford University Press, 2012.

———. "The Prophet Elias Puzzle." *Dialogue* 39, no. 3 (Fall 2006): 1–17.

Bushman, Richard L. *Joseph Smith: Rough Stone Rolling*. New York, Knopf, 2005.

———. "Joseph Smith and Power." In *A Firm Foundation: Church Organization and Administration*. Edited by Arnold K. Garr and David J. Whittaker, 1–13. Salt Lake City and Provo, UT: Deseret and the Religious Studies Center, Brigham Young University, 2011.

———. *Joseph Smith and the Beginnings of Mormonism*. Urbana: University of Illinois Press, 1984.

———. "The Visionary World of Joseph Smith." *BYU Studies* 37, no. 1 (January 1997): 183–204.

Campbell, Alexander. *Christian Baptism: With Its Antecedents and Consequents*. Bethany, VA: printed by author, 1851.

———. *Debate on Christian Baptism, between Mr. John Walker, a Minister of the Secession, and Alexander Campbell*. Pittsburgh, PA: Eichbaum and Johnston, 1822.

———. *Delusions: An Analysis of the Book of Mormon; with an Examination of Its Internal and External Evidences, and a Refutation of Its Pretenses to Divine Authority*. Boston: Benjamin H. Greene, 1832.

Cannon, Brian Q. "Seventy Contemporaneous Priesthood Restoration Documents." In *Opening the Heavens: Accounts of Divine Manifestations 1820–1844*. Edited by John W. Welsh, 215–63. Salt Lake City and Provo: BYU Press and Deseret, 2005.

Cannon, Donald Q., and Lyndon Cook. *Far West Record: Minutes of the Church of Jesus Christ of Latter-day Saints, 1830–1844*. Salt Lake City: Deseret, 1983.

Clark, Adam. *The New Testament of Our Lord and Savior Jesus Christ*. New York: J. Emory and B. Waugh, for the Methodist Episcopal Church, 1831.

Coleman, William. *Georges Cuvier, Zoologist: A Study in the History of Evolution Theory*. Cambridge, MA: Harvard University Press, 1962.

Compton, Todd. *In Sacred Loneliness: The Plural Wives of Joseph Smith*. Salt Lake City: Signature, 1997.

Cook, Lyndon W. *Revelations of the Prophet Joseph Smith: A Historical and Biographical Commentary of the Doctrine and Covenants*. Provo, UT: Seventies Mission Bookstore, 1981.

Corrill, John. *A Brief History of the Church of Christ of Latter Day Saints*. St. Louis: printed by the author, 1839.

Cowdery, Oliver. "The Following Communication." *Messenger and Advocate* 1, no. 1 (1834): 7–8.

Darowski, Joseph F. "King after the Ancient Order: Conferences and Councils in Early Church Governance. 1830–34." In *A Firm Foundation: Church Organization and Administration*. Edited by David Whittaker and Arnold Garr, 97–113. Salt Lake City: Deseret; Provo, UT: Brigham Young University Religious Studies Center, 2001.

———. "School of the Prophets: An Early American Tradition." *Mormon Historical Studies* 9, no. 1 (Spring 2008): 1–14.

———. "Seeking after the Ancient Order: Conferences and Councils in Early Church Governance, 1830–1834." *Mormon Historical Studies* 11, no. 1 (Spring 2010): 27–39.

Davidson, Karen Lynn, David J. Whittaker, Mark Ashurst-McGee, and Richard L. Jensen, eds. *The Joseph Smith Papers, Histories*. 2 vols. Salt Lake City: Church Historian's Press, 2012.

Davidson, Karen Lynn, Richard L. Jensen, and David J. Whittaker, eds. *Joseph Smith Papers, Histories*. Vol. 2, *Assigned Histories, 1831–1847*. Salt Lake City: Church Historian's Press, 2012.

Daynes, Kathryn. *More Wives Than One: Transformation of the Mormon Marriage System*. Urbana: University of Illinois Press, 2001.

Delbourgo, James. *A Most Amazing Scene of Wonders: Electricity and Enlightenment in Early America*. Cambridge, MA: Harvard University Press, 2006.

De Pillis, Mario S. "The Quest for Religious Authority and the Rise of Mormonism." *Dialogue* 1, no. 1 (1966): 68–88.

Derr, Jill Mulvay, Carol Cornwall Madsen, Kate Holbrook, and Matthew J. Grow, eds. *The First Fifty Years of Relief Society: Key Documents in Latter-day Saint Women's History*. Salt Lake City: Church Historian's Press, 2016.

Dirkmaat, Gerrit J., et al., eds. *The Joseph Smith Papers, Documents*. Vol. 3, *February 1833–March 1834*. Salt Lake City: Church Historian's Press, 2014.

Duffy, Eamon. *The Stripping of the Altars: Traditional Religion in England 1450–1580*. New Haven, CT: Yale University Press, 2002.

Ehat, Andrew. "Joseph Smith's Introduction of Temple Ordinances and the 1844 Mormon Succession Question." MA thesis, Brigham Young University, 1982.

Ehat, Andrew F., and Lyndon W. Cook, eds. *The Words of Joseph Smith: The Con-*

*temporary Accounts of the Nauvoo Discourses of the Prophet Joseph*. 3rd ed. Orem, UT: Grandin, 1994.

Enders, Donald L. "A Snug Log House." *Ensign* 15, no. 8 (August 1985): 14–23.

Esplin, Ronald K. "The Emergence of Brigham Young and the Twelve to Mormon Leadership, 1830–1841." PhD diss., Brigham Young University, Provo, 1981.

———. "Joseph, Brigham and the Twelve: A Succession of Continuity." *BYU Studies* 21, no. 3 (June 1981): 301–41.

Faulring, Scott H., Kent P. Jackson, and Robert J. Matthews, eds. *Joseph Smith's New Translation of the Bible: Original Manuscripts*. Provo, UT: Religious Studies Center, Brigham Young University, 2004.

Flake, Kathleen. "From Conferences to Councils: The Development of LDS Church Organization, 1830–1835." In *Archive of Restoration Culture: Summer Fellows' Papers, 1997–1999, 1–8*. Provo, UT: Joseph Fielding Smith Institute of Latter-day Saint History, 2000.

———. "Ordering Antinomy: An Analysis of Early Mormonism's Priestly Offices, Councils, and Kinship." *Religion and American Culture* 26, no. 2 (2016): 139–83.

Flegg, C. Graham. *Gathered under Apostles: A Study of the Catholic Apostolic Church*. New York: Clarendon, 1992.

Fluhman, Spencer J. "Authority, Power, and the 'Government of the Church of Christ,' 1835." In *Joseph Smith: The Prophet and Seer*. Edited by Richard Neitzel Holzapfel and Kent P. Jackson, 195–231. Provo, UT: Brigham Young University Religious Studies Center, 2010.

———. *A Peculiar People: Anti-Mormonism and the Making of Religion in Nineteenth-Century America*. Chapel Hill: University of North Carolina Press, 2012.

Foster, Lawrence. *Women, Family, and Utopia: Communal Experiments of the Shakers, the Oneida Community, and the Mormons*. Syracuse, NY: Syracuse University Press, 1992.

Givens, Terryl. *By the Hand of Mormon: The American Scripture That Launched a New World Religion*. New York: Oxford University Press, 2002.

———. *Feeding the Flock: The Foundations of Mormon Practice: Sacraments, Authority, Gifts, Worship*. Oxford: Oxford University Press, 2017.

———. *Wrestling the Angel: The Foundations of Mormon Thought: Cosmos, God, Humanity*. Oxford: Oxford University Press, 2014.

Glenn, Myra C. "Troubled Manhood in the Early Republic: The Life and Autobiography of Sailor Horace Lane." *Journal of the Early Republic* 26, no. 1 (Spring 2006): 59–93.

Godfrey, Matthew. "Seeking after Monarchal Power and Authority: Joseph Smith and Leadership in the Church of Christ, 1831–1832." *Mormon Historical Studies* 13, nos. 1–2 (Spring–Fall 2012): 15–37.

Godfrey, Matthew C., Mark Ashurst-McGee, Grant Underwood, Robert J. Woodford, and William G. Hartley, eds. *The Joseph Smith Papers, Documents*. Vol. 2, *July 1831–January 1833*. Salt Lake City: Church Historian's Press, 2013.

Godfrey, Matthew, Brenden W. Rensink, Alex D. Smith, Max H. Parkin, and Alexander L. Baugh. *Joseph Smith Papers, Documents*. Vol. 4, *April 1834–September 1835*. Salt Lake City: Church Historian's Press, 2015.

Grasso, Christopher. "The Religious and the Secular in the Early American Republic." *Journal of the Early Republic* 36, no. 2 (2016): 358–88.

Green, Steven K. *Second Disestablishment: Church and State in Nineteenth-Century America*. New York: Oxford University Press, 2010.

Grow, Matthew J., Ronald K. Esplin, Mark Ashurst-McGee, Gerrit J. Dirkmaat, and Jeffrey D. Mahas, eds. *The Joseph Smith Papers, Administrative Records, Council of Fifty, Minutes, March 1844–January 1846*. Salt Lake City: Church Historian's Press, 2016.

Guyatt, Nicholas. *Providence and the Invention of the United States, 1607–1876*. New York: Cambridge University Press, 2007.

Hadley, Jonathan. "Golden Bible." *Palmyra Freeman*, August 11, 1829, 1.

Hales, Brian C. "'A Continuation of the Seeds': Joseph Smith and Spirit Birth." *Journal of Mormon History* 39, no. 4 (2012): 105–30.

———. *Joseph Smith's Polygamy*. 3 vols. Salt Lake City: Greg Kofford, 2013.

Hamburger, Philip. *Separation of Church and State*. Cambridge, MA: Harvard University Press, 2004.

Handy, Robert T. "Biblical Primitivism and the American Baptist Tradition." In *The American Quest for the Primitive Church*. Edited by Richard T. Hughes, 142–53. Urbana: University of Illinois Press, 1988.

Hardy, Carmon. *Doing the Works of Abraham: Mormon Polygamy: Its Origin, Practice and Thought*. Norman, OK: Arthur H. Clark, 2007.

Harper, Reid L. "The Mantle of Joseph: Creation of a Mormon Miracle." *Journal of Mormon History* 22, no. 2 (1996): 35–71.

Harper, Steven C. "Dictated by Christ: Joseph Smith and the Politics of Revelation." *Journal of the Early Republic* 26, no. 2 (2006): 275–304.

———. "Evaluating the Book of Mormon Witnesses." *Religious Educator* 11, no. 2 (2010): 37–49.

———. "Oliver Cowdery as Second Witness of Priesthood Restoration." In *Days Never to Be Forgotten Oliver Cowdery*. Edited by Alexander Baugh, 73–91. Provo, UT: Brigham Young University Religious Studies Center, 2009.

———. "A Pentecost and Endowment Indeed": Six Eyewitness Accounts of the Kirtland Temple Experience." In *Opening the Heavens: Accounts of Divine Manifestations 1820–1844*. Edited by John W. Welsh, 321–71. Provo, UT and Salt Lake City: BYU Press and Deseret, 2005.

Hartley, William G. *My Fellow Servants: Essays on the History of the Priesthood*. Provo, UT: BYU Press, 2010.

Hatch, Nathan O. *The Democratization of American Christianity*. New Haven, CT: Yale University Press, 1989.

Haws, John B. *The Mormon Image in the American Mind: Fifty Years of Public Perception*. New York: Oxford University Press, 2013.

Hewitt, Hugh. *A Mormon in the White House? 10 Things Every American Should Know about Mitt Romney*. Washington, DC: Regnery, 2007.

Heyrman, Christine Leigh. *Southern Cross: The Beginnings of the Bible Belt*. New York: Alfred A. Knopf, 1998.

Hill, Marvin S. *Quest for Refuge: The Mormon Flight from American Pluralism*. Salt Lake City: Signature, 1989.

Holifield, E. Brooks. *God's Ambassadors: A History of the Christian Clergy in America*. Grand Rapids, MI: Eerdmans, 2007.

———. *Theology in America: Christian Thought from the Age of the Puritans to the Civil War*. New Haven, CT: Yale University Press, 2003.

Holland, David F. *Sacred Borders: Continuing Revelation and Canonical Restraint in Early America*. Oxford: Oxford University Press, 2011.

Homer, Michael. "'Similarity of Priesthood in Masonry': The Relationship between Freemasonry and Mormonism." *Dialogue* 27 (Fall 1997): 1–113.

Horne, Thomas. *Introduction to the Critical Study and Knowledge of the Holy Scriptures*, Vol. 1. Philadelphia: E. Littell, 1825.

Howe, Eber D. *Mormonism Unvailed*. Painesville, OH: printed by the author, 1834.

Huddleston, Lee E. *Origins of the American Indians: European Concepts, 1492–1729*. Austin: University of Texas Press, 1967.

Hughes, Richard T. *Reviving the Ancient Faith: The Story of Churches of Christ in America*. Abilene, TX: Abilene Christian University Press, 1996.

Jenson, Andrew, ed. *Latter-day Saint Biographical Encyclopedia*. Salt Lake City: Deseret News Press, 1901.

———. "Plural Marriage." *Historical Record* 6 (May 1887): 232–33.

Jensen, Robin Scott, Robert J. Woodford, and Steven C. Harper, eds. *Joseph Smith Papers, Revelations and Translations*. Vol. 1, *Manuscript Revelations Books*. Salt Lake City: Church Historian's Press, 2011.

Jessee, Dean, Mark Ashurst-McGee, and Richard L. Jensen, eds. *Joseph Smith Papers, Journals*. Vol. 1, *1832–1839*. Salt Lake City: Church Historian's Press, 2008.

Jessee, Dean C. "The Earliest Documented Accounts of Joseph Smith's First Vision." In *Opening the Heavens: Accounts of Divine Manifestations 1820–1844*. Edited by John W. Welsh, 1–76. Provo, UT: Brigham Young University Press, 2005.

Johnson, Paul E., and Sean Wilentz. *The Kingdom of Matthias: A Story of Sex and Salvation in 19th-Century America*. New York: Oxford University Press, 1994.

Juster, Susan. *Doomsayers: Anglo-American Prophecy in the Age of Revolution*. Philadelphia: University of Pennsylvania Press, 2006.

Kenney, Scott, ed. *Wilford Woodruff's Journal*. 6 vols. Midvale, UT: Signature, 1984.

Kern, Louis J. *An Ordered Love: Sex Roles and Sexuality in Victorian Utopias—the Shakers, the Mormons, and the Oneida Community*. Chapel Hill: University of North Carolina Press, 1981.

Larson, Stan, and Samuel J. Passey, eds. *The William E. McLellin Papers, 1854–1880*. Salt Lake City: Signature, 2007.

Leonard, Bill. *Baptist in America*. New York: Columbia University Press, 2005.

Lively, Robert L. "The Catholic Apostolic Church and the Church of Jesus Christ of Latter-day Saints." PhD diss., Oxford University, 1977.

MacKay, Michael Hubbard. "'Git Them Translated': Translating the Characters on the Gold Plates." In *Joseph Smith and the Ancient World*. Edited by Lincoln H. Blumell, Matthew J. Grey, and Andrew H. Hedges, 79–112. Provo, UT: Brigham Young University Religious Studies Center; Salt Lake City: Deseret, 2015.

MacKay, Michael Hubbard. *Sacred Space: Exploring the Birthplace of Mormonism*. Provo, UT: Brigham Young University Religious Studies Center, 2016.

MacKay, Michael Hubbard, and Gerrit Dirkmaat. *From Darkness unto Light: Joseph Smith's Translation and Publication of the Book of Mormon*. Salt Lake City: Deseret and Brigham Young University Religious Studies Center, 2015.

MacKay, Michael Hubbard, Gerrit J. Dirkmaat, Grant Underwood, Robert J. Woodford, and William G. Hartley, eds. *The Joseph Smith Papers, Documents*. Vol. 1, *July 1828–June 1831*. Salt Lake City: Church Historian's Press, 2013.

MacKay, Michael Hubbard, and Nick Frederick. *Joseph Smith's Seer Stones*. Salt Lake City: Deseret and Brigham Young University Religious Studies Center, 2016.

MacKay, Michael Hubbard, and William G. Hartley. *Rise of the Latter-day Saints: The Journals and Histories of Newel Knight*. Salt Lake City: Deseret and Brigham Young University Religious Studies Center, 2019.

Marks, David. *The Life of David Marks to the 26th Year of His Age*. Limerick, ME: Morning Star, 1831.

Marquardt, H. Michael "An Appraisal of Manchester as Location for the Organization of the Church." *Sunstone* 16, no. 1 (February 1992): 49–57.

———, ed. *Early Patriarchal Blessings of the Church of Jesus Christ of Latter-day Saints*. Salt Lake City: Smith-Pettit Foundation, 2007.

———. "Ezra Booth on Early Mormonism: A Look at His 1831 Letters." *John Whitmer Historical Association Journal* 28 (2008): 65–87.

Matthews, Robert J. *"A Plainer Translation": Joseph Smith's Translation of the Bible; A History and Commentary*. Provo, UT: Brigham Young University Press, 1985.

McBride, Spencer. *Pulpit and Nation: Clergymen and the Politics of Revolutionary America*. Charlottesville: University of Virginia Press, 2017.

Moore, Wendy. *The Knife Man: Blood, Body-Snatching and the Birth of Modern Surgery*. New York: Bantam, 2005.

Moorhead, James H. "Between Progress and Apocalypse: A Reassessment of Millennialism in American Religious Thought, 1800–1880." *Journal of American History* 71, no. 3 (December 1984): 524–42.

Nevin, John W. "Early Christianity." In *Catholic and Reformed: Selected Writing of John Williamson Nevin*. Edited by Charles Yrigoyen Jr. and George H. Bricker, 177–310. Eugene, OR: Pickwick, 1978.

Nibley, Hugh. "The Early Christian Prayer Circle." *BYU Studies* 19, no. 1 (Fall 1978): 41–78.

Noll, Mark A. *The Rise of Evangelicalism: The Age of Edwards, Whitefield and the Wesleys*. Downers Grove, IL: IVP Academic, 2003.

Outler, Albert C. "Biblical Primitivism in Early American Methodism." In *The American Quest for the Primitive Church*. Edited by Richard T. Hughes, 134–42. Urbana: University of Illinois Press, 1988.

Outram, Dorinda. *Georges Cuvier: Vocation, Science, and Authority in Post-Revolutionary France*. Manchester, UK: Manchester University Press, 1984.

Parkin, Max. "Joseph Smith and the United Firm: The Growth and Decline of the Church's First Master Plan of Business and Finance, Ohio and Missouri, 1832–1834." *BYU Studies* 46, no. 3 (July 2007): 4–66.

Parry, Donald W. "Temple Worship and a Possible Reference to a Prayer Circle in Psalm 24." *BYU Studies* 32, no. 2 (September 1992): 57–62.

Petrey, Taylor G. "Purity and Parallels: Constructing the Apostasy Narrative of Early Christianity." In *Standing Apart: Mormon Historical Consciousness and the Concept of Apostasy*. Edited by Miranda Wilcox and John D. Young, 174–95. New York: Oxford University Press, 2014.

Phelps, William W. "Letter No. 6." *Latter Day Saints' Messenger and Advocate* 1 (April 1835): 21–26.

Porter, Larry C. "Odyssey of William Earl McLellin." In *The Journals of William E. McLellin*. Edited by Jan Shipps and John W. Welsh, 290–378. Urbana: University of Illinois Press; Provo, UT: BYU Studies, 1994.

———. "The Restoration of the Aaronic and Melchizedek Priesthood." *Ensign* 26 (December 1996): 30–47.

Porterfield, Amanda. *Conceived in Doubt: Religion and Politics in the New American Nation*. Chicago: University of Chicago Press, 2012.

Pratt, Orson. "Distinguishing Characteristics between the Latter-day Saints and the Various Religious Denominations of Christendom." *Journal of Discourses* 16 (November 2, 1873): 284–300.

———. *Divine Authority; or, The Question Was Joseph Sent of God?*. Liverpool, UK: R. James, 1848.

———. "Experience in Missionary Labors—Ancient Prophecies concerning the People of God in the Last Days." *Journal of Discourses* 12 (August 11, 1867): 85–93.

Pratt, Parley P. *The Autobiography of Parley Parker Pratt*. New York: Russell Brothers, 1874.

———. "The Millennium, A Poem: To Which Is Added Hymns and Songs." Boston, for Elder Parley P. Pratt, 1835.

———. *Proclamation of the Twelve Apostles of the Church of Jesus Christ of Latter-day Saints*. Liverpool: Wilford Woodruff, 1845.

———. *Voice of Warning and Instruction to All People, or An Introduction to the Faith and Doctrine of the Church of Jesus Christ of Latter-day Saints, Commonly Called Mormons*. New York: W. Sanford, 1837.

Prince, Gregory A. *Power from On High: The Development of Mormon Priesthood*. Salt Lake City: Signature, 1995.

Quinn, D. Michael. "Latter-day Saint Prayer Circles." *BYU Studies* 19, no. 1 (September 1978): 79–105.

———. *The Mormon Hierarchy: Extensions of Power*. Salt Lake City: Signature, 1997.
———. *The Mormon Hierarchy: Origins of Power*. Salt Lake City: Signature, 1994.
———. "The Mormon Succession Crisis of 1844." *BYU Studies* 16, no. 2 (January 1976): 187–234.
———. "Mormon Women Have Had the Priesthood since 1843." In *Women and Authority*. Edited by Maxine Hanks, 365–409. Salt Lake City: Signature, 1992.
Rakestraw, Joseph. *Some Extraordinary Instances of Divine Guidance and Protection, and Awful Warnings of a Just Retribution, through Dreams and Visions*. Philadelphia: printed by author, 1814.
Ralston, Samuel. *A Review of a Debate on Christian Baptism: Between Mr. John Walker, a Minister of the Secession, and Mr. Alexander Campbell, a Baptist Minister, Published by Mr. Campbell; in a Series of Letters*. Pittsburgh, PA: Eichbaum and Johnston, 1822.
Randolph, Robert M. "We Speak Where the Bible Speaks: Religious Authority in Churches of Christ." In *By What Authority: The Vital Questions of Religious Authority in Christianity*. Edited by Robert Millet. Macon, GA: Mercer University Press, 2010.
Ricks, Stephen D. "The Appearance of Elijah and Moses in the Kirtland Temple and the Jewish Passover." *BYU Studies* 23, no. 4 (October 1983): 483–86.
Rivett, Sarah. *The Science of the Soul in Colonial New England*. Chapel Hill: University of North Carolina Press, 2011.
Roberts, Allen D., Richard S. Van Wagoner, and Steven C. Walker. "The 'Lectures on Faith': A Case Study in Decanonization." *Dialogue* 20, no. 3 (Fall 1987): 71–77.
Roberts, Brigham H. *A Comprehensive History of the Church of Jesus Christ of Latter-Day Saints*. 6 vols. Salt Lake City: Deseret New Press, 1930.
Robinson, Elwin C. *The First Mormon Temple: Design, Construction, and Historic Context of the Kirtland Temple*. Provo, UT: Brigham Young University Press, 1997.
Romney, Mitt. "Faith in America." In *The Mormon Quest for the Presidency*. Edited by Newel Bringhurst and Craig Foster, 353–59. Independence, MO: John Whitmer, 2008.
Rowe, David L. *God's Strange Work: William Miller and the End of the World*. Grand Rapids, MI: Eerdmans, 2008.
Rowley, Dennis. "The Ezra Booth Letters." *Dialogue* 16, no. 3 (Autumn 1983): 133–39.
Schmidt, Leigh Eric. *Hearing Things: Religion, Illusion, and the American Enlightenment*. Cambridge, MA: Harvard University Press, 2000.
Sehat, David. *The Myth of American Religious Freedom*. New York: Oxford University Press, 2011.
Shaw, Plato E. *The Catholic Apostolic Church Sometimes Called Irvingite: A Historical Study*. New York: King's Crown, 1946.
Shipps, Jan. *Mormonism: The Story of a New Religious Tradition*. Urbana: University of Illinois Press, 1987.
Smith, Emma. *A Collection of Sacred Hymns for the Church of the Latter Day Saints*. Kirtland, OH: F. G. Williams, 1835.

Smith, Ethan. *View of the Hebrews. Or, The Tribes of Israel in America*. Poultney, VT: Smith and Shute, 1825.

Smith, George A. "Historical Discourse." *Journal of Discourses* 11 (November 15, 1864): 1–12.

Smith, George D., ed. *An Intimate Chronicle: The Journals of William Clayton*. Salt Lake City: Signature, 1995.

Smith, Heman H. "Biography of David Whitmer." *Journal of History* 3 (July 1910): 303–4.

Smith, Joseph Fielding. "Magnifying Our Calling in the Priesthood." *Improvement Era* 73, no. 6 (June 1970): 65–66.

Smith, Merina. *Revelation, Resistance and Mormon Polygamy: The Introduction and Implementation of the Principle, 1830–1853*. Logan: Utah State University Press, 2013.

Smith, Timothy L. "Righteousness and Hope: Christian Holiness and the Millennial Vision in America, 1800–1900." *American Quarterly* 31, no. 1 (Spring 1979): 21–45.

Smith, William. *William Smith on Mormonism*. Lamoni, Iowa: Herald Office, 1883.

Spencer, Joseph M. *For Zion: A Mormon Theology of Hope*. Salt Lake City: Greg Kofford, 2014.

Staker, Mark. *Hearken, O Ye People: The Historical Setting of Joseph Smith's Ohio Revelations*. Salt Lake City: Greg Kofford, 2009.

Stapley, Jonathan. "Last Rites and the Dynamics of Mormon Liturgy." *BYU Studies* 50, no. 2 (April 2001): 96–128.

Stephanson, Anders. *Manifest Destiny: American Expansion and the Empire of Right*. New York: Hill and Wang, 1995.

Stevenson, Joseph Grant. *Richards Family History*. 5 vols. Provo, UT: Stevenson's Genealogical Center, 1991.

Taves, Ann. *Revelatory Events: Three Case Studies of the Emergence of New Spiritual Paths*. Princeton, NJ: Princeton University Press, 2016.

Thomas, Keith. *Religion and the Decline of Magic*. New York: Oxford University Press, 1997.

Underwood, Grant. *The Millenarian World of Early Mormonism*. Urbana: University of Illinois Press, 1999.

Van Wagoner, Richard. *Mormon Polygamy: A History*. 2nd ed. Salt Lake City: Signature, 1992.

Vogel, Dan. *Indian Origins and the Book of Mormon: Religious Solutions from Columbus to Joseph Smith*. Salt Lake City: Signature, 1986.

———. *Religious Seekers and the Advent of Mormonism*. Salt Lake City: Signature, 1989.

Wacker, Grant. "The Holy Spirit and the Spirit of the Age in American Protestantism, 1880–1910." *Journal of American History* 72, no. 1 (June 1985): 45–62.

Walker, Ronald W. "The Persisting Idea of American Treasure Hunting." *BYU Studies* 24, no. 4 (September 1984): 429–59.

———. "Six Days in August: Brigham Young and the Succession Crisis of 1844." In

*A Firm Foundation: Church Organization and Administration*. Edited by Arnold K. Garr and David J. Whitaker, 161–96. Salt Lake City: Deseret, 2011.

Weber, Max. *The Theory of Social and Economic Organization*. Edited by Talcott Parsons. Translated by A. M. Henderson and Talcott Parsons. New York: Free Press, 1947.

Welsh, John W., ed. *Opening the Heavens: Accounts of Divine Manifestations, 1820–1844*. Provo, UT: Brigham Young University Press and Deseret Book, 2005.

Whitmer, David. *Address to All Believers in Christ*. Printed by the author, Richmond, MO, 1887.

———. *Address to All Believers in the Book of Mormon*. Printed by the author, Lamoni, IA, 1887.

Wood, James. *A Dictionary of the Holy Bible*. New York: Griffin and Rudd, 1813.

Worthen, Molly. *Apostles of Reason: The Crisis of Authority in American Evangelicalism*. New York: Oxford University Press, 2014.

Wuthnow, Robert. "Democratic Renewal and Cultural Inertia: Why Our Best Efforts Fall Short." *Sociological Forum* 20, no. 3 (September 2005): 343–67.

Young, Brigham. "Discourse by President Brigham Young, Delivered in the Third Ward Meeting House, Salt Lake City, Sunday Evening. June 23, 1874." *Journal of Discourses* 18 (June 23, 1874): 235–49.

———. "Priesthood." *Journal of Discourses* 9 (May 7, 1861): 86–93.

———. "The Temple Corner Stones—The Apostleship, &c." *Journal of Discourses* 1 (April 6, 1853): 131–37.

Zeitlin, Solomon. "The Liturgy of the First Night of Passover." *Jewish Quarterly Review* 38, no. 4 (April 1948): 431–60.

# Index

Michael Hubbard MacKay is an associate professor at Brigham Young University and a former historian for the Joseph Smith Papers Project. He is the author of *Sacred Space: Exploring the Birthplace of Mormonism* and coauthor of *Joseph Smith's Seer Stones.*

The University of Illinois Press
is a founding member of the
Association of University Presses.

Composed in 10.5/13 Adobe Minion Pro
with Optima display
by Jim Proefrock
at the University of Illinois Press
Cover designed by Dustin Hubbart
Cover image: Lt. General Joseph Smith
In Nauvoo Legion Uniform by Sutcliffe
Maudsley (1809-1881). Courtesy of the
Church of Jesus Christ of Latter-day Saints.
Manufactured by Sheridan Books, Inc.

University of Illinois Press
1325 South Oak Street
Champaign, IL 61820-6903
www.press.uillinois.edu

Michael Hubbard MacKay is an associate professor at Brigham Young University and a former historian for the Joseph Smith Papers Project. He is the author of *Sacred Space: Exploring the Birthplace of Mormonism* and coauthor of *Joseph Smith's Seer Stones.*

The University of Illinois Press
is a founding member of the
Association of University Presses.

Composed in 10.5/13 Adobe Minion Pro
with Optima display
by Jim Proefrock
at the University of Illinois Press
Cover designed by Dustin Hubbart
Cover image: Lt. General Joseph Smith
In Nauvoo Legion Uniform by Sutcliffe
Maudsley (1809-1881). Courtesy of the
Church of Jesus Christ of Latter-day Saints.
Manufactured by Sheridan Books, Inc.

University of Illinois Press
1325 South Oak Street
Champaign, IL 61820-6903
www.press.uillinois.edu